GURU ARJUN DEV

THE GREAT GURUS OF THE SIKHS SERIES

GURU ARJUN DEV

Editor-in-Chief

O. P. RALHAN

ANMOL PUBLICATIONS PVT. LTD.
NEW DELHI-110002 (INDIA)

ANMOL PUBLICATIONS PVT. LTD.
4374/4B, Ansari Road, Daryaganj
New Delhi-110 002

Guru ArjunDev

First Edition 1998

ISBN 81-7488-672-9

PRINTED IN INDIA

Published by J. L. Kumar for Anmol Publications Pvt. Ltd., New Delhi-110 002 and Printed at Mehra Offset Press, Delhi.

Preface

'Great Gurus of the Sikhs' in six volumes is a monumental work by the editor drawing every succinct information on each of the ten Gurus from unapproachable historical and religious sources.

These volumes should not be treated simply in biographical sketches of their lives or travelogue of their lives, but an account of their teachings, philosophies, travelogue, their sufferings and sacrifices for the country, their mythological and theological aspects, socio-economic reforms, their political contention and wars with the autocracy at their times and many more touching incidents of their lives, miracles which they manifested on several occasions—all have been contained in them. These volumes are treasures of religious wealth enshrined in their sacred *Vanis*—viz. Guru Granth Sahib and on political scenario of their times.

The sufferings of the Gurus were immense during Mughal period. Guru Arjun Dev, Guru Teg Bahadur and Guru Gobind Singh sacrificed every thing for the sake of their sincere love for humanity and reforming zeal. Repressive policies and numerous maneuvre could not bend them, instead. The rulers have to bow before them for their unparallelled and unmatched chivalry shown by them in spite of great emotional hurdles.

These volumes are faithful and sincere narration of the political conditions, social conditions, religious fanaticity of the rulers, prevailing at that times and how all those Great Gurus not only fought against heavy odds but simultaneously never allowed to fade away the spiritual lamp lighted by them which even today imparts eternal peace to thousands of people not only of Sikh people but all other religions.

These volumes on Great Gurus of the Sikhs advocate tenaciously a superb, enchanting study for each and every one. Highly recommended for teachers, students, social reformers, historians. A useful and worthy of acquisition for each library. Section of Sikh history in each library remain incomplete with without such a marvellous set.

[illegible]

[illegible]

[illegible] of [illegible]

[illegible]

[illegible]

[illegible]

[illegible]

Contents

1

Early Career

GURU ARJAN DEV
(1581-1606 A.D.)

Guru Arjan, the Fifth Guru, is the central most figure of the Sikh Theocracy and by virtue of his unique personality, he is the most brilliant star in the galaxy of seers, saints and sages.

Guru Arjan was born poet and composer of music. He was a saint and scholar of rare piety and literary attainments. His compositions bespeak the great depth of his mind and sublimity of his thought, full of Divine Love and human sympathy. But above all we find in him a paramount Saviour, carrying the Torch of Divine Light which sets the dead soul awake.

Guru Arjan Dev's hands were always full with matters spiritual which aimed at dispelling the forces of darkness, and ushering in Light into this Land of Five Rivers. Many-fold as were his activities in his busy life of about 40 years, yet there were three outstanding works connected with him, any one of which, by itself, would be sufficient to make his name immortal. They were: the compilation of the Holy Granth, the construction of the Golden Temple and above all his own sacrifice in up-holding Truth and righteousness.

Complication of Holy Granth

It was an Himalayan task which Guru Arjun Dev took on his shoulders and he carried it through, as he alone could. Mere words are inadequate to pay tribute to the extent of work put forth and of the labour involved in compiling this sacred book. It was indeed an Herculean task accomplished and to which generations of seekers of truth and devotees would continue to pay their homage.

Holy Granth is by no means a Sikh Bible alone, but it is the universal Bible of Man. For its spirit is so large and profound and there is nothing sectarian in it. It contains only universal Truth. It is the lyric of divine love, and all the people of the earth subsist on such glowing lyrical prayer.

Along with the hymns of the Gurus, we find Psalms of Kabir, Ravidas, Namdev, Jaidev and of many others who were inspired by the Divine Spirit. Although the hyms of fifteen saints have been included in Granth Sahib yet it is a single great book in which there is a remarkable unity of outlook, sincerity of purpose and beauty of poetry and realism of vision. It has really one theme—man's search for

God, his longing and yearning after God, his intense love for Him, and to feel His presence and live mentally and spiritually healthy life on earth. Guru Grantha is but One Song, One Idea and One Life.

Guru Arjan's personal contribution to Granth Sahib is by far the greatest of all the Bhagatas combined together. There are 2218 hyms contributed by Guru Arjan himself. The hymns are set to music. There is a wide range of mystical emotions, intimate expressions of the personal realizations of God and rapturous hymns of divine love.

To convey their message of love, light and life, the Gurus employed both music and poetry in the writings of Guru Granth. For you can speak Truth uncontradicted in verse, you cannot in prose. The hymns of Guru Granth are set to measures of thirty-one classical Indian ragas. In this way each hymn acquires a specific emotional evocation and a distinctive spiritual aura.

Guru Nanak's poetry displays a remarkable freedom of expression. The pastrol beauty, the ripening cornfields, the break of dawn and the awakening of birds; the comely leap of deer in the woodlands the awesome majesty of monsoon clouds and the music of rainfall aroused him to religious and poetic frenzy. The fifth Guru Arjan, expresses the same deep sentiments in his poetry as Guru Nanak. His verses abound with beautiful phrases and has an enchanting melody, produced by the use of alliteration and repetition of words. How beautifully worded hymns crave for union with God:

"O blissful night, long be thy hours,
O wretched sleep, be brief,
I have a tryst with the Lord I love,
I long to touch the Lotus Feet of the Lord."

(Guru Arjan: Rag Behagri)
(translated.)

One who reads this Divine Book is undoubtedly stirred to the depth by the spirit which pervades the whole poetry. Each verse sparkles with divine refulgence, each line tingles us with rare joy. There is no human chord that is not struck, there is no depth that is not stirred. It imparts the Spark of Life that kindles the "Extinguished-Ones" and makes whole the 'Broken-Ones'.

In the pages of holy Grantha, we do feel man comes into his own, developed to his full stature of manhood, when man is no longer a mere man, but one with the Supreme Self. No longer are forces of nature, the object of worship, but only the Timeless Spirit. The arid desert of philosophy has been replaced by mountain-heights of love-lit meditation.

Guru Granth Sahib is not a book of cold wrangling philosophy, but it is pulsating with the warm blood of the heart. Sweet humility has taken the place of inflated egoism.

In Guru Granth Sahib, there is the first genuine attempt to completely take off the veil from the Spirit. Above all, Guru Granth is the only Bible which gives you complete information about NAM—the Word or Logos, which is the Key to the Kingdom of Heaven within us, and but for which all poetry is verbiage and all philosophy illusory. This Divine Poetry brings the man face to face with this Dazzling, Eternal all All-Pervading Reality, Golden State ultimate, reaching which all is one.

Each psalm of the Guru, is a beautiful piece which can well be termed the Gems of the Spirit. The following is one such inspired psalm which depicts the state of mind, when Truth dawns on man:

"The shell of the egg of illusion has burst,
My mind is illumined;
The Guru has broken the fetters
The captive soul is freed.

No more cycles of life and death,
No more fretting and fuming
The steaming cauldron of desires has cooled down
No sooner the Guru showered the blessings of NAM on me.

My enemies—the senses that assailed me,
Are under my control since I found the Saint's company.
The Lord in His mercy has now removed
All the temptations that once stood in my way.

The load of 'Karma' is taken off my breast
And I soar like a bird, free on its wings,
No more restraint,
I now act without any desire for reward.

I have crossed the sea of life
And have reached the shore.
The Guru hath done this act of mercy
Now truth is my Resting Ground,
Truth is the Rock on which I stand, I dwell in Truth
Truth is my Capital and Stock-in-Trade,
Saith Nanak, Yea, I have found My House within me."

(Guru Arjan: Rag Maru)
(translated)

Guru Arjan's Sukhmani (The Song of Eternal Peace)

His Sukhmani is the most popular and widely chanted hymn. It is veritably the Kohi-Noor of the Spiritual Diamonds. It is joy infinite which is beyond the span of words; for words are volatile, but the joy which emanates from this Song of songs is eternal.

Sukhmani came out from the heart of Guru Arjan as a river flows out from a snow covered mountain. It is a great healer of all the ills of the mind. When worries seize you, and troubles burden you and outweigh your spirit, plunge into Sukhmani, the ever-flowing River of Peace and you will be soothed and comforted. It makes you fearless and joyous. You will feel refreshed, stimulated and anew.

The Golden Temple of Amritsar (Darbar Sahib)

It is said that Guru Nanak, the founder of Sikh religion, during his missionery tours once halted by a natural pond in the midst of a thick jungle in the Punjab. This secluded spot afforded great peace and he stayed there for some time to enjoy the crystal clear waters and to commune with God in the midst of this cool, quiet place.

Because Guru Nanak had been so fond of this spot, it naturally took on a hallowed significance to his disciples and followers. When Emperor Akbar visited Guru Amar Das and received spiritual satisfaction, he made a presentation of this land to Bibi Bhani, the daughter of Guru Amar Das. At any rate, Guru Ram Das established his residence in the area where Guru Nanak first halted and in 1577 the city was founded with the construction of the tank which was to be called Amrit-Sar. The construction of the tank and the temple was at first commenced by Guru Ram Das, but the subsequent modelling and finish was due entirely to the Fifth Guru. It was the task of Guru Arjan, to crystalize the spiritual aspect of the religion and its metropolis. He not only compiled the Guru Granth Sahib, the holy book, but he also established the Golden Temple as the religious centre of the Sikh community.

Blind ritualism had smothered the essence of the religion of the Hindus and the peculiar forms of eating and drinking had become the ultimate in ritualism So Guru Nanak and his successors, to hit at the heart of artificiality, established a free kitchen and decreed that all who come to see them must first sit side by side with other pilgrims and eat food prepared by the devotees. Thus each man had to shed his ritualistic beliefs by sitting by the side of men and women of other castes. In this way the Guru abolished superficialities and showed the people that under the ritualism lay an inner sameness. Thus Sikhism opened its doors to all and gave men simple basic beliefs which all could follow.

The Golden Temple was designed as a symbol of such a faith and, to demonstrate its universality, Guru Arjan asked his dear Muslim friend, Mian Mir, to lay the foundation stone.

A marble synthesis of the arts and cultures that had passed through the Punjab, the Hari Mandir, as the temple was originally called, grew out of the waters and floated like a lotus on the crystal pool. The pool of water around the temple not only isolates it from a temporal environment but also adds considerably to its majesty and beauty. The temple's glimmering reflection in the myriad ripples of the holy water, dancing around it, is an unforgettable memory. By day, under the blue sky, dazzling in the sunlight, the temple looks like a garnished ornament. By night, when the temple and its causeway are lit with lights of different colours they resemble a miniature fairyland. Connected to the shores by a single bridge, its surrounding water bordered by a wide walk, this temple is accessible to men and women of all faiths, castes and nationalities.

Where Indian places of worship normally had one door opened towards the direction of that faith's conception of God's abode, the Golden Temple was built with four doors opening to the cardinal points to show that God is everywhere at all times. Where Hindu temples were open only to those of chosen castes, the Golden Temple opened its doors to all who would seek God. Where Muslim mosques were open only to men, the Golden Temple received also women, giving them dignity and equality with men and making them personally responsible to God. Where Hindu temples enshrined idols of gods for worship, no image found a place in Golden Temple and worship of only one God was done. God who is formless all-pervading, who is the creator of the universe, who is not an abstraction but a reality, Immortal, unborn and Self-existent. And He is worshipped through love and righteousness by singing odes and hymns in praise of Him.

Thus the establishment of the Golden Temple was a revolutionary step in Indian history.

But those, who look on merely the alabaster and the gold of the temple, miss the inner spirit which pervades the whole building. The whole atmosphere is surcharged with Divine Light and no one who enters the sacred precinets of the Golden Temple would fail to perceive its sacred influence.

Everyday, Guru Arjan, chanted the life giving hymns, playing the Tambura exquisitely with his own deft fingers; his melodious voice, and with his disciples gathered round him listening to his divine lyrics in wonder and worship. The lovely music rose from under the dome of Hari Mandir and was absorbed and reabsorbed by the thirsty lake which surrounded it. His divine voice still lingers on and its reverberating echoes still awaken the sleeping souls. The mystics and the 'Living Ones' know and appreciate the sacred influence of the atmosphere there.

Akbar, the Emperor of India Pays a Visit

Akbar paid a visit to the Guru in order to see the Temple and its architectural beauty. He asked the Guru, as was his wont, the way to acceptance by God. The Guru said, "Through Service and Love." Akbar wished to make a contribution towards the maintenance of the Golden Temple. But the Guru declined the offer, saying that it was being well supported by the people. But when the Emperor insisted, the Guru said, "There is an acute famine in the country; it would be best if the Imperial visit were to be marked by the remission of this year's land revenue to the poor farmers."

Akbar gave orders accordingly.

Social Reforms

Arjan felt that there could be no hope for the social and political regeneration of our people as long as they did not take interest in the development of arts and industries. Men of high castes kept aloof and left the hard work to be done by the so called lower classes. All those who were spiritually minded shunned work, as it was looked upon by them as mean, degrading and worldly. Guru Arjan said that every man must work. It is only those that work and earn and share their earnings with others that find the true path.

Renunciation of the world was against the teachings of the Gurus. He preached that retirement from the world was a confession of failure, like a run-away soldier from the battle field.

The Guru recognised that the reform of a nation meant the reform of its masses. A nation is as great as its rank and file. It is the common man that was of utmost significance and therefore the Guru left no stone unturned to care for him. All classes were declared equal. All occupations that were honest were glorified as sacred. There was to be no prejudice against any trade and profession. Worldly riches were no longer to be considered 'Maya.' These could be helpful in the conduct of human affairs.

For a religious man, it was not irreligious to acquire wealth, provided he makes use of his wealth beneficially to give comfort and derive comfort.

So now the intelligentsia also began too take active part in all arts and industries. The Guru patronised and encouraged them, as this was one of the noblest ways of serving the country. At the same time, centres of commerce and industries like Amritsar and Tarn Tarn were founded by the Guru.

Centuries of Mohammedan rule had demoralised the Hindus so much so, that in desperation they had come to believe that all pain and suffering was meted out to them by God because of their sins and that virtuous men would never suffer. They said that king Dasrath, Rama's father, suffered agony in the exile of his son, because he had caused pain to the father of Sarwan. So all actions that involved pain and suffering began to be shunned. The concept of sacrifice and patriotism were thrown to the winds.

Guru Arjan Dev laid great stress on the service of love and self-sacrifice for a virtuous cause. His purpose was to show that whatever suffering one had to undergo in the cause of doing good to others, is not the outcome of one's sins, but a necessary co-relative of virtue. How can a conscientious man can remain at ease as long as his fellow brethern are suffering before his eyes. Guru Arjan enjoined upon the Sikhs to voluntarily contribute atleast One Tenth of their income as a love-full offering for the advancement of the social, national and 'Dharmic' causes.

Views of Contemporary Poets, Mystics and Scholars About Guru Arjan Dev

Some contemporary poets, mystics and scholars who personally saw the Master and came in close contact with him wrote about him thus:

> "Unfathomable, pure, serene and immortal is the spirit of Guru Arjan Dev. The light of his soul is brighter than the moon and more resplendent than sun. He is imbued with the love of God and in him burns the undying Flame of the Eternal. Every-one acknowledges the spiritual greatness of Guru Arjan, and the wise and enlightened sing songs about his virtues and spiritual granduer. Guru Arjan personal life and his spiritual ideals attracted people of divergent faiths, men and women belonging to all the four different castes, those who were devout followers of Vedas and those belonging to the Six Schools of Philosophy.
>
> Guru Arjan's heart vibrates with Celestial Music. His inner self is the abode of perennial joy and bliss, as he is deeply absorbed in the love of God. His personality emanates Truth.
>
> From the North and South, from the East and West, seekers of truth flock to Guru Arjan and accept the discipleship of his faith. He maintains a free Kitchen giving bodily food as well as spiritual food to all those who seek it."
>
> (Bhai Gurdas: *Translated)*

> "I relate from my personal experience, the virtues of Guru Arjan Dev. He was born in the house of Guru Ram Das. His birth fulfilled the great expectations of the house of the Guru. He had the divine, illumination from his very birth. He is a great seer who loveth God truly and liveth a detached life in this world. He has given the widest expression to the Holy Word. The Name of the Lord is ever on his lips. His mind is ever at peace. He has perfect realization of God.
>
> Ever since I have felt the moral and spiritual influence of Guru Arjan, my mind has experienced Truth through the Guru's Word. My thirst for true knowledge of God has been appeased and my search has ended in this supreme realization.
>
> Immortal and invaluable is the inherent divinity in Guru Arjan. His inner spirit is the very image of God and is everlasting. The supreme Light of the Holy Word passed from Guru Nanak to Angad, then to Amardas and from him to Ram Das. With the transmuting touch of Ram Das, Guru Arjan became the torch-bearer of Guru Nanak.
>
> Guru Arjan ever remains united with God. So impressive and pure is his personality that whosoever comes in contact with him praises his virtues. He has come to bear the burden of the world. Through his moral and spiritual influence he dispells all fears and does everything to remove the sorrows and sufferings of others. He is gracious and compassionate like God Himself.

Guru Arjan is an embodiment of patience, tolerance and calm endurance. He is also a profound scholar. By his very touch all ego departs. He is the perennial fountain of charity. The greatest gift which he freely gives to others is the divine wisdom. He preaches Truth, loves Truth and stands by Truth. He is the King of kings and the most perfect living being. Great is Guru Arjan indeed as he fills to the brim the empty, spiritless souls with the Light and Love of God."

(Kalya Sahar—a Poet and scholar of Banaras)
ranslated.

Mathura's Observations about Guru Arjan

Mathura, a mystic and a scholar makes observations about Guru Arjan which are briefly as under:

"God is Supreme Light. The same Divine Light manifested itself in human form and was known as Guru Nanak. The Divine Spirit of Guru nanak came to be passed on the Guru Arjan. Blessed am I to see the Light of the Perfect Guru shining in Arjan Dev with my own eyes. This Light radiates from his personality and spreads in all realms. In this dark age, Guru Arjan is a ship to save humanity from the tumultuous and the stormy waters of this dark ocean—our world.

Hear, ye people, I seek the Light that shines in Guru Arjan. His mind is imbibed with a genuine love for humanity and God. Ah! who can measure the spiritual greatness of Guru Arjan. He has come to enlighten the seekers of truth and to save suffering humanity. Ah! who else can bestow peace and light on mankind, plunged in darkness except the great Guru Arjan. Those who have drunk deep from the cup of nectar which he alone at present holds out to humanity, have overcome all sorrows and sufferings.

Pure is the life of Guru Arjan and pure are his principles, whoever treads his path becomes pure like him. On the earth and in sky and in worlds, the light of God pervades. That resplendent light of God can be visibly seen in Guru Arjan."

(Translated)

The Great Sacrifice

Hundreds of thousands of people equally from amongst the Hindus and Muslims flocked to Guru Arjan, fascinated by the beauty of his spirit, his purity and saintliness. A great number of villages with hundreds of Muslim inhabitants bowed before the Guru and became his disciples.

Up to the time of Akbar, and Mughal Emperors had not greatly interfered with this peaceful movement. But the ever growing popularity and influence of Sikhism perturbed Jahangir, who had little of the mildness and tolerance of his father. As a Mohammedan, he thought it was his duty to bring the infidels to the fold of Islam.

Thus the bigotry of Emperor Jahangir was stirred up. He himself writes in his autobiography:

> "On the banks of the river Beas, there stands a village Goindwal, where dwells a person Arjan by name. He is known as Guru. He has taken into his folds quite a number of Hindus, as also simple Mohammedans by influence of his ways and manners. His purity and saintliness is being loudly proclaimed on all sides and worshippers from all parts of the country rally round him. They manifest complete faith in him and pay their homage to him. This movement has been going on for the past three to four generations. I have been contemplating for a long time either to end this movement or to convert the Guru to Islam."

A pretext was soon created for hauling up the Guru on charge of sedition. Chandu, the Dewan, conspired with servile informers and invented the story that the Guru had helped Khusrau, the rebellous son of the Emperor Jahangir, while he was passing through Goindwal and that the Guru had applied a 'tilk' on his forehead as a token of his blessings. The Emperor grabbed this opportunity of giving vent to his pent-up feelings and rage.

Referring to these allegations, Jahangir writes in his autobiography: "I was already fully aware of his heresies and as I was now informed of him, I ordered that the Guru be brought into my presence and I conferred all his belongings to Murtza Hussain Khan and further ordered that he should be tortured to death under the Law of Yusa." Power-mad Monarchs are often blind to truth and reason. The following day the Emperor left Lahore of Kashmir, with no effort to know or seek the truth behind all these allegations against the Guru; and even before the Guru could be brought to Lahore:

> Jehangir's son, Khusrau, had rebelled against him. He was fleeing towards Lahore and the Emperor was closely pursuing him. On the way he mercilessly massacred all those who were reported to have helped Khusrau in any way. The Emperor's diary shows that on the 16th Zeeulhaj he was at Serai Qaziwali. On the 17th he reached Goindwal starting the same morning from Sultanpur. He knew that Guru Arjan lived at Goindwal. If the Guru had really helped Khusrau in any way, the Emperor would have surely dealt with him then and there. But there was no report against him.
>
> From there, the emperor marched on the Jaipal, a village seven miles from Lahore and stayed there till the 28th. He heard nothing against the Guru till then.
>
> On the 3rd of Maharram, Khusrau was arrested and 700 of his companions were impaled alive on spikes pitched outside the Lahore gates. Some of them were sewn up in wet cowhides and asshides. The Emperor remained at Lahore till the 8th. It was not until the 7th that he was suddenly informed that Guru Arjan had applied a tilak on Khusrau's forehead in token of his blessings.
>
> Now in the house of Guru Nanak, Tilak was never applied to anyone except on the forehead of the succeeding Guru when he was installed on the spiritual

throne. Even when the Emperor Akbar visited the Guru Amar Das and then also Guru Arjan himself, no Tilak was applied to his forehead.

It was an utterly false charge that was brought against the Guru. Chandu, the Dewan had conspired with some fanatic Mohammedans and fabricated the whole story.

Chandu bore a grudge against the Guru. His malice was due to the Guru's refusal to accept his daughter in marriage to his son Har Gobind. Chandu had spoken contemptuously of the house of Guru Nanak and therefore the Guru refused his offer.

But Jehangir, who for reasons of his own, had long since been contemplating to take some strong action against the Guru, now found a good excuse to order that he should be arrested and tortured to death.)

After the Emperor left for Kashmir, the Guru was brought to Lahore. Murtza Hussain Khan handed him over to Chandu, the Dewan who devised the tortures inflicted upon the Guru. Guru Arjan was made to sit on red hot iron and burning sand was poured over his bare body. But the Guru remained calm and tranquil throughout, and his face flushed with divine glory.

When Hazrat Mian Mir, a Muslim saint, who had laid the foundation-stone of the Golden Temple, heard this tale of sorrow, he rushed to see the Guru. Tears trickled down the cheeks of the aged Mian Mir when he saw the ghastly scene. He cried like a child and said: "Master! I cannot bear to see these horrors inflicted on you." But the Master comforted him and asked him to look up. When lo! the hosts of Heaven were seen hovering around the Guru and angels stood awaiting his commands. But the Guru was unruffled, quite calm and tranquil and full of ineffable peace.

He completely resigned himself to the Will of God, and submitted cheerfully to the most agonising physical, torture, and said: "Sweet be Thy Will, My Lord, Thy Grace alone I beseecheth."

Main Mir then bowed and left in silence.

At last Chandu made up his mind to kill Guru Arjan by suffocating him in a fresh cowhide, in which he was to be sewn up. The Guru asked for a bath in Ravi River. He was permitted to bathe, as Chandu revelled in the thought that the Guru's body full of blisters would undergo greater pain when it would be dipped in cold water.

He was led out to the river which flowed embracing the walls of the Lahore fort. The Master's disciples saw him. He looked at them still forbidding any action. "Such is the Will of my God, submit to the Divine Will," said he, "move not, stand calm against all woes."

Crowds of people watched him, calm but deeply afflicted while the Master stood in water and had a dip and disappeared. The Light blended with Light and his body was to be found nowhere.

The testimony of Bhai Gurdas on Guru Arjan's martyrdom is of great importance. Particularly note worthy are the comments of this saint-scholar who lived during that period. He does not brood over the horrors of torture, but elucidates the superhuman endurance, equanimity and calmness of Guru Arjan under the severest torments and extreme agony. He writes:

> "Profound indeed was Guru Arjan's martyrdom. As a fish swims into the depth of flowing water, so Guru Arjan lived deep into the Eternal Stream of Lord's presence. As the moth flings its body into flame sacrificing itself on it, so Guru Arjan submitted his body to the torture of fire and heat and blended his soul with the Undying Flame of God.
>
> As a deer, cares not for the deadly arrows of the hunter but runs heedlessly towards the call of the drum, Guru Arjan cared not for the cruel hands of the murderer but marched on fearlessly to face a martyr's death, keeping all the time his mind absorbed in the Celestial Music within his soul. Even at the severest torture and at the most tragic moment of his end, he thought not of anything else but the enchanting of Heaven's symphony within his mind.
>
> As a butterfly, when trapped in the petals of the lotus flower dies in the joy of its fragrance and honey, so Guru Arjan cared not for any physical torture but kept his mind unsullied in the fragrance of the Lord's Love.
>
> Like a rainbird, thirsting only for a drop of rain and no other water, Guru Arjan abandoned all worldly opportunities offered to him and desired but an abiding repose in the Love and Will of God. So deeply was he absorbed in the undisturbed and unbroken vision of the Lord, that his enlightened and elevated spirit conquered all sorrow and pain and his soul rested peacefully in the eternal embrace of God's love. I am a sacrifice unto Guru Arjan, the Perfect One."

2

Foundation of Darbar Sahib

It was on the 1st of Magh, Sambat 1645 (A.D. 1589), the Guru laid the first brick of the masonry foundation of the Har Mandar, or the Darbar Sahib, now known to Europeans as the Golden Temple. A mason afterwards accidentally displaced the brick, whereupon the Guru prophesied that the foundation should again have to be laid. His words were subsequently fulfilled. Ahmad Shah Abdali, in Sambat 1819, destroyed the temple and desecrated the tank. Two years afterwards the great army of the Khalsa recovered possession of the temple, relaid its masonry foundation, and reconstructed it.

The Guru had given orders that only kiln-dried bricks should be employed. Some masands who had charge of the bricks, resolved to cheat the Guru and scamp the work. They smeared sun-dried bricks with plaster and laid them. The Guru heard of their dishonesty and ordered them to desist. They disobeyed his orders three times. He then dismissed them, and said that, when he became tenth Guru, he would visit them with condign punishment.

When the Sikhs in large numbers contributed their assistance, and the tank and temple were approaching completion, the Guru felt that God Himself had assisted in the work, and in joy and gratitude composed the following:

God Himself came, and stood up to do the work of the saints.

Into the beautiful land and the beautiful tank He poured nectareous water.

He poured nectareous water, completed the work, and all our desires are fulfilled.

There are rejoicings in the world, and all anxiety is at an end.

The Veds and the Purans sing the praises of Him who is fixed and imperishable.

God hath been mindful of His usual function; Nanak hath meditated on His name.

The Creator gave me the nine treasures, wealth, and supernatural power; I have not been in want of anything.

I have obtained happiness eating, spending, and living comfortably; God's gifts ever increase:

His gifts increase, are never exhausted, and I have found the Searcher of hearts.

Millions of obstacles have been removed and trouble hath not approached me.

Peace, composure, and happiness in abundance are mine, and all my craving is satisfied.

Nanak singeth the praises of the Lord; wonderful is His praise.

He did it whose work it was; what is wretched man?

The saints are adorned by singing God's praises, and ever wishing Him victory.

Pleasure is produced by singing God's praises and forming an alliance with His saints.

How shall his praises be recounted who exerted himself in the *construction* of the tank?

Bathing in this tank is equal to bathing in the sixty-eight places of pilgrimage, to the bestowal of alms, and the performance of great purifications.

The purification of sinners is the function of the Lord; His word is Nanak's support.

Treasury of excellences, my God, Creator, what praises of Thine may I utter?

The prayer of the saint is —'O Lord, grant us the great elixir of Thy name.

Give us the Name; grant us this boon, forget us not for a moment.'

O tongue, repeat God's praises; let us ever sing them night and day.

The mind and body of him who loveth the Name shall be filled with ambrosial essence.

Nanak representeth, may desires have been fulfilled. I live by a sight to Thee.

The following also was composed on the same occasion:

The Creator stood in the midst *of the work,*
And not a hair *of any man's head* was touched.
The Guru will render ablution herein very profitable,
And by repeating Go's name sins shall depart.
O saints, Ram Das's tank is excellent:
He who batheth in it shall save his family; his own soul too shall be saved.
He who here below singeth a song of rejoicing *over this work,*
Shall obtain the fruit his heart desireth.
He who while meditating on his God
Cometh to bathe here shall be made safe and whole.
He who batheth in the saints' tank
Shall obtain final salvation.
Meditating on God's name,
He shall not die or suffer transmigration.
He to whom God is merciful
Knoweth divine knowledge.

His cares and anxieties shall depart
Who seeketh the protection of Baba Nanak and God.

The Guru thus described the advantages of the tank:

By bathing in the tank of Ram Das
All the sins that man committeth shall be done away,
And he shall become pure by his ablutions.
The perfect Guru hath given us this boon.
When we meditate on the Guru's instruction,
God bestoweth all comfort and happiness,
And causeth the whole cargo to cross over safely.
In the association of the saints uncleanness departeth,
And the supreme Being abideth with us.
Nanak by meditating on the Name
Hath found God the primal Being.

When the tank and temple were completed there were great rejoicings. The enormous exertions and personal sacrifices made by Bhais Budha, Bhagtu, and Bahilo are specially mentioned. One day as they were all bathing, Guru Arjan shed tears on seeing the state of their bodies as the result of their labours. The Guru said with mournful voice, that, as the tank had been constructed by such devout and sincere Sikhs, all sins should be removed and all desires fulfilled by bathing in it and duly worshipping God.

He who batheth herein, having meditated on his God,
Shall be completely restored to health.
He who batheth in the tank of the saints
Shall obtain salvation.
He who meditateth on God's name
Shall not die or suffer transmigration.
He to whom God is merciful
Is thoroughly acquainted with divine knowledge.
Guru Nanak hath entered God's sanctuary;
He hath removed all my cares and anxieties.

The following was composed by the Guru on the same occasion:

God Himself hath given the support of His lotus feet.
He who entereth God's asylum shall ever be renowned.
God is the Preserver, unequalled; holy is His service.
The divine Guru hath made Ramdaspur God's empire.
Ever and ever meditate on God, and no obstacle shall thwart you.

Nanak, by praising the Name the fear of enemies fleeth away.

The Guru wrote the following on the completion of the Har Mandar.

By repeating God's name I have made God's temple: ye saints and worshippers, sing God's praises.

Remember, remember the Lord your God, and ye shall be released from all your sins.

By singing God's praises the supreme position is obtained; His word is the best.

The savour of divine knowledge is very sweet when the tale of the Ineffable is told.

Good the juncture, true the time and moment when I had the immovable foundation laid.

O slave Nanak, when God was merciful everything was completed.

The instruments of joy continually play; the supreme being hath taken His abode in my heart.

The performance of the work of the True One under the Guru's instruction is best of all; by it false doubts and fears are dispelled.

The Guru hath spoken the divine Word; on continually hearing it the mind and body are refreshed.

He whom God hath made His own, hath obtained all happiness;

In his house are the nine treasures, his garners are filled with God's name which he loveth.

Nanak, the servant who is fully fortunate shall never forget God.

When God, the Lord of the umbrella, affordeth shelter, all trouble departeth;

The abode of sorrow and sin hath fallen and the work hath succeeded.

When the Lord God ordered it, misfortune was averted, and true religion and charity flourished.

Ever meditate on this God whether sleeping, sitting, or standing.

The Treasure of excellences, the Sea of happiness, the Lord is in sea and land, in the nether and upper regions.

O slave Nanak, there is no shelter except in God.

My house hath been constructed; my garden and tank have been constructed; may God enter therein!

My heart hath become glad; my friends and associates rejoice, and sing songs of praise and gladness to the Lord.

They have sung the true God's praises, meditated on Him, and obtained all their desires.

They who are attached to the Guru's feet are ever awake; in their hearts resound God's praises.

When the Lord who dwelleth in happiness casteth a look of favour, this world and the next are arranged.

Nanak representeth—ever repeat His name who supporteth soul and body.

The Emperor Akbar's new prime minister, Raja Birbal, a learned and accomplished man, was on religious grounds hostile to the Guru and jealous of his daily increasing influence and popularity. The minister was a great favourite of the Emperor, who desired to have him always by his side. He is said to have been capable by the force of his intellect of telling the Emperor his secrets at any time. His energy blazed for a while, but it was only the expiring flicker of the lamp. On account of his hostility to the Guru evil days came upon him. On the failure of Zain Khan Kokah in his expedition against the Yusufzais, Birbal was ordered to proceed to him with reinforcements. Before his departure he received a written permission from the Emperor to levy a tax of a rupee on the house of every Khatri on the way. He crossed the Bias and sent his agents to collect the tax in Amritsar. The Khatris there refused payment and complained to the Guru. He represented to the Prime Minister's agents: 'The tax is on Khatris. We are Sikhs and look for exemption. Up to the present the government hath never imposed forced labour or taxes on the Guru's house. My kitchen is kept open by the offerings of Sikhs and saints. No one is refused access to it. Take as much corn and food as you require, but I have no money to give you. I live on confidence in God.'

The agents repeated this speech to the Prime Minister, who became furious on hearing it. He said: 'I am a commander of many men; how dareth the Guru disobey me? Moreover I bear the Emperor's order. Even if it be the Guru's house, it is for Sikhs and not for me to reverence it.' Upon this Birbal sent some soldiers to the Guru with the following message: 'Thou art a Khatri, a subject, and in every way subordinate to the state. If thou come to meet me, it will be well; otherwise I will sack the whole of thy city.' The soldiers went, but were dumb-founded in the presence of the Guru. Divining their object he thus addressed them: 'My friends, I care not for any one, nor do I fear any one. Let Raja Birbal come and do what he pleaseth. The Creator will protect me.' The soldiers, fearing the Guru's words and also their master's wrath, went and falsely told him that the Guru would come on the morrow. Raja Birbal said: 'What mattereth it is he be a saint or an object of reverence, or even very old, if he have not fear of me? Well, if he come not tomorrow, I will sack Amritsar. That night the Raja never slept through perturbation of mind.

Meanwhile another order arrived from the Emperor telling the Raja to make haste and proceed with his troops by forced marches to unite with Zain Khan against the Yusufzais. The Raja was much disappointed on receiving this peremptory command, as it left him no time to wreak his vengeance on the Guru. He ordered his staff to remind him of the Guru on his return, and said that if he did not then get a rupee from each house in Amritsar, he would raze the city to its foundations. As the sacrificial fire flames up when clarified butter is thrown on it, so did the Raja's spirit burn at the recollection of the Guru's language. When the Sikhs communicated to the Guru the Raja's wrathful words he merely said, 'If the Raja return he will give us trouble.' Zain Khan the Commander-in-Chief and Raja Birbal held divided councils. They were attacked and defeated by the Yusufzais. Zain Khan escaped with difficulty, but Birbal was slain.

Prithi Chand in alliance with Sulahi Khan found ample opportunities of annoying the Guru. Wazir Khan, the Emperor's assistant Prime Minister, interposed on the Guru's behalf and prevailed on Sulahi Khan to bring the contending brothers to a compromise. The reason why Wazir Khan espoused the Guru's cause is said to have been the following: Once as he was lying ill in his house in Lahore, suffering from dropsy, a Sikh passed by singing the Guru's Sukhmani. As Wazir Khan listened his pain decreased. When the Sikh had gone beyond hearing, the pain appeared again. When he returned by the same route singing the same strain, Wazir Khan's pain was again allayed. He called the Sikh and requested him to continue to sing the Sukhmani for him. He then distributed sacred food in the Guru's name, and was soon restored to perfect health. When he found an opportunity he visited the Guru, told him the whole circumstance, and became a devout follower of his. Wazir Khan until his death retained Sikhs in his service to sing the Guru's hymns for him every morning before day-break, a time which the Sikhs call the ambrosial hour. When Wazir Khan solicited the Guru to give him instruction the Guru addressed him the following:

O servant of God the Inscrutable,

Cease to think of worldly occupations.

Become the dust of the feet of poor travellers; thus shall the darwesh be accepted at God's door.

Make truth thy prayer, faith thy prayer-carpet;

Chasten desires and subdue thy feelings.

Make thy body the mosque, thy conscience the Mulla, and the very pure God thy creed.

Make thy shariat the practice of *real* sacred law.

Make thy tariqat the search for God and abandonment of the world;

Make thy marifat, O devotee, the chastening of thy mind; and thy haqikat the meeting of God, by which thou shalt not die again,

Make the restraint of thine organs of action and perception from evil ways.

Thy hearty practice of the precepts of the Quran and sacred books,

Make subjugation of the five thieves thy sidaq, charity thy saburi, and thou shalt be accepted.

Make kindness thy Makka, humility thy fasting,

Implicit obedience to the word of thy priest thy heaven,

The service of God thy huris, thy nur, and thy perfume; and God thy lofty hujra.

He who practiseth truth is a Qazi;

He who chasteneth his heart is a Haji;

He who banisheth Satan is a Mulla, and he who praiseth *God* is a darwesh.

At every time and on every occasion

Remember God, the Creator, in thy heart.

Make the subjection of thy ten organs the rosary by which god is remembered in thy heart;

Good conduct and great restraint *over thyself,* thy circumcision.

Know in thy heart that everything is for the moment.

Sports, banquets, and sodalities are all entanglements.

Kings, rulers, and nobles are perishable; God's gate alone is the stable place.

Let first God's praises, second patience,

Third mildness, fourth almsgiving,

Fifth the five evil passions restrained in one place be thy five most precious times of prayer.

Make the knowledge that God is everywhere thy daily worship;

The abandonment of evil deeds the water-pot in thy hand;

The knowledge that there is but one God thy call to prayer; such a Muazzin shall have an excellent reward.

What is honestly obtained eat thou as thy food;

Wash away thy filth in the river of thy heart.

He who recognizeth his Pir is the man for heaven; Azrail will not keep him in hell.

Make good works thy body, faith thy spouse,

And obedience to God thy pleasures and spectacles.

Purify what is impure, make God's presence thy Hadis; let a complete body be the turban on thy head.

Let a Musalman be soft-hearted,

And wash away the filth of his heart.

Let not the pleasures of the world approach him; and let him be pure as flowers, silk, clarified butter, or deer-skin.

He is the object of the kindness of the Kind One,

Who is a man, the manliest of men:

He is a Shaikh, a chief of Shaikhs, and a Haji; the man on whom God's look of favour falleth is His slave.

Power belongeth to the Omnipotent, kindness to the Kind One;

The attributes and love of the Merciful are unfathomable.

Understand God's order which is true, O Nanak, and thou shalt be released from thy prison.

When the buildings around the Guru's tank had increased, the Guru ordered his Sikhs and worshippers to take up their abode in them. Thus did the city of Amritsar gradually extend. A Sikh called Bhai Salo, who appears to have possessed much local influence, materially assisted the Guru in the accomplishment of his design. After a little time, however, the Sikhs finding there was no worldly advantage to them in living in Amritsar presented a humble address to the Guru: 'True king, there is here no trade or commerce of any sort, by which we may gain our livelihood and support our families. There are very few inhabitants, and consequently as yet no buying or selling.' The Guru in reply told them not to despair, that Amritsar, should yet become a great city and possess a large population. He counselled them to depend on prayer and divine worship for their prosperity. They were to rise early, bathe and go to the temple to hear expositions of the Guru's hymns. After that they were to attend to their worldly affairs till evening, when their worship should begin anew by the repetition of the Rahiras and Sohila.

Notwithstanding the compromise that had been effected, the Guru's quarrelsome brother Prithia continued to give him every form of annoyance. Consequently the Guru decided to leave Amritsar and make a tour in the Manjha, or country between the Ravi and Bias. He first visited Khadur and Goindwal, and then proceeded to the village of Sarhali, where he sought to obtain land whereon to build himself a dwelling.

A Sikh of the village of Bhaini invited the Guru to visit him, and the Guru knowing his devotion consented. When he arrived in the village the day was far advanced. The Sikh's wife saw that the Guru was hungry, but at the same time it would take too long to cook vegetables for his dinner. She therefore prepared a dish of broken bread mixed with butter and sugar, and laid it before him. Having satisfied himself he inquired the name of the village. She said, 'Bhaini.' The Guru replied, 'The name of this village shall be Cholha, that is, tit-bit, or dainty dish.' Upon this he composed the following:

I am a sacrifice to my Guru who implanted God's name in my heart;

Who pointed out to me the straight road when I was in a great wilderness and darkness.

God is my life;

He feeleth anxiety for me regarding everything in this world and the next.

By remembering Him I obtain all treasure, respect, greatness and perfect honour.

By repeating His name, the dust of whose feet all saints desire, millions of sins are erased.

Let him who desireth all desirable things worship the one supreme Treasure.

The Lord is the supreme Being, limitless; by remembering Him man crosseth over *the world*.

By abiding in the association of the saints man obtaineth comfort, peace, and great happiness, and his honour is preserved.

To amass God's wealth and make God's name my food—Nanak hath made these things his cholha (dainties).

On the same occasion the Guru composed the following :

God's name is priceless;

It is naturally comfortable.

God abideth with me and helpeth me; He forsaketh me not; He is unfathomable and unrivalled.

He is my beloved brother, my father, my mother, and the shelter of the saints.

The Invisible is seen when He is obtained from the Guru, who, O Nanak, is God's cholha (dainty).

The name Bhaini was duly changed into Cholha in the government records of the period.

A Jat inhabitant of the village of Cholha represented to Guru Arjan that the inhabitants of the village of Buh would not allow his cattle to graze on their lands, though he had an ancient right of pasturage. The Guru replied, *'Buh juh howega,,'* that is, 'Buh shall become sterile,' a prediction which was subsequently fulfilled.

Guru Arjan on this tour visited a village called Khanpur, between Goindwal and the present Tarn Taran. He was accompanied by five Sikhs, including Bidhi Chand and Gur Das, men famous in different ways, of whom we shall hereafter have much to say. He remained the whole day engaged in his devotions. In the evening it rained heavily and wintry winds were blowing. Bidhi Chand said to the Guru. 'The Guru objected, and said it would be better to remain where they were than associate with the evil people who dwelt there. Bidhi Chand, however, prevailed on him to let him go into the village and endeavour to secure shelter, as the night was piercingly cold. Bidhi Chand begged the people to let his party have even one room in which they could all sleep together. The villagers only laughed at him, and called the Guru and his Sikhs hypocrites. Bidhi Chand went and duly informed the Guru of the character of his reception. The Guru replied: 'Pay no heed, I told thee they were foul-tongued people. Whoever hath devotion in his heart will come to us of his own accord, and give us accommodation for the night.'

As Guru Arjan had anticipated, Hema, a devout Sikh of the village, arrived and said, 'O true Guru, I have a tattered hut made out of grass and twigs which is at thy service. It will be hallowed by receiving thee.' Hema, who had been made a Sikh by Guru Ram Das, lived by grinding corn for the villagers. His leisure time he employed in repeating the Guru's hymns. Though he was extremely poor, and possessed only a coarse blanket to wear, his hut was ever open to the stranger. The Guru seeing his love and devotion gladly accepted his hospitality. He then cooked and supplied his distinguished guest with the best food in his possession. Before retiring he took off his sole blanket, and put it under the Guru as bedding, so that he might enjoy sweet repose. The Guru, seeing his devotion, composed the following:

Very beautiful is that hut in which God's praises are sung,

While the mansion in which God is forgotten is of no avail.

There is a pleasure even in poverty when in the company of the saints God is remembered.

May that grandeur which is bound up with mammon perish!

Even when turning a handmill or wearing a coarse blanket, the heart may be happy and contented.

That empire is of no avail which conferreth not satisfaction.

They who wander even naked in the love of the one God obtain honour.

While vain are silks and satins, attachment to which maketh man covetous.

Everything is in Thy power, O God; Thou actest and causest to act.

May Nanak obtain the gift of remembering Thee at every breath he draweth!

On the same occasion the Guru composed the following:

The place where the name of the beloved God is repeated,

Is like a mansion of gold;

The city in which the name of God is not repeated is like a wilderness.

He who eating dry bread remembereth God,

Shall behold Him whether at home or abroad.

Know that he who through pampering his belly committeth bad deeds is planting for himself a garden of poison.

The spiritually ignorant man who loveth not the saints,

And committeth sins in company with the infidel,

Loseth his human body so difficult of attainment, and uprooteth himself.

I have entered Thine asylum, O compassionate to the poor.

O ocean of comfort, my great God,

Nanak singeth Thy praises, mercifully preserve his honour.

The Guru remained for sometime in Khanpur. During his stay Hema obtained his desire, and went to his heavenly abode. After the Guru's departure, the Emperor's viceroy, who had some reason to be dissatisfied with the inhabitants of Khanpur, sent an army against it, razed it to the ground, and massacred its chief inhabitants. The survivors had reason to reflect on the words of Kabir:

> Kabir, the house in which God and His saints are not served,
> Is like a cremation-ground and ghosts dwell therein.

The Guru thence proceeded to the village of Khara, where he was pleased with the prospect around him—the flowering woods and glades, the limpid water, and the fresh and exhilarating atmosphere. On entering the village he received a friendly reception from the headmen. They afterwards assisted him in obtaining land from the villagers on which he laid the foundation of what is now the famous Sikh city of Tarn Taran, and proceeded to construct a tank for the devotional ablutions of his Sikhs. The year in which these events occurred is stated to be A.D.

1590. The name Tarn Taran means a raft to take men across the world's ocean. The Guru, at great expense, built lime-kilns and caused bricks to be baked. When these were seen by Nur-ul-Din, the local Muhammadan governor, they were, according to the tyrannical custom of the age, seized by him for the construction of a seraglio designed by the Emperor for the public use. The Sikhs on seeing this suggested to the Guru to write to the Emperor to allow the tank to be finished and to inspire fear in Nur-ul-Din. The Guru, who was the essence of humility, refused to take notice of the outrage. He said that God had not yet ordered the tank to be made, wherefore they were to stop its construction altogether. 'Mercy,' continued the Guru, 'is the basis of religious worship; wherefore we should have mercy on every one. All the acts of him who hath not mercy in his heart are vain.'

In the Sambat year 1832 (A.D. 1775) Sardar Khushal Singh of Faizullapur and Sardar Jassa Singh of Ramgarh destroyed Nur-ul-Din's edifice, and employed the bricks, of which Nur-ul-Din had robbed the Guru, in the construction of the tank.

> (The tank at Tarn Taran is larger than that at the Golden Temple at Amritsar. At one corner is a tall minaret built by Ranjit Singh. He intended to build three others, but died before he could accomplish his project. The money collected for the construction mysteriously disappeared from its custodians.
>
> The approach to the temple has lately been opened by the demolition of some houses, to whose proprietors large sums of money have been paid by willing subscribers as compensation).

The Guru then went into the Jalandhar district, where he purchased land to build another city, Kartarpur, or the city of the Creator, which has since risen to considerable spiritual and temporal eminence. It lies in what is called the Jalandhar Doab between the Bias and Satluj rivers.

The Guru with his own hands cut the first sod for the construction of the city and its necessarily accompanying well to supply water to the inhabitants. The well he called Gangsar, or the Ganges tank, for the following reason: A man called Baisakhi, who used every year to visit the Ganges, once called upon the Guru on his way. The Guru asked him not to go, but bathe in his well worship God, repeat the true Name, and he should worship God, repeat the true Name, and he should thus obtain all the advantages of bathing in the Ganges. Baisakhi respectfully represented that he had made a vow to go to the Ganges, and must accordingly proceed thither. The Guru, on seeing his determination, allowed him to continue his journey. When Baisakhi on the point of returning sought to fill a vessel with Ganges water, it slipped from his hand and was taken away by the current. He did all in his power to recover it, but in vain. When he returned to the Guru, and related the untoward incident, it is said that the Guru to his astonishment produced in his presence from the new well the very vessel that had fallen from his hands at the Ganges. Baisakhi was then convinced that his pilgrimage to Hardwar had been in vain. On this account the well at Kartarpur was called the Gangsar.

The guru went to the country of Nakka at the invitation oi Bhai Bhuria, Chaudhri Chuhar Mal, and other pious Sikhs. He visited Khemkaran, Chunian, and other villages, where he preached with great success. He then went to Jambar, where he remained for sometime, during which he converted Kidara, Kheda, Samdu, Mukanda, Tulsa, Lalu and others.

The Guru then proceeded to Lahore at the request of the Sikhs who raised there. He rested in the Dabbi Bazar on the side of the present 'Guru's Bawali,' and planned its construction. People of all classes hearing of his fame flocked to see him, receive his instruction, and make provision for their future salvation. Thither came the Jogi Sambhunath and the Hindu saints Kahna and Chhajju; the Moslem saints Shah Husain, Shah Sulaiman, Shah Inayat Qadari, Shaikh Wali Shah, and others, all humbling themselves before the Guru and beseeching soul-saving religious instruction. The Guru fixing his thoughts on God uttered the following hymn:

O wise men, think of the Lord in year hearts.

The true King, the Releaser from bondage, dwelleth in the heart by the mind's affection.

Nothing is equal in value to the sight of God.

Thou art the pure Cherisher; Thou Thyself art the Lord great and incomparable.

Give me Thy hand, O Brave One, Thou art the only one to *assist* me.

O Creator, by Thy power didst Thou create the world; Thou art Nanak's prop.

This hymn, when heard by the Viceroy of Lahore, produced a great impression on his mind. It is said that he reformed his life, and devoted himself to God's service. He invited the Guru to ask him a favour. The Guru did so, and the result was the excavation of the Bawali at the Viceroy's expense.

3

The Challenge

When the priest and the barber returned to Dehli then told Chandu everything they had heard and seen in Amritsar—the Guru's refusal and the reason thereof, the abuse of Chandu uttered by the Sikh in Darbar, the betrothal of Har Gobind and the actual appointment of a time for his marriage. Chandu was naturally very much incensed, but he wrote the Guru a letter, in which as a matter of policy he concealed his resentment. He began by magnifying the Guru and demeaning himself, and then continued: 'It is certainly true that I said thou art of inferior caste to me. This expression thoughtlessly escaped my mouth, and some one hath written and exaggerated it, and made thee displeased with me. Thou art now the most worshipful Guru in the world, and it is right for thee to consider everything. It is not proper for thee to fall out with me for what lunatics and base people tell thee. If I interest myself for thee with the Emperor, he too will be at thy service. I can give a large dowry to my daughter. Retain for thy son the other girls with whom thou hast formed alliances, and accept mine also. Great people contract many marriages. If thou tell me I used overbearing language, I may or may not have done so; but it was in my own private house and not meant for others to hear. Your people in public darbar have called me a dog. Well, let bygones be bygones, and I will have many favours conferred on thee by the Emperor. Thou art already on bad terms with thy brother Prithi Chand. Thou oughtest too make me an ally. If thou fall out with me too, thou shalt nowhere find an abiding-place. There are now sparks flying about. If they increase there will be a blazing fire which it will be difficult to extinguish. Thou shalt not again have this opportunity. And if thou hast called me a dog I may become mad, and do thee harm contrary to my saner judgement.

Chandu dispatched this letter by the hands of the Brahman. The Guru having read it said: 'It is pride that ruineth men. Pride of wealth is the basis of all ills. Man must suffer for his acts. Now know that Chandu must not form an alliance with us. They whom the Creator joineth are united; but they whom man joineth are not. It is the Guru's rule to comply with the wishes of his Sikhs. Their words are immutable. What they once reject, it is not proper again to accept. Even were I to consent to Chandu's alliance, no good could result. He tempteth me with gain, but who would forfeit his soul therefor? As for his threats, I have no fear of them. God alone is the guardian of all.' The priest returned with this message without being able to prevail on the Guru to alter his determination.

The Guru then made all preparations, and invited guests to his son's wedding with Narain Das's daughter. He even invited his own brother Prithi Chand, but the invitation was refused. The marriage was duly celebrated with all suitable ceremony and rejoicing.

The women of Narain Das's household sang the following composition of the bridegroom's father on the occasion of the marriage:

It is a time of rejoicing, I sing my Lord;

I have heard of the imperishable Bridegroom, and joy hath arisen in my heart.

My mind longeth *to know* when I shall be fortunate enough to meet the perfect Lord.

Grant me, O my friend *Guru*, understanding to *know* when I shall meet God and be absorbed in Him.

Day and night I stand and wait *to find* by what way I may obtain the Lord.

Nanak prayeth, have mercy and attach me to the hem of Thy garment.

Prithia addressed himself to the qazis and pandits who bore enmity too the Guru on account of his compilation of the Granth, and induced them to complain to the Emperor Akbar that Guru Arjan had compiled a book in which the Muhammadan priests, prophets, and leaders, and the Hindu incarnations and gods, were spoken of with contempt. Akbar was at that time touring in the Punjab and the complaint of the qazis and the pandits was placed before him by Chandu on his arrival in Gurdaspur. Chandu supported the complaint by saying that he knew the charges were based on facts. Upon this the Emperor ordered that Guru Arjan and his Granth should be produced before him. The Guru did not go himself, but sent Bhai Budha and Bhai Gur Das to read to him from it. The first hymn which caught the Emperor's eye was the following of Guru Arjan's own composition in the Persian language:

From earth and light God made the world:

The sky, earth, trees and water are God's creation.

O man, whatever the eye can behold is perishable.

The world is an eater of carrion, neglectful *of God* and greedy of *mammon*.

Like an ogre or a beast it killeth and eateth forbidden food.

Restrain thy heart, or the Omnipotent will take and punish thee in hell.

When Azrail shall seize thee, of what avail

Shall patrons, brothers, courts, possessions and mansions be?

The pure God knoweth thy condition.

Slave Nanak, utter thy prayer to the holy man *to guide thee*.

The Emperor on hearing this said it was a very proper hymn. The qazis and pandits represented that the hymn was specially selected for the Emperor's hearing, and begged him to procure some one else to read the Granth to him, none among them being acquainted with the Gurumukhi characters in which the sacred volume is written. The Emperor turned over its pages himself, and pointing to a particular spot asked Gur Das to read from there. On this, the hymn already given, beginning 'O servant of God the Inscrutable,' was read to His Majesty.

The Emperor on hearing this was much pleased. Chandu, however, was not to be thwarted. He said that Gur Das had repeated this from memory. The Emperor must have the Granth read to him by some one else who knew Gurumukhi. Chandu found a man called Sahib Diyal, who possessed the necessary knowledge. Chandu turned over the leaves of the Granth and told him to read the hymn he pointed out. The hymn was the following:

Thou fastenest a stone to thy neck,
And seest not God who dwelleth in the heart.
O infidel, thou wanderest astray in error:
Thou churnest water and shalt die in agony.
The stone which thou callest God
Shall take thee with it and drown thee.
O sinner, untrue to thy salt,
It is not a boat of stone which will ferry thee over.
On meeting the Guru, Nanak recognizeth the Lord.

The Arranger is contained in the water, the dry land the nether regions, and the firmament.

When the Emperor heard this, he was still more pleased with the teaching of the Granth, and displeased with the Guru's slanderers and enemies. He then gave his decision: 'Excepting love and devotion to God I so far find neither praise nor blame of any one in this Granth. It is a volume worthy of reverence.' He then made an offering to it of fifty-one gold muhars, and gave Bhai Budha and Bhai Gur Das dresses of honour for themselves and a third for Guru Arjan. He told them to give his respectful salutations to the Guru, and promised to go to visit him when he was returning from Lahore whither he was then proceeding.

When Chandu and his party heard the Emperor's decision and his message to the Guru, their faces became pale and they hung down their heads through shame. All good people cursed Chandu, and his evil reputation spread from house to house. The Emperor, true to his word, visited the Guru on his return journey to Dehli, and was charmed with his saintly bearing. He was also so pleased with the imposing and beautiful temple which the Guru had constructed, and the delightful melodies to which the hymns of the Gurus had been set, that words failed him to express his gratification. He called himself the Guru's slave and asked for instruction to render him happy and secure peace for his soul. The Guru then repeated for him the following hymn:

One man invoketh Ram, another Khuda;
One man worshippeth Gosain, another Allah;
Some speak of the Cause of causes, *others of* the Benevolent.
Some talk of the Extender of mercy, *others of* the Merciful.
Some bathe at the Hindu sacred places, others visit Makka.
Some perform the Hindu worship, others bow their heads *in the Muhammadan fashion*.
Some read the Veds, others the Musalman books.
Some wear white, others blue.
Some call themselves Hindus, others Musalmans.
Some aspire to the heaven of the Hindus, others to the heaven of the Muhammadans;
But he who recognizeth God's will, saith Nanak,
Knoweth the secret of the Lord God.

The Emperor partook of the Guru's hospitality, and prayed to be allowed to make a contribution to his large expenditure, so that thereby he might secure spiritual and temporal welfare and happiness. The Guru replied, 'The welfare and happiness of monarchs depend on cherishing their subjects and doing justice. The monarch whose subjects are happy shall himself be happy in this life, and in the next obtain praise, glory and honour.'

The Emperor remitted the revenues of the Punjab for that year in compliment to the Guru, who represented that there was a severe famine in the land and the cultivators required His Majesty's consideration. The Guru's fame and influence largely increased owing to the respect the Emperor had shown him. This, in the words of the chronicler, was the cause of such agony to Prithia as would last till it had taken his life with it.

Badaoni states that on another occasion, namely, the thirteenth of the month of Azur (Jamadi ul sani), Akbar, with a gorgeous military retinue, crossed the Bias and went to Goindwal to visit Guru Arjan, whose teaching and character he appreciated. Badaoni also writes that people reverenced the successive Gurus as spiritual leaders, and solicited their benedictions.

Unfortunately for the Guru the tolerant Emperor Akbar died soon after, and was succeeded by his son Jahangir. Jahangir's son Khusro, nominated to the throne by Akbar in supersession of Jahangir, claimed the Punjab and Afghanistan, which his father was unwilling to concede him. Jahangir accordingly desired to obtain possession of Khusro's person, but Khusro escaped from Agra pursued by the Imperial army, and directed his steps towards Afghanistan. On the way he visited the Guru at Tarn-Taran and begged him to grant him pecuniary assistance. The Guru said he had money for the poor, but not for princes. Khusro replied with great humility that he himself was now very poor, needy, and unfriended, and had not even travelling expenses.

Guru Arjan, seeing the Prince's evil plight and humility, took compassion on him. He, moreover, felt friendly to the Prince, who had visited him a few times previously with the Emperor Akbar; and he also felt a debt of gratitude to the Prince's grandfather, the late monarch, so he gave him five thousand rupees to defray his expenses to Kabul. Khusro, however, was seized by the imperial troops as he was crossing the Jhilam and taken in chains to his father.

Prithia managed to retain Sulahi Khan's assistance and co-operation to ruin the Guru. Sulahi, on the pretext of having to collect revenue in the Punjab, obtained leave from the Emperor to proceed thither. On his way he visited Prithia in his village of Kotha. Under the pretence of hunting they spent their time concocting plans for the Guru's destruction.

The Guru, on hearing of the further conspiracies of his enemies, composed to following:

Death laugheth over man's head, but, brute that he is, he knoweth it not.

Involved in quarrels, pleasures, and pride, he thinketh not of death.

Serve thy true Guru; why wander, O luckless one?

On beholding the brilliant safflower, why make the mistake of attaching thyself to it?

Constantly sinning thou hast accumulated wealth to use it thyself;

But thou shalt depart naked, and thy dust shall be blended with dust.

They for whom thou didst take trouble are at variance and enmity with thee.

At the last hour they will flee from thee; why burnest thou with wrath?

He on whose forehead such destiny hath been written, becometh the dust of the holy man's feet.

Saith Nanak, *by seeking* the protection of the true Guru man is released from his bonds.

One day Prithia took Sulahi to admire some brickkilns he had made. On arriving, Sulahi's horse started at the accidental flight of a bird from under his feet, and ran with his rider straight into a kiln in full blast. In a few minutes horse and rider became a mass of cinders. On hearing of this event the Guru composed the following:

If any one *flout the* poor by stroking his beard at them,
The supreme God will burn him in the fire.
The creator who protecteth His servant
Hath administered perfect justice.
Before and through the ages His glory was manifest—
The calumniator died in great agony.
None saveth him who is accursed of God:
In this world and the next evil shall be his reputation.

God embraceth and protecteth His servant:

Nanak, meditate on God's name, and seek His shelter.

The Guru composed the following also on the same subject:

God preserved me from Sulahi.

Sulahi by no means succeeded; Sulahi died unclean.

God drew forth His axe and smote off his head, and in a moment he became ashes.

He was consumed ever meditating evil; He who created him thrust him *into the fire.*

Son, friend, wife, nothing remaineth for him now; his brethren and relations have all abandoned him.

Saith Nanak, I am a sacrifice to that God who fulfilled the words of His servant.

The following was uttered by the Guru on the same occasion:

The slanderer by the Guru's favour hath been turned away. God the supreme Being was merciful: He killed him with unerring arrow.

Death and death's noose cannot affect me since I have established the sect of the True One.

The jewel of God's name I have earned as wealth, which will never decrease by eating and spending.

In one moment the slanderer became ashes and obtained his deserts.

Nanak foretold what was hidden; the whole world saw the truth of his prophecy.

Prithi Chand was naturally most displeased at the death of his faithful ally in evil. In the meantime Chandu was considering how he could procure the marriage of his daughter with Har Gobind or avenge himself on the Guru. He accordingly wrote to Prithia to request him to use all his influence to bring about the marriage, and in the event of his failure threatened to confiscate the fief he had recently obtained from the Emperor. Prithia, however, required no threats; he was only too willing to assist Chandu in his nefarious designs. He wrote in reply that Arjan, who had deprived him of his rights, was already his enemy; and he would be only too happy to assist in meting him adequate punishment. He begged Chandu to use his influence with the Emperor to bring the Guru to justice. On receiving this letter Chandu summoned Prithia to Dehli. There they both concocted a plan to induce the Emperor by some means to visit the Punjab, where they would have an opportunity of entering into some conspiracy against the Guru. Chandu informed the Emperor of the abundance of game in the Lahore district, and also explained that Lahore would be a convenient place to rest on the Emperor's way to Kashmir, where he ought to spend the summer on account of the beauty of its scenery and the salubrity of its climate. Upon this Prithia returned home.

Chandu's scheme proved successful. In a short time the Emperor proceeded to the Punjab. On reaching the Bias he encamped on its banks and went a—hunting. Chandu, in conversation with him, represented that there were several thieves in the country who, during the night, had stolen some of the Emperor's property. The Emperor inquired how thieves could exist in his empire. Chandu replied that the Emperor had a rival in the Panjab, namely Guru Arjan, who entertained thieves and exercised independent authority. Upon this the Emperor issued an order to the Guru through Sulabi Khan, nephew of the late Sulahi Khan, to abstain from such practices. The Guru's business, he said, was to restrain others from evil, and it behoved him not to do evil himself. Chandu wrote on his own account to Sulabi Khan to endeavour to induce the Guru to consent to the marriage alliance, and also to grant a more liberal distribution of property and offerings to Prithia than had been formerly agreed on. Sulabi Khan went to Amritsar to endeavour to carry out these measures.

When the Sikhs heard of Sulabi Khan's intention they proposed that they should be allowed to kill him, but they were dissuaded by the Guru. He was already sufficiently armed and protected against his enemies. On that occasion he composed the following:

Humility is my mace,
And being the dust of the dust of all men's feet my two-edged sword:
These no evil doer can withstand.
The perfect Guru hath arranged this matter.

On Sulabi's journey to Amritsar his party fell in with a Saiyid who was accompanied by several Pathans. The Saiyid represented to him that these Pathans had been in his uncle Sulahi Khan's service, and that a year's salary was due to them. Sulabi put them off with excuses, whereupon an affray arose. Sulabi's escort, reverencing the Saiyid as a descendant of the Prophet, did not strenuously defend their master, and he was killed. When Chandu heard of Sulabi Khan's death he represented to the Emperor that it had been done through the machinations of the Guru. He added that the Guru had perpetrated many other misdeeds. For instance, he had deprived his elder brother Prithia of the Guruship, and had endeavoured to deprive the Hindus and Muhammadans of their religions. Prithia had made complaints in person to the late Emperor, who promised to summon the Guru when he visited the Panjab. When His Majesty on one occasion did visit the Panjab, he had not time to make the necessary inquiry into the charges against Guru Arjan, but now was the time to do so. The Guru only became bolder with delay and impunity. Upon this the Emperor ordered Chandu to send for Prithia, and he accordingly did so. Prithia was overjoyed on receiving the invitation. On the way he for some business of his own visited Tarn Taran, where the Sikhs invited him to bathe. He said that the Guru's tank there was only a common pool, and he would only bathe in his own tank at Hehar. Thither he accordingly proceeded, and after bathing in it and eating a surfeit at dinner, he got cramp in the stomach, and died the same night.

Mihrban, son of Prithia, took advantage of the Guru's gift to Khusro to rouse the ire of the Emperor against the Guru. He informed Chandu of it, and Chandu informed the Emperor, adding that the Guru had blessed Khusro and promised him that he should become Emperor. Chandu also represented to the Emperor that, if he did not have Khusro quickly arrested, the pretender would receive great military assistance from the followers of the Guru. The people of the Panjab, he said, were all highway robbers. The Pandits and the qazis also thought it a favourable opportunity to institute new proceedings against the Guru on the old charge of having compiled a book which blasphemed the worship and rules of the Hindus and the prayers and fastings of the Muhammadans. By such accusations Chandu induced the Emperor to summon Guru Arjan. Chandu's heart was now gratified, for he knew he had at last secured his revenge.

The Guru now felt that his enemies were victorious and that his end was near, but he was confident at the same time that the vials of God's wrath would burst on their heads. Before his departure for Lahore he appointed his son Har Gobind his successor with all ancient ceremony and formality, and gave him injunctions suitable for the occasion. The Guru then addressed his wife Ganga: 'This body abideth not for ever. Wherefore a wise person should not love it. Whatever is born perisheth, and whatever is high falleth sooner or later. This is nature's law. To love the body is a grievous error. All bodies daily grow old and preserve not their original strength. From a child one groweth to be a man, and then cometh old age, which seizeth on the body and causeth it to waste away until it falleth into its final sleep. Live thou when I am gone, mourn not for me and make no effort of thine own to separate thy soul from thy body.' The latter was an injunction not to cremate herself on his death.

The Guru took with him Bhai Bidhi Chand, Bhai Langaha, Bhai Paira, Bhai Jetha and Bhai Pirana. The Emperor Jahangir was at first disposed to treat the Guru with respect, but Chandu reminded him of the Guru's pecuniary assistance to Khusro. The Emperor then addressed him: 'Thou art a saint, great teacher, and holy man; thou lookest on all, rich and poor, alike. It was therefore not proper for thee to give money to my enemy Khusro. The Guru replied: I regard all people, whether Hindu or Musalman, rich or poor, friend or foe, without love or hate; and it is on this account that I gave thy son some money for his journey, and not because he was in opposition to thee. If I had not assisted him in his forlorn condition, and so shown some regard for the kindness of thy father the Emperor Akbar to myself, all men would despise me for my heartlessness and ingratitude, or they would say that I was afraid of thee. This would have been unworthy of a follower of Guru Nanak, the world's Guru.'

The conclusion of this speech was not calculated to soothe the Emperor's feelings. He ordered the Guru to pay a fine of two lakhs of rupees, and also to erase the hymns in his Granth which were opposed to the Hindu and Musalman religions. The Guru replied: 'Whatever money I have is for the poor, the friendless, and the stranger. If thou ask for money thou mayest take what I have; but if thou ask for it by way of fine I shall not give thee even a kauri, for a fine is imposed on wicked worldly persons and not on priests and anchorets. And as to what thou hast said regarding the erasure of hymns in the Granth Sahib, I cannot erase or alter an iota. I am a worshipper of the Immortal God, the Supreme Soul of the world. There is no monarch save Him; and what He revealed to the Gurus, from Guru Nanak to Guru Ram Das, and afterwards to myself, is written in the holy Granth Sahib. The hymns which find a place in it are not disrespectful to any Hindu incarnation or any Muhammadan prophet. It is certainly stated that prophets, priests, and incarnations are the handiwork of the Immortal God, whose limit none can find. My main object is the spread of truth and the destruction of falsehood; and if, in pursuance of this object, this perishable body must depart, I shall account it great good fortune.'

The Emperor made no reply, but rose and left the hall of audience. After this a magistrate informed the Guru that he must pay the fine or be imprisoned in default. When the Sikhs of Lahore heard this decision, they proposed to unite and raise a subscription to discharge the Guru's obligation. The Guru would not agree, and sent them word, that whoever contributed to pay the fine imposed on him should be deemed a pervert, and would for the sake of momentary gratification imperil his future salvation. Men devoted to religion, the Guru said, never paid fines. Fines were for thieves, adulterers, slanderers and robbers. As the Guru would not allow the fine to be paid, he was placed under the surveillance of Chandu. The qazis and Brahmans offered the Guru the alternative of being put to death or of expunging the alleged objectionable passages in the Granth Sahib and inserting the praises of Muhammad and of the Hindu deities.

The Guru replied, 'The Granth Sahib hath been compiled to confer on men happiness and not misery in this world and in the next. It is impossible to write it anew, and make the omissions and alterations you require.' On hearing this the Guru's enemies concluded that he would yield to no ordinary threats, so they put fetters on him, and began to torture him in various ways. They poured burning sand on him, seated him in red-hot caldrons, and bathed him in boiling water. The Guru bore all this torture with equanimity and never uttered a sign or groan. He was given another opportunity to recant and comply with the demands of his enemies. He replied, 'O fools, I shall never fear this treatment of yours. It is all according to God's will; wherefore this torture only affordeth me pleasure.' On this occasion the Guru repeated the following:

The egg of superstition hath burst; the mind is illumined:

The Guru hath cut the fetters off the feet and freed the captive.

My transmigration is at an end.

The heated caldron hath become cold; the Guru hath given the cooling Name.

Since the holy man hath been with me, *Death's myrmidons,* who lay in wait for me, have left me.

I have been released from him who restrained me; what shall the judge do to me now?

The load of my karma is removed; I am freed therefrom.

From the sea I have reached the shore; the Guru hath done me this favour.

True is my place, true my seat, and truth I have made my special object.

Truth is the capital; truth the stock-in-trade which Nanak hath put into his house.

When Chandu threatened to put the Guru to further torture he addressed him as follows:

The earth, the firmament, and the stars *are under the influence* of fear; over their heads is unchanging law.

Wind, water, and fire are under the influence of fear; so, too, is helpless Indar.

There is only the one God without fear, as I have heard.

He who meeting the Guru singeth God's praises, is happy and ever at peace.

Corporeal beings and gods are under the influence of fear; Sidhs and their disciples have died through fear.

The eighty-four lakhs of beings which die and are born, which again and again are yoked to wombs, *are under the influence of fear*.

All beings which Thou, *O God,* hast created *subject to the qualities* of passion, goodness, and darkness are under the influence of fear.

The helpless Lakshmi *who produceth* illusion is under the influence of fear, and greatly so is Dharmraj.

All things are filled with fear—it is only the Creator who is devoid of it.

Saith Nanak, God is the Companion of saints; saints adorn His court, *and are therefore without fear*.

Several Jogis and religious men who had met the Guru and appreciated his sincerity and exalted doctrines, went to condole with him in his afflictions. Mian Mir, the Moslem saint of Lahore, also went and contributed his sympathetic tears. He found the Guru's body all blistered and suppurated, and requested his permission to appeal to the Emperor for his release and the punishment of his torturers. The Guru requested him to cast his eyes towards heaven. On Doing so, it is said, Mian Mir saw angels begging the Guru's permission to destroy the wicked, the proud, and the perverse. Mian Mir on beholding this supernatural vision asked the Guru why, when he possessed superhuman power, he consented to endure suffering at the hands of such vile sinners. The Guru replied, 'I bear all this torture to set an example to the teachers of the True Name, that they may not lose patience or rail at God in affliction. The true test of faith is the hour of misery. Without examples to guide them ordinary persons' minds quail in the midst of suffering. In the second place, if he who possesseth power within him defend not his religion by the open profession thereof, the man who possesseth no such power will when put to the torture abjure his faith. The sin will light on the head of him who hath the power but showeth it not; and God will deem him an enemy of religion. In the third place, the body is naturally subject too woe and weal, but not the spirit. The body is perishable, the soul imperishable. To set aside by the exercise of supernatural power the law of nature which applieth to all things perishable, and thereby to engender pride in the heart, would be supreme folly.' Mian Mir on hearing this departed commending the Guru's fortitude and singing his praises.

Upon this the Guru's enemies again applied themselves to his torture. They kept him for three hours seated in a caldron heated by a blazing fire. The Guru's life was well-nigh extinct, but he would not even submit to Chandu's conditions, namely, to allow his son Har Gobind to marry Chandu's daughter.

The Guru repeated the following also during the period of his torture:

Sir Rag Ashtapadi

When very great troubles befall, and nobody receiveth one;

When enemies pursue, and relations flee away;

When all from whom man *looked for* assistance have fled, and all succour is at an end,

If he then remember God, no hot wind shall strike him.

God is the strength of the strengthless.

He neither cometh nor goeth; He is permanent ever; by the Guru's instruction know Him as the True One.

If man be weak from the pangs of nakedness and hunger,

If he have not a paisa in his purse, and there be none to console him,

If no one gratify his aims and desires, and he be never successful,

Yet, if he remember God, he shall obtain a permanent kingdom.

If any one have excessive anxiety and bodily suffering,

If bound up in household and family, he feel alternate joy and sorrow,

If he wander in every direction, and cannot rest even for a moment,

Yet if he think upon God, his body and soul shall be happy.

Man may be in the power of lust, wrath, and covetousness; he may become a miser through love of greed;

He may have committed the four great sins and *all venial* sins; he may be a demon to destroy;

He may never have listened to *sacred* books, hymns, and poetry;

Yet shall he be saved if he think upon God and repeat His name even for a moment.

Even though man repeat by heart the Shastars, the Simritis, and the four Veds;

Though he be a penitent, a leader of penitents, or a Jogi and have made all pilgrimages;

Though he perform the six duties twice over, though he bathe and perform worship,

Yet if he love not the supreme God, he shall assuredly go to hell.

Man may have empire, dominion, and principality; enjoyments may be scattered *around him;*

He may have delightful and beautiful gardens, and his orders may be such as cannot be disobeyed;

He may have merriment and spectacles of many descriptions, and he may continue devoted to pleasure;

Yet if he think not of the supreme God, he shall be born again as a serpent.

May may be very wealthy; he may be attentive to ceremonial duties; his reputation and conduct may be ostensibly spotless;

He may love his mother, father, children, brothers and friends;

Armies in full panoply and all men may show him honour;

Yet if he think not of the supreme God, he shall be taken and consigned to the abode below.

Man's body may have no disease or blemish; he may have no heart-burning or grief;

He may not think of death, but day and night enjoy himself;

He may have made everything his own and fear no one;

Yet if he think not of the supreme God, he shall fall into the power of Death's myrmidons.

He to whom the supreme God is merciful obtaineth the society of the saints.

The more that *association* increaseth, the greater his love for God.

He is the Lord of both worlds; there is no *resting* place but in Him.

If the true Guru be pleased, Nanak shall obtain the true Name.

A daughter-in-law of Chandu, daughter of a pious Sikh, who had heard of the Guru's torture, considered what she could do to save him whom her father had ever reverenced, and from whom he had ever obtained the object of his desires. She said to herself, 'The Guru hath eaten nothing, and not even drunk water or slept for several days. Accursed is my life in this house that I hear of the Guru's torture, and still see the light of day!' She prepared some sharbat and took it in the dead of night secretly to the Guru's prison. When stopped by the sentry on guard, she drew forth a piece of jewellery and gave it to him. He allowed her to pass with strict injunctions to return quickly. She told the Guru who she was: 'Recognize in me the daughter of a Sikh of thine. I am wife of the sinner's (Chandu's) son, but I ought never to have been married to him. I must have committed some great sin in a previous existence, and this is the result of it. Hence I desire to live no longer. Take this sharbat and also eat something. Look on me as thy slave, and have pity on me.'

The Guru replied, 'Hail to thee who hast so much devotion! Thou hast now but few days to live and thou mayest accompany me. Keep thy secret to thyself. I cannot take food or drink from Chandu's house.' On hearing this, the lady begged him to take her as his companion to the unknown world.

Chandu was all night meditating further torture for the Guru. He said to himself, 'The Guru manifesteth no pain under ordinary torture, therefore I will cause him further suffering.' Notwithstanding all the tortures employed, the Guru would not abate a jot of his determination.

For five days the Guru suffered torture and then asked permission to bathe in the Ravi and take his five Sikh companions with him. Chandu might afterwards order what he thought fit. Chandu was very pleased at the Guru's proposal and said, 'When the guru's body is cool after bathing, he will certainly consent to his son's alliance with my daughter.' He accordingly granted the Guru's request and said, 'Thy life shall be saved, if thou hearken to my words.'

Chandu sent with his prisoner an escort of soldiers armed with swords and matchlocks. He ordered them to keep a close watch on the Guru. They were not to speak to any one on the way lest they should reveal the Guru's sufferings. They also received orders not to allow the Guru to make any detour, but proceed straight on, and not halt before he had arrived at the bank of the river. While the Guru was bathing and subsequently drying himself, the soldiers were not to address him or interrupt him in any way. They were then to return with him and keep him and his Sikhs in front of them so that he might not escape.

The Guru enveloped himself in a long sheet and set forth. The whole of his body was blistered, and the soles of his feet sore and festered. Looking where he might tread with the least pain he proceeded very slowly. Seeing his servant Pirana near him he leaned on his shoulder, and emerged from the city by a wicket opening towards the river. Several people bowed as he passed. The bystanders were astonished on seeing him weak from hunger and suffering, and said, 'In what a state the Guru is travelling!' His mind however appeared collected and fixed on divine meditation as in his earlier and happier days. His devotion like a mountain which cannot be moved was in no way affected by his bodily pain.

On arriving with very slow and painful steps at the Ravi he took up some of its cold water—recently melted from Himalayan ice—and bathed his feet and hands therewith. He then went into the water and bathed his whole body. Meanwhile he recited with great devotion the Japji, which confers salvation on Sikhs. His men, who were like a halo round him, followed his example. The Guru bowed at the end of his devotions and thus addressed his Sikhs: 'I have succeeded in effecting the object of my life. Go to my son the holy Har Gobind, and give him from me ample consolation. Bid him not mourn or indulge in unmanly lamentations but sing God's praises. Let him also restrain from grief the other members of my family. Let him sit fully armed on his throne, and maintain and army to the best of his ability. Let him affix the patch of Guruship to his forehead according to ancient custom, and ever treat his Sikhs with the utmost courtesy. Let him hold Bhai Budha in honour, and in all respects, except the wearing of arms hereby enjoined, adopt the practices of the preceding Gurus. Cremate not my body, but let it flow on the bosom of this river.

Having thus spoken the Guru observed a minstrel approach with a two-stringed instrument, and invited him to take a seat on a pleasant spot near the river, sing the Guru's hymns, and accompany himself on his instrument. The minstrel accordingly stated to sing with great feeling and expression, whereupon the heavenly hosts thronged to listen, to witness the Guru's departure, and to congratulate him on his victory over torture and tyranny. Some recounted the Guru's deeds, while others listened with admiration. They vowed that the earth itself had not such patience as the Guru. There was nothing animate or inanimate to be compared with him. 'He hath shown extreme patience and endurance, though, had he chosen to exercise his miraculous power, he might have averted his sufferings. He hath never meditated retaliation on his enemy; his praise suits none but himself for having endured extreme suffering and heeded it not. He now cometh to us to abide in glory and bliss after his earthly misery.'

The Guru's death occurred on the fourth day of the light half of the month Jeth, Sambat 1663 (June, A.D. 1606).

When Chandu's daughter-in-law heard of the Guru's death she too abandoned her body, as if it were a worthless blade of grass. Her corpse remained concealed in her chamber and none knew that her spirit had accompanied the Guru's in its heavenly flight.

Thus did Guru Arjan for his sanctity, his conversion of the Hindus and Muhammadans, his compilation of the Granth Sahib and his assistance to the grandson of his former benefactor, fall a victim to the bigotry and inhumanity of a Muhammadan emperor.

The temple dedicated to the Guru in Lahore bears the following inscription of his own composition:

Perform ablution, remember your God, and your minds and bodies shall be free from disease.

Millions of obstacles shall be removed by God's protection, and good fortune shall dawn on you.

I have uttered the compositions and the hymns of God.

O my brethren, ever sing, listen, and read them, and the perfect Guru will preserve you.

4

Hymns

Sri Rag

Life is uncertain and man ought to repent be-times:

Though only a guest for a ghari or two, man arrangeth his affairs.

He is absorbd in mammon and Lust; and, fool that he is, knoweth not *that he is but a guest*.

He only repenteth after his departure, and so falleth into the power of Death the executioner.

O blind man, thou art sitting on a falling bank.

If thou art so fated from the beginning, then act according to the Guru's instruction.

The Owner may gather the crop whether it be green, half-ripe, or ripe and fit to be cut.

The reapers make preparations, bring sickles, and arrive on the ground.

They cut the crop as it is measured out to them when the Landlord giveth orders.

The first watch of night is gone in business; during the second man sleepeth his fill;

The third is passed in idle discourse; and at the fourth the morning dawneth.

He who gave soul and body never entereth into man's mind.

I sacrifice and devote my life to the society of the saints,

Through whom understanding entered my heart, and I met God the Omniscient.

Know that Nanak hath ever seen God who is the Searcher of hearts with him.

The attributes of God:

I love that true One who dieth not or suffereth transmigration;

Who, being contained in everything, will not be separated from me though I separate from Him;

Who removeth the pain and sorrow of the poor, and truly loveth His servant.

Wonderful is the form of the Pure One; the Guru hath caused me to meet Him, O my mother.

O my brethren, be friends with such a God.

Accursed is the love of worldly things; no one attached to them appeareth happy.

God is wise, generous, mild, beautiful and infinite;

He is the companion, the helper, exceeding great, exalted, and altogether without limit;

He is not known as young or old; everlasting is His court.

What we ask Him we obtain; He is the support of the weak.

On beholding Him sins vanish, and the soul and body are at peace.

If man with single mind meditate on Him, mental doubts shall be dispelled.

He is the treasury of excellences; every new and complete are His gifts.

Ever and ever adore Him; forget Him not by day or night:

He is the companion of those who are so destined from the beginning.

Devote your body, your soul, and your wealth all unto Him; sacrifice your whole life unto Him.

He beholdeth, He heareth, He is ever present, He pervadeth every heart.

He cherisheth even the ungrateful; O Nanak, God is ever the Pardoner.

God's beneficence:

Ever and ever remember God and clasp Him to thy heart, who gave thee soul, body, and wealth, and adorned thee;

Who constructed all the materials *of the body* and infused into it immortal light.

O my soul, there is none but God.

Ever remain under God's protection and thou shalt feel no sorrow.

Jewels, wealth, gems, gold, and silver are all dust.

The affinities of mother, father, sons, and kinsmen are all false.

The perverse man, unclean beast that he is, knoweth not Him who made him:

He deemeth that God who is within and around him is distant;

Avarice clingeth to him, and his heart is attached to pride and falsehood.

Boatfuls of persons without devotion or God's name come and go.

O God, the Creator, mercifully preserve man and Thine other creatures.

There is no protector but Thee; very unfeeling is the God of death.

Saith Nanak, O God, have mercy on me that I may not forget Thy name.

Nothing can be concealed from the omnipotent God:

In the dust of the saints' feet are found the merits of hundreds of thousands of pilgrimages, fastings and mortifications.

From whom canst thou hide thine evil deeds, since God ever present beholdeth thee?

My God pervadeth and filleth every place.

True is His empire, true His authority, and truest of the true His seat.

The true One exerteth true power in the creation of the world.

Nanak, repeat the true Name to which I am for ever and ever a sacrifice.

The Guru counsels the rejection of worldly pleasures:

Deeming the *pleasures of the world* sweet, man partaketh of them, but they prove to have a bitter taste.

He causeth his brethren and friends to love him heartily; he is vainly devoted to sinful pleasures.

These shall pass away in a trice, and he shall be astonished without the Name.

O my soul, apply thyself to the service of the true Guru. Whatever is seen is perishable, abandon thy perversity.

As a mad dog runneth in every direction,

So the avaricious man distinguisheth not, but eateth both what is allowed and what is forbidden.

He who feeleth lust, wrath, and pride shall enter the womb again and again.

Mammon hath spread out her net and placed a bait within it:

The greedy bird is snared and cannot escape, my mother.

Man knoweth not Him who made him; wherefore he shall suffer transmigration again and again.

This world hath in many ways and forms bewitched man.

He who is preserved by the omnipotent and enternal Being shall be saved.

The people of God are saved by their love for Him; to them Nanak is ever a sacrifice.

Man during his brief measure of life ought to practice devotion:

When the herdsman goeth *only for a few days* to the pasture ground, why should he prefer *a claim to it?*

When thy time is completed, thou must depart; yet thou art arranging thy household affairs.

O man, sing God's praises and serve the true Guru with love.

Why art thou proud of a trifle?

Like the guest of a night thou shalt depart in the morning.

Why art thou attached to thy family? Everything is *short-lived* as the flowers of the garden.

Why ever speak of thy property? Long for the God who gave it thee.

Thou must assuredly depart and leave thy lakhs and karors.

Having wandered among the eighty-four lakhs of existences, thou hast at last obtained human life so difficult to obtain.

Nanak, remember thou the Name; the day *of thy departure* is near.

While life remains learn wise conduct:

O body, as long as *the soul* thy companion is with thee, so long thou livest happily.

When thy companion departeth, thou shalt be blended with the dust.

If thou have felt love of God and a desire to behold Him, blest shall be thine abode.

As long as the soul dwelleth with thee, every one will say 'Sir, Sir,' to thee;

But when it departeth no one will care for thee.

Serve thy Bridegroom in thy father's house, and thou shalt abide in happiness in thy father-in-law's.

Having met the Guru, learn wise conduct; and sorrow shall never befall thee.

All must go to their father-in-law's; God taketh every one away.

Nanak, blest is that happy wife who loveth the Bridegroom.

Some moral injunctions:

Store up God's wealth, worship the true Guru, and renounce all sin.

Remember that God who made and adorned thee, and thou shalt be saved.

O man, repeat the name of the one eternal God,

Who gave thee soul, mind, and body, and who is the support of the heart.

The world is intoxicated with the prevailing lust, wrath and pride.

Enter the asylum of the saints, fall at their feet, and thy misery and mental blindness shall be removed.

The practice of truth, patience, and mercy is the best work *man can accomplish*.

He to whom God the Formless One granteth grace, renounceth pride and becometh the dust of all men's feet.

Whatever is seen, the extension of creation, is all Thou, O God.

Saith Nanak, the Guru hath cut away doubt; and I consider all things God.

The Guru addresses God as a child his father:

Relying on Thee, O Beloved, I have been made happy.

Even if I have gone astray, I am Thy child, O God, Thou art my father and mother.

It is easy to talk,

But to act as Thou pleasest is difficult.

In Thee I repose mine honour and my strength; I know thee as mine.

Thou art within and without everything; Thou needest nothing, O Father.

O Father, I know not Thy ways.

God freeth me from entanglements, O saints, and cherisheth love for me.

The Lord hath been merciful, and my transmigration is at an end.
On meeting the Guru, Nanak hath recognized the Supreme God.

Ashtapadi

Better seek God's protection than join any of the current Indian religious sects:
I know not what things please *the Lord;*
O my soul, seek His way.
The meditator practiseth meditation.
He who is possessed of knowledge may employ his knowledge,
Yet few know God.
The Bhagauti acteth according to the rules *of his sect;*
The Jogi claimeth that he *alone* is emancipated;
The Penitent is absorbed in his penance;
The Silent observe silence;
The Sanyasi, the Brahmachari,
And the Hermit are devoted to their lonely lives;
The Bhagats worship in nine ways;
The Pandits shout the Veds;
The householders who practise household duties,
The Eksabdis, Bahurupias, the Audhuts,
The Kaprias, the Kautas, the Jagutas *all plume themselves on their religious merits.*
Some bathe at places of pilgrimage.
The Nirahars, fast; the Aparasas touch nothing they deem impure;
Some hide and do not allow themselves to be seen.
Some in their own estimation know everything:
Nobody admitteth any deficiency in himself.
All say that they have found God;
But it is only the saint whom God uniteth with Himself.
All the above-mentioned efforts
I abandon, and seek God's protection;
Nanak, I fall at the Guru's feet.
The Guru confesses the benefits he has received from God:
In fall at *God's* feet to conciliate Him;
The true Guru hath blended me with God' there is none so great as He.
The Lord of the earth is my Beloved;
He is dearer to me than mother, father,
Sisters, brothers, and all friends; there is none like Thee, O God

By Thine order Sawan hath come,

And I have yoked the plough of truth.

I begin to sow the Name in the hope that God in His beneficence will cause it to yield heaps of corn.

Having met the Guru, I recognize the one God;

I know nothing of any else.

God appointed me to the one duty; as it pleaseth Him so I perform it.

Do you, my brethren, eat and enjoy yourselves;

The Guru hath invested me with a robe of honour in God's court.

I have become master in my own village; I have taken its five claimants captive.

I have entered Thine asylum, O *God*.

The five claimants have now become my tenants.

None of them can interfere with me; Nanak, the village is *now* thickly populated.

I am a sacrifice and devote myself to Thee,

O my Sovereign; on Thee alone I meditate.

Thou hast re-peopled a ruined village: I am a sacrifice unto Thee.

I continually meditate on God, the Beloved,

And thus obtain the fruit my heart desireth.

God hath arranged all mine affairs and appeased the hunger of my soul.

I have abandoned all mine avocations,

And I serve the true God.

God firmly tied the Name, the receptacle of the nine treasures in my robe.

I have found the comfort of comforts.

The Guru hath implanted his instruction in my heart.

The true Guru placing his hand on my forehead hath shown me God.

I have built a true temple:

I search for and bring into it the disciples of the Guru.

I bathe their feet, fan them, and ever prostrate myself before them

Having heard of the Guru I went to him:

He implanted in my heart the *virtues* of the Name, of charity, and of ablutions.

The whole world, Nanak, having embarked on the true boat hath been saved,

The whole creation waiteth on Thee, O Lord, day and night.

Lend Thine ear and hear my supplication.

I have seen and examined every one; it is Thou alone who graciously deliverest us.

The order of the Merciful hath now been issued

That no one should annoy another;

That all should dwell in peace, and that this should be a benign reign.

Nectar falleth in torrents.

I speak as the Master inspireth me.

I am very proud of Thee, O Lord; do Thou accept me.

Thy saints ever hunger for Thee;

O God, fulfil my desires.

Giver of comfort, grant me a sight of Thee and embrace me:

I have found none so great at Thou.

Thou art in the earth, the heavens, and the nether regions;

Thou art contained in every place, saith Nanak; Thou art the true support of the saints.

I am the wrestler of the Lord:

Having met the Guru I put on a tall turban.

All are assembled for the wrestling; God Himself is seated to behold it.

The music of the drums and clarions striketh up;

The wrestlers enter the arena and walk round.

I have vanquished the five youth—*The deadly sins;* —the Guru patted me on the back.

All came together *to see the wrestling,*

And they shall take their various ways homewards.

The holy have obtained profit; the perverse have lost even their capital.

Thou art devoid of colour and marks;

O God, Thou appearest ever present.

O Lord of excellences, Thy saints hear *Thy praises,* meditate on Thee, and love Thee.

I am God's servant in every age.

The Guru cut the rope of *ignorance which bound me.*

I will not again engage in wrestling; Nanak hath searched and found this opportunity *of deliverance.*

Chhant

The happiness of the saints:

When the Lord is merciful, men bathe in the dust of the saints' feet.

Nanak hath obtained all things in God who is wealth and property.

Beautiful, O Lord, is Thy house; the saints live in the hope of rest in it.

Their souls and bodies dissolve in love on remembering God's name, and they drink its nectar;

They drink its nectar, live immortal lives, and while drinking deem the water of sin insipid.

When my God the Lord of the earth became merciful, I deemed the saints' society a treasure.

O beloved saints, all happiness and abundant joy are theirs who have sewed God's jewel in their hearts.

They forget not for a moment the support of life; O Nanak, they live by repeating God's name.

Majh

Gratitude to God who treats all men as equal.

That season is pleasant when I remember Thee, O God;

That work is pleasant which is done for Thee.

O Thou who bestoweth on all, that heart is happy in which Thou dwellest.

Thou art our universal Father.

In Thine inexhaustible storehouse are all treasures.

He on whom Thou bestoweth is satisfied and satiated, and he is Thy worshipper.

Every one reposeth his hopes in Thee.

Thou abidest in every heart,

All are partners in Thee; Thou disownest none.

Favour with God is likened to a woman's happy married life:

In the house where the Beloved celebrated His marriage Female friends sang songs of rejoicing,

Where the Spouse hath adorned the bride, there reign joy and pleasure.

The woman who is dear to her husband, is beautiful, clever, skillful,

Well conducted, and distinguished:

She is accomplished, and very fortunate;

She possesseth sons and is a virtuous wife;

She hath all decorations, and it is she who is wise.

She who is adorned with the love of her Spouse, is of good family and a queen.

The greatness of her whom her Spouse

Hath embraced cannot be described.

The married life of her who hath the support of the love of the Unapproachable and Inapprehensible Spouse shall be eternal.

The Hindu Shastras and religious ceremonies are of no avail:

I have searched and searched in the desire to behold Thee, O God;

I have traversed every variety of forest.

Is there any one who will bring me my God—who is devoid of qualities, and yet possesseth all qualities — and introduce me to Him?

Man may recite aloud the wisdom of the six Shastars;

He may worship, apply frontal marks, and bathe at places of pilgrimage;

He may perform the nivali feat, and sit in the eighty-four postures of the Jogis, but he shall obtain no comfort therefrom.

Man many perform devotion and penance for many years;

He may travel and roam over the earth;

Yet peace shall not enter his heart for a moment, and his soul shall wander again and again.

God being merciful hath caused me to meet the saint.

My soul and body are refreshed, and I have obtained consolation.

The immortal God resideth in my heart, and Nanak singeth to God a song of rejoicing.

Praise and prayer to the Almighty:

Darling God, merciful, joyous,

Deep, profound, endless, Sustainer of the earth,

Lofty, unfathomable, eternal Lord, I live by remembering Thee.

Destroyer of sorrow, priceless treasure,

Without fear or enmity, unfathomable, unequalled,

Deathless, unborn, self-existent; the mind becometh refreshed by remembering Thee.

O God, Thou joyous One, be ever with me.

Thou art the Cherisher of high and low.

Thy name is the elixir which satisfieth my heart; under the Guru's instructions let me drink the nectar.

In pain or pleasure I meditate on Thy name, O dear One:

This wisdom have I obtained from the Guru.

Thou art Nanak's support, O God; by Thy love I shall be saved.

The Guru expresses his love for God by familiar similes:

Thou art, O God, an ocean of water; I am Thy fish:

I a chatrik thirst for the drops of Thy name.

In Thee is my hope, for Thee I thirst, my heart is absorbed in Thee.

As a child is satisfied by drinking milk,

As a poor man is happy on finding wealth,

As a thirsty man is refreshed by drinking water, so is my soul happy with God.

As a lamp shineth in the darkness,

As *a woman's* hopes are fulfilled on beholding her spouse,

As one becometh happy on meeting one's beloved, so is my soul gladdened with God's love.

The saints have put me on God's road,

And being merciful have made me intimate with Him.

God is mine; I am His slave; Nanak, the Guru hath given me the true Word.

God's name is the sweetest and most potent of all relishes:

The ambrosial Name is ever pure.

God is the bestower of comfort and the Destroyer of sorrow.

I have tasted and tried all other relishes, but to my mind God is the sweetest dainty of all.

They who drink the nectar of His name are satisfied,

And become immortal on possessing it.

The treasure of the Name is obtained by him in whose heart the Guru's word abideth.

He who obtaineth the essence of God's name is satisfied and cloyed.

He who hath obtained God's sweets wavereth not.

God's name is obtained by him on whose forehead favourable destiny *was recorded*.

God hath come into the possession of one man, the Guru, from whom many receive favours.

On meeting him many obtain salvation.

The pious obtain the treasure of the Name, but few, O Nanak, are they who have seen them.

God's praises:

God is my ocean, God is perfection, God is my wealth;

O deep and profound One, Thou art the boon of my life. he who toucheth the Guru's feet enjoyeth countiess pleasures and delights.

They who have seen God are pure,

And save all their brethren and friends.

My Lord is inaccessible, and inapprehensible; I meditate on Him, the True One, by the kindness of the Guru.

A few by great good fortune have obtained a sight of Him,

Whom men make every effort to find.

His palace, exalted, infinite, and invisible, the Guru hath shown me.

Deep and profound is Thine ambrosial name, O God;

He in whose heart it dwelleth deliverance.

Nanak, they whose bonds are all cut off by the Guru are absorbed in God.

The Guru delights in his devotion:

By God's favour I meditate on His name,

And by His mercy I sing a song of joy.

All your lives whether standing, sitting, sleeping, or waking, meditate on God,

The holy man hath given me the Name as medicine; He hath cut off my sins, and I have become pure:

All my pains have departed, all my pangs have been assuaged, and I have become happy.

He whown my Beloved assisteth

Shall be delivered from the ocean of the world.

Why should he who recognizeth the Guru as true be afraid?

Since I have obtained the society of the saints

And met the Guru, the demon of pride hath departed.

At every breath Nanak singeth God's praises; the true Guru hath cast a veil over his sins.

The condition of God's worshipper:

God pervadeth His worshipper as warp and woof: God, the Bestower of comfort, Cherisheth His worshipper.

I draw water, I fan, I grind corn for him, and am ever ready to do the work of the Lord.

God hath cut off my chains and applied me to His worship.

The order of the Lord is pleasing to the worshipper's heart.

He acteth as is pleasing to the Lord; he becometh versed in spiritual and wordly knowledge.

Thou art wise, O God; Thou knowest all things.

God's worshippers enjoy His love.

What belongeth to God belongeth to His worshipper; the worshipper is distinguished in the company of his Lord.

He whom God hath clothed with His robe of honour,

Shall not again be called on for his account.

Nanak is a sacrifice to that worshipper; he is a gem of the Deep and Unfathomable.

The devotion of the householder is superior to that of the anchoret:

Everything is found at home, nothing abroad:

He who searcheth abroad is lost in doubt.

He who by the Guru's favour hath found God in his heart, is happy in mind and body.

A stream of nectar raineth *on him* in torrents.

The man who drinketh it after hearing and reflecting on the Word,

Rejoiceth and is glad day and night, and ever sporteth with God.

Separated from God through many births, I have now found Him,

And though dried up have revived by the Guru's favour.

Having met pious men I have obtained excellent wisdom, and meditated on the Name.

As waves blend with water,

So light is blended with light.

Saith Nanak, the doors of error have been opened for its escape, and there shall be no more wandering.

The Guru's devotion to the holy:

I am a sacrifice to him who hath heard Thy praises;

I am a sacrifice to him who uttereth Thy name;

I am ever a sacrifice to him who worshippeth Thee with heart and soul.

I will wash his feet and behold

That merciful person who walketh in Thy path.

I will bestow my heart on that friend of mine who meeting the Guru hath found God.

Greatly fortunate are they who know Thee;

Among crowds they live apart unaffected by them;

In the company of the saints they subdue all passions and cross the terrible ocean.

Having renounced pride, insolence, and the darkness of worldly love,

My soul hath entered their asylum.

Ye saints, grant Nanak the gift of the name of that inaccessible and unfathomable God.

God pervades creation:

Thou art the tree; Thy branch hath blossomed;

From being small Thou hast become great.

Thou art an ocean, Thou art its foam and its bubbles; there is nothing seen besides Thee.

Thou art the string, Thou art the beads *of the rosary,*

Thou art its knots, Thou art its chief bead.

God is in the beginning, the middle, and the end, and none besides is seen.

O Bestower of comfort, Thou possessest no attributes, and yet Thou possessest all.

Thou dwellest at Case; Thou art the Enjoyer; Thou art saturated with love.

Thou knowest Thine own affairs; it is Thou who rememberest Thyself.

Thou art God, and again Thou art Thine own worshipper;

Thou art concealed, O God, and again manifest.

The slave Nanak ever singeth Thy praises: look on him with a little kindness.

Man is happy on meeting the Guru and hearing his universal instruction:

O God, Thy Word is nectar

On hearing it may final emancipation is obtained.

On hebolding the true Guru the burning of my mind hath been quenched, and it hath become cool;

Happiness is obtained and sorrow fleeth far away.

When the saints repeat God's name,

Water, dry land, and lakes are completely filled with it; there is no place without it.

The Creator showing mercy

Cherisheth all men and lower animals.

By the kind, merciful, and compassionate One all living things are satisfied and satiated.

God made the forests, the glades, and the three worlds:

He created them all in a moment.

Under the Guru's instruction, Nanak, adore Him who fulfilleth the desires of the mind.

God's relationship to man:

Thou art my father, Thou art my mother,

Thou art my kinsman, Thou art my brother;

Thou art everywhere my protector; then why should I feel fear and anxiety?

By Thy favour I recognize Thee;

Thou art my shelter, Thou art mine honour.

Besides Thee there is none other; the whole world is the arena of Thy play.

Men and lower animals all hast Thou created;

Thou didst appoint them to whatever duties pleased Thee.

Everything Thou hast created is Thine; there is nothing ours.

I have obtained great comfort by meditating on Thy name,

And my heart is refreshed by singing Thy praises.

The perfect Guru hath congratulated me; Nanak hath overcome his difficulties.

Divine instruction refreshes the mind:

By God's order the rain beginneth to fall.

Let us, my friends, having met the saints, repeat His name.

I have obtained coolness, peace, composure, and comfort, since God Himself infused coolness into my heart.

By God's grace the Guru's instruction has been promulgated:

The Lord God hath become merciful;

Rain hath fallen everywhere.

The Creator, compassionate and ever merciful to the poor, hath bestowed comfort on us,

And cherished His human beings and lower animals,

As a mother taketh care of her child.

Thou, O Lord, art the Destroyer of grief, and Ocean of comfort, and Thou givest sustenance to all.

The Kind One filleth sea and land:

I ever devotee myself and am a sacrifice to Him;

I ever meditate on Him night and day, who in one moment saveth all beings.

Since God Himself preserveth them,

All their sorrows and afflictions depart.

When the Name is repeated,

And God looketh on us with favour, O Nanak, the soul and body are refreshed.

The universal happiness produced by the diffusion of the Guru's instruction:

Rain hath fallen; God made it fall:

He hath caused all men and animals to dwell in comfort:

Their sufferings have departed, and they have obtained true happiness by remembering God's name.

He whose they are cherisheth them;

The supreme God hath become their Protector.

My God hath heard my supplication, and my labour hath been successful.

By the Guru's favour I have beheld Him

Who is the Benefactor of all living things.

The things that dwell in sea and land, beneath the earth, and in the firmament, are all satisfied, and I shall now wash the fact of holy men.

I ma ever and ever a sacrifice to Him

Who fulfilleth the heart's desires.

O Nanak, the Destroyer of pain hath bestowed this boon on me, and I am dyed with the love of Him who is the abode of pleasure.

Praise and Thanksgiving:

My soul and body are Thine; my wealth also is Thine;

Thou art my Lord and Master;

My soul and body are all Thy capital; my power is from Thee, O God.

Ever and ever Thou alone art the Giver of happiness.

I bow and bow and touch Thy feet.

If it please Thee, and Thou give me work, O Merciful One, I will perform it.

O God, it is from Thee alone I receive; Thou art mine ornament.

Whatever Thou gives I treated as happiness.

Wherever Thou placest me, there shall be heaven for me:

Thou art the Cherisher of all.

Nanak having remembered Thee hath obtained happiness.

He hath sung Thy praises all day long;

All his heart's desires have been fulfilled, and he shall never more be unhappy.

God sent the Guru to comfort the world:

The supreme God hath sent the cloud,

And hath caused it to rain on sea and land in all directions. Comfort hath ensured, all thirst is quenched, and there is joy everywhere.

An exhortation to holiness:

My soul and body are dyed with the beloved God.

Sacrifice to Him all that thou hast:

Sing God's praises the live-long day, and forget Him not even for a moment.

He who meditateth on God's name in the company of holy men,

Is my beloved saint and friend:

In the company of holy men thou shalt cross over the world's ocean and cut death's noose.

By God's service the four boons are obtained.

Repeat His name who is the Tree of Life unseen and inscrutable.

The Guru hath cut off my sins of lust and anger, and my hopes have been fulfilled.

The mortal who hath perfect good fortune

Shall meet God in the company of holy men.

Nanak, he within whose heart the Name abideth shall be acceptable, whether a householder or an anchoret.

Prayers ought *only* to be offered for worthy objects:

If any one pray for worldly objects,

He shall not take long to perish.

He whoever worshippeth the Supreme Being, shall on meeting the Guru abide everlasting.

He in whose heart there is love and devotion,

Ever waketh day and night singing God's praises.

God will take his arm and blend with Himself him whom
He hath destined to receive from Him.
God's lotus feet dwell in the hearts of the saints.
Without God's *assistance* all men are robbed.
Ever desire the dust of the saints' feet: the name of the True One is their ornament.
Whether standing or sitting sing God's name :
By remembering it a permanent boon is obtained.
O God be merciful to Nanak; what Thou doest must be endured.

Majh Ashtapadi

The Guru replies to several questions of his Sikhs:
Who is saved? Who hath found the right way?
Who hath divine knowledge? Who is the preacher?
Who is householder? Who is anchoret? Who hath found God's price?
How is man bound? How is he set free?
How shall he escape from transmigration?
Who doeth good works? Who doeth unselfish works?
Who speaketh of God and causeth others to speak of Him?
Who is happy? Who afflicted?
Who turneth towards the Guru? Who turneth away from him?
How is God met? How doth man separate from Him? Who shall explain this to me?
What is that word by which the mind's wandering ceaseth?
What is that instruction by which man may bear weal and woe alike?
What is that way by which man may meditate on the Supreme God?
What is that way by which man may sing His praises?
The following are the replies seriatim to the above questions:
The believer is saved: the believer hath found the right way;
The believer possesseth divine knowledge; the believer is the preacher.
Blest is the believer, whether householder or anchoret; the believer hath found God's price.
By pride man is bound; by the Guru's instruction he is freed.
The believer escapeth from transmigration.
The believer performeth good works; the believer performeth unselfish works; whatever the believer doeth is acceptable.
The believer is happy; the unbeliever is afflicted.
The believer listeneth to the Guru; the unbeliever turneth away from him.

The believer meeteth God; the unbeliever is separated from Him—the Guru hath explained this.

The Guru's instruction is the Word by which the mind's wanderings cease;

By the Guru's instruction woe and weal are borne alike.

The Guru's teaching is the way by which the supreme God is meditated on, and man singeth His praises.

Thou Thyself hast made the whole creation.

Thou art the Cause of causes, and hast established everything.

Saith Nanak, from being one Thou hast become endless, and in the One *the Endless* is absorbed.

God's praises:

God is indestructible, then what anxiety can there be?

God is Omnipotent, so His slave is perfectly happy.

O Giver of life, soul, honour, and happiness, we obtain happiness from what Thou doest for us.

I am a sacrifice and my life is a sacrifice to that holy man to whose soul and body Thou art pleasing.

Thou art my mountain; Thou art may shelter; none can rival Thee.

He to whom Thy works are agreeable

Hath seen Thee, O Supreme God, in every heart.

Thou art the one sole God contained in every place.

Thou gratifiest all the heart's desires:

Thy storehouses are filled with devotion and love.

He whom Thou mercifully protectest shall be absorbed in Thee by perfect good works.

God hath brought man to the surface out of the blind well.

He mercifully regardeth His servant with a favouring eye.

The servant singeth the perfect and immortal God's praises in repeating and hearing which there is no end.

In this world and the next Thou art the Protector, *O Lord;*

Thou cherishest the child in its mother's womb.

The fire of Maya cannot affect those who are dyed with God's love and sing His praises.

What excellences of Thine can I remember and relate?

In any soul and body I behold Thee.

Thou art my Friend, my Saint, and my Lord; I know none but Thee.

He whose helper Thou art, O God,

Feeleth no hot wind.

Thou art the Lord; Thou givest comfort to those who seek Thy protection; By repeating Thy name in the company of the saints, Thou becomest manifest.

Thou art exalted, unfathomable, infinite and inestimable.

Thou art the true Lord; I am Thy servant and slave;

Thou art the King, true is Thy sovereignty. Nanak is a sacrifice unto Thee.

The Twelve Months of Guru Arjan

Majh

O God, mercifully unite with Thee those who by their past acts are separated from Thee!

Weary of wandering in the four corners of the world and in every direction, we have come to Thy protection.

A cow without milk is of no avail:

Without water the tree withereth and beareth no fruit.

If we meet not the Lord God, the Friend, how shall we find rest?

The city or village or house where God is not seen is as a furnace.

All decorations, betel, and tasteful viands are unstable together with the body.

Without the Lord God all friends are as the dod of death.

Nanak's supplication is, 'Mercifully grant me Thy name;

'O Lord God, whose abode is immovable, unite me with Thee.'

In Chet worship God and you shall greatly rejoice.

You shall obtain Him by meeting saints and repeating His name.

It is only those who have found their God, whose advent into the world is of account:

Vain is his birth who liveth even for a moment without Him.

God is equally contained in sea and land, the nether regions the firmament, and the forests.

With how much pain shall man reckon if God enter not his heart?

They who repeat God's name are very fortunate,

Nanak, my mind desireth, my mind thirsteth for a sight of God.

I shall touch his feet who causeth me to meet God in the month of Chet.

In Baisakh how can they find consolation who are separated from God, in whose hearts there is no love,

Who forget Him the Friend, and attach themselves to deceitful mammon?

Son, wife, wealth remain not; God alone perisheth not.

The whole world is strangled in its love of false occupations.

All but the name of the one God shall be lost on man's last journey.

He who forgetteth God is ruined; there is none but Him.

Pure is the fame of those who are attached to the feet of the Beloved.

Nanak's prayer, O God, is—'Unite me with Thee that I may obtain Thee.'

Baisakh is then delightful when the saints cause man to meet God.

In Jeth man should unite with God before whom all bow.

He who clingeth to the skirt of God, the Friend, shall never be bound by any one.

God's name is like gems and pearls which none may steal.

In God are all the loves which delight the mind.

What God desireth He doeth, and creatures act according to His will.

They whom God hath made His own are blest.

Could men on their own account meet God, why should they weep in separation?

Nanak, God is obtained by association with the saints; and they who obtain Him are happy.

In Jeth the playful God is obtained by the fortunate for whom it hath been so recorded.

Asarh is a burning month for him to whom the Lord God is not near.

He who forsaketh God the life of the world and resteth his hopes on man,

Shall be ruined by his love of mammon, and shall wear Death's halter around his neck.

As man sowed, *in a previous life,* so was the destiny recorded on his forehead, and so hath he reaped.

When the night *of human life* hath passed, man regretteth and departeth without hope.

They who meet the saints shall be released in Gods' court.

O God, show Thy mercy unto me that I may thirst for a sight of Thee.

Nanak representeth—O God, there is none but Thee.

Asarh is pleasant for him in whose heart dwell God's feet.

In Sawan happy is the woman who loveth God's lotus feet.

Her mind and body are imbued with true love, and her one support is the Name.

The love of worldly pleasures is false; everything we see shall become ashes.

Pleasant are the drops of God's nectar; he shall drink them who meeteth saints.

The woods and glades rejoice with God the omnipotent and unequalled.

My mind longeth to meet God; His favour shall cause me to meet Him.

I am ever a sacrifice to my companions who have met God.

Nanak, God mercifully regenerateth men with the Word.

Sawan is pleasant for those who clasp God's name to their hearts.

In Bhadon she who loveth mammon is lost in doubt.

Though she have hundreds of thousands of decorations, they are of none avail.

They whom man loved leave him in a moment.

He wringeth his hands, his body trembleth, and changeth from black to white.

On the very day his body perisheth men call out 'ghost!'

The myrmidons of Death seize and take away *the soul,* and tell no one their secret.

As man soweth, so shall he reap the field of his works.

Nanak, God giveth His feet as a boat to him who hath sought His protection.

They who love the Guru, their saviour, shall not go to hell in Bhadon.

In Assu ariseth the pang of love—how man can meet God.

The mind and body greatly thirst for a sight of some one to come and cause us to meet God.

I fall at the feet of the saints who support me in my love.

How can any one obtain happiness but in God? There is no place beside.

They who have tasted the juice of love are satiated and cloyed.

Humbling thyself make this supplication, 'O God, attach me to Thy skirt!'

They whom God the Spouse united with Himself shall never be separated from Him.

Nanak, there is no other shelter than God.

In Assu they dwell happy to whom God showeth mercy.

In Kartik they who do bad acts cannot impute the blame to others.

They who forget God suffer from every disease.

They who have turned their faces from God, are separated from Him at every birth.

All the sweets of mammon become bitter for them in a moment.

No one will mediate for them; to whom shall they make their daily complaints?

Nothing resulteth from man's own efforts; *he obtaineth* what was recorded in his original destiny.

My Lord is found by good fortune; then shall all pains of separation depart.

O God, saved Nanak, and release him from this prison.

If in Kartik man obtain the society of the saints all his anxieties shall depart.

The month of Maghar is beautiful for those who sit with their beloved God.

How can their glory be told whom God blendeth with Himself?

The bodies and minds of those who have the saints for their companions rejoice in the Lord.

They who are deprived of the society of the saints dwell alone;

Their pain never departeth; they are bound in the thrall of Death.

They who have enjoyed their Lord are seen ever standing in His service.

Their necklaces are set with God for gems, jewels, and rubies.

Nanak desireth the dust of the feet of those who fall for shelter at God's door.

They who worship God in Maghar shall never be born again.

In Poh cold shall never be felt by those whom the Lord God hath embraced.

God's lotus feet have entered my heart, and I desire to behold Him.

Take shelter in God and His service shall be thy gain.

On meeting the holy sing God's praises and sin shall not affect thee.

Thou shalt be blended with what thou hast sprung from; wherefore be absorbed in true love.

He whom the Supreme Being hath taken by the hand shall never be separated from Him.

I am a hundred thousand times a sacrifice to God the Friend, the unapproachable and unfathomable.

Nanak hath fallen at God's door: it is to His honour *to protect him.*

Poh is agreeable and bringeth all happiness to him whom God pardoneth.

In Magh bathe in the dust of the saints' feet;

Meditate on God's name, and bestow it upon all;

So shall the filth of the sins of births be washed away, and pride vanish from thy heart.

Lust and anger shall not seduce, and the dog covetousness shall be destroyed.

The world praiseth those who walk in the true way.

Mercy to human beings is more acceptable than bathing at the sixty-eight places of pilgrimage, and then all alms *offered there:*

He on whom God mercifully bestoweth it is a wise man.

Nanak is a sacrifice to those who have met their Lord.

In Magh they to whom the perfect Guru is kind are called the pure.

In Phagun they enjoy happiness to whom God hath manifested Himself.

The saints who render man assistance with God have mercifully blended me with Him.

Since then my couch is beautiful; I possess all happiness, and there is no room for sorrow.

My desires have been fulfilled; I am very fortunate in having obtained God as my Spouse.

My companions, come to me, sing a song of rejoicing and chant the hymns of the Lord.

Nobody appeareth like God; no one is equal to Him.

He hath prepared for me this world and the next, and given me a stable position.

He hath rescued me from the ocean of the world, and I shall not again have to run through births.

My tongue is but one, while manifold are His attributes:

Nanak is saved by falling at His feet:

In Phagun ever praise Him who hath not a particle of avarice.

The affairs of those who meditated on the Name have been adjusted.

They who adore God the perfect Guru shall be found genuine in His court.

God's feet are the basis of all comforts; through them man crosseth over the terrible and dangerous ocean.

They who have obtained love and devotion burn not in sin.

Their falsehood hath vanished, their worldliness hath disappeared, and they are filled to the brim with the truth.

They serve God the supreme Being, and put Him alone in their hearts.

All months, days, and minutes are good for him on whom God looketh with favour.

Nanak craveth the boon of a sight of Thee, O God' be Thou merciful unto him.

Gauri

An inquirer asked the Guru in the first two lines of the following how final rest and God were obtained. The Guru duly replied:

How is comfort found, O my brother?

How shall God the helper be obtained?

There is no comfort in the house *whose master saith* 'All this wealth is mine;'

Nor *in dwelling in* a lofty and beautifully built mansion.

In such deceptive avarice man loseth his human life.

He his pleased on beholding his elephants and his horses,

The assemblage of his army, his mace-bearers, and his servants;

But on their account, there is a halter of pride round his neck.

Were man to rule over the whole world,

Enjoy pleasures and embrace many women,

It would be as if a beggar became a king in a dream.

One comfort the true Guru hath pointed out to me—

'Whatever God doeth is pleasing to His saints.'
Slave Nanak, he who destroyeth his pride shall be absorbed in God.
In this way comfort is found, O my brother;
Thus God the Helper is obtained.

Since God is everywhere contained, man may lead a holy life as a householder:

Why wander? Who would wander
When God is contained in the water, dry land, the earth, and in the firmament?
The holy are saved; the perverse lose their honour.
Non can equal him
Whom the merciful God protecteth.
Since the one infinite Being pervadeth all things,
Be thou free from care and sleep happy:
God knoweth everything which happeneth,
The perverse are dying of thirst for mammon;
They wander through many births on account of their destiny writ from the beginning.
As man soweth, so shall he eat.
On beholding God, the heart delighteth;
The light of God is everywhere manifested.
God hath fulfilled all Nanak's desires.

Man after long transmigration having obtained human birth, ought to endeavour to utilize it and work out his deliverance:

In how many births wert thou a worm or a moth!
In how many births an elephant, a fish, or a deer!
In how many births a bird or a serpent!
In how many births wert thou yoked as a horse or an ox!
Meet the Lord of the world—this is the time to meet Him.
After a long period this human body hath been formed for thee.
In how many births wert thou created in rocks and mountains!
In how many births wert thou aborted from the womb!
In how many births wert thou born as a vegetable!
Thou didst wander through the eighty-four lakhs of existences.
Human birth having now been obtained by thee, associate with the saints,
Perform service, repeat God's name under the guidance of the Guru,
And renounce pride, falsehood and insolence.
If thou be dead when alive, thou shalt be acceptable in God's court.

O God, whatever hath been or shall be is Thy work.
There is none other fit to perform it.
Man shall meet Thee, O Lord, if Thou cause him to do so.
Saith Nanak, sing God's praises.

Man in his present state of probation ought to practise holiness:

Sow the Name in this productive soil,
And thy desires shall be accomplished;
Thou shalt obtain the fruit of thy labour and the fear of Death shall be dispelled.
Ever sing God's attributes and praises;
Clasp His name to thy heart,
And thou shalt quickly attain thine object.
Fix thine attention upon God,
And thou shalt obtain honour at His court.
Abandon all thy tricks and devices of speech,
And cling to the feet of holy men.
He in whose power all men are,
Shall never be separated from us, but shall be with us alway.
Abandon shifts; grasp His protection,
And in a moment thou shalt obtain deliverance.
Know that He is ever near thee.
Receive God's commands as true and obey them.
Under the Guru's instruction efface thyself
And repeat God's name, O Nanak.

Man ought to show gratitude to God for His many favours:

During the eight watches of the day meditate on that God
Who made thee a jewel out of earth,
Who carefully preserved thee in the womb,
And who bestowed on thee renown and greatness.
O All-pervading, may I obtain the dust of Thy saints' feet!
O men, meet the Guru and meditate on my Lord.
My mind forgetteth not that God,
Who turneth of foolish man into a preacher,
Who turneth a senseless into a sensible man,
And by whose favour the nine treasures are obtained.
May I day and night at every breath remember Him
Who giveth a home to the homeless,

Who giveth honour to the unhonoured,
Who fulfilleth all desires,
And by whose favour the chains of mammon are cut off!
By the favour of the Guru poison hath become nectar.
Saith Nanak, nothing is accomplished by man—
Praise ye the Preserver.

The advantages of devotion:

Hear the Word of God and thy uncleanness shall depart;
Thou shalt become very pure and obtain enduring happiness.
By good fortune the society of holy men is obtained,
And love to the Supreme Being produced.
God saveth His servants who repeat His name,
And conducteth them across the great sea of fire.
By singing God's praises the heart is refreshed,
And the sins of many births blotted out.
I behold in may heart God's whole treasure;
Why should I now go searching for it abroad?
When the Master is kind,
His servant's labour is already accomplished.
Remember, remember, remember the attributes of Him,
Who having cut off thy shackles hath made thee His servant.
There is but one God in the heart and in every place:
He filleth the whole world.
The perfect Guru hath dispelled all may doubts.
By remembering God, Nanak hath obtained comfort.

The human race tends to degenerate:

They who are dead have passed away;
They who survive stand with their loins girded:
Looking to the occupations in which the former were engaged,
The later have contracted twice their load of mammon.
They are entangled in things which are perishable,
And think not of the last hour.
The foolish person is bound by desire,
And involved in lust, anger, and worldly love:
Dharmraj standeth over him:
He eateth poison deeming it to be sweet, *and saith*

'I shall take mine enemy captive and punish him;
Who shall dare set foot on my soil?
I am a pandit, I am clever and wise.'
Attached to the world man knoweth not the Creator:
Only God knoweth His own state and condition.
What can one say? How can any one describe Him?
Man is engaged in whatever duties God appointed for him.
Every one prayeth to secure his own advantage.
Everything is Thine; Thou art the Creator.
Thou hast no end or limits.
Bestow this boon upon Thy slave Nanak,
That he may never forget Thy name.

They who without service to God are attached to mammon shall regret when it is too late:

Man is not satisfied with vast wealth.
It is not sufficient for him to see many phases of life; *he desireth to see more;*
He is entangled with children and wife, deeming them his own;
But his *wealth* shall perish, and his *children and wife* become heaps of ashes;
Then shall you behold him lamenting without God's name.
Accursed the bodies, accursed the wealth of the lovers of mammon.

All wealth is God's' it is but given to man for brief use:

As when one putteth a bag of money on the head of a forced labourer;
The money reacheth the master's house, but the labourer suffereth pain.
As when *a beggar* in a dream sitteth on a king's throne,
On opening his eyes *he findeth it* a baseless phantom.
As when a watchman is placed over another's field,
The field belongeth to its owner, and the watchman leaveth *when his business is done.*
Even though the watchman strive vigorously,
He shall not become owner of the field.
He to whom the empire *of the world* belongeth hath sent it as a dream.
He who made Maya hath infused avarice *into mankind.*
God Himself destroyeth, He himself restoreth.
Nanak, offer thy supplication unto Him.

Men in previous births held high positions, but are not now happy until saints tell them of God:

I have seen many forms and species of mammon;
With my pen I have written ingenious things on paper;
I have known what it is to be a chief, a king, a lord;
But with all that my mind was not satisfied.
O, ye saints, show me that comfort,
By which my thirst may be quenched and my mind satisfied.
I had fleet horses and elephants to ride on,
Distilled aloe wood, sandal, couches, and beautiful women.
Actors sang for me at performances in the arena,
Yet with all that my heart was not satisfied.
Mine were thrones, courts, jewels and carpets,
All fruits, beautiful gardens,
And the occupation of the chase, the sport of kings,
Yet my heart was not happy; all was illusion and deception.
The saints of their kindness told me of the True One,
And in Him I found all comfort and joy.
Sing God's praises in the company of the saints;
Saith Nanak, they are met by great good fortune.
He who hath God as his wealth is happy.
By God's mercy the company of the saints is obtained.

Men are entangled in mammon as birds in a net:

Man thinketh that his body is his own;
Again and again he clingeth to it.
Children, wives, and household are entanglements;
Which prevent man from becoming the servants of God.
What is that way by which God's praises may be sung?
What is that skill by which man may escape from mammon?
What is for man's good he deemeth evil.
If one tell him the truth, he regardeth it as poison.
He knoweth not what is for his profit or his loss.
That is how the infidel is entangled in the world.
The fool drinketh what is deadly poison for him.
And deemeth bitter the ambrosial Name.
He never approacheth the company of the saints;
He wandereth through the eighty-four lakhs of existences.
Birds after enjoying pleasures of various descriptions.

Are all caught in the same net.
Saith Nanak, the perfect Guru hath cut the net
For whomsoever he is merciful.

God's mercy and man's supplication:

By Thy mercy, O God, the way is found;
By Thy mercy the Name is meditated on;
By Thy mercy man is released from his fetters;
By Thy mercy pride is dispelled.
If Thou appoint me to Thy service I will perform it.
I can do nothing of myself, O God.
If it please Thee, I sing Thy word;
If it please Thee, I call Thee the True One;
If it please Thee, the true Guru is kind.
All happiness, O God, is obtained from Thy mercy.
Pure is the act which pleaseth Thee;
True is the faith which pleaseth Thee.
The treasury of all excellences is with Thee.
Thou art the Lord, Thy servant *maketh Thee this* supplication—
'May my soul and body become pure through the love of God!
May I obtain all happiness in the society of the saints!
May my soul be dyed with Thy name!'
This Nanak deemeth supreme happiness.

Of all relishes none so sweet as God's name:

O my tongue, thy thirst departeth not for an instant,
However many sweets thou tasteth.
If thou now taste the sweetness of God,
Thou shalt be astonished on tasting it.
My beloved tongue, drink the nectar of *God's name:*
Steeped in this relish thou shalt be satiated.
O my tongue, sing thou God's praises;
Every moment meditate on God.
The association of the saints is obtained by good fortune;
Go to none but them, and hear no words but theirs.
During the eight watches, O my tongue, adore
The supreme God, the unfathomable Lord,
And thou shalt be ever happy in this world and the next.

By singing His praises, O my tongue, thou shalt by beyond all price.
Plants and trees may burst into flower and fruit *and sweet may be their flavour,*
But God's name once tasted thou shalt never forsake.
No other relish can equal it.
Saith Nanak, the Guru hath become my succourer.

God who resides in the heart is the great merchant with whom the saints deal:

The heart is a building, the body is a fence constructed round it;
Within it are countless things;
Within it, we hear, dwelleth the Merchant.
Who are the dealers who enjoy credit with Him?
Few there are who deal in the precious Name,
Who eat its nectar as food,
And devote their soul and body to God's service.
What is the way by which God will be pleased?
Who is the man who will introduce me to that traffic?
I will touch his feet and renounce all ideas of mine and thine.
How shall I reach the Merchant's palace?
How shall I be invited to enter it?
Thou art the great Merchant who has millions of dealers.
Who is that benefactor who will associate me with them?
Searching and searching I have found my home.
The true one hath shown me the priceless jewel.
Saith Nanak, by faith in the Guru
He will mercifully blend us with the Merchant.

The saint's occupation, attributes and praises:

Night and day *the pious* abide in the love of the one *God.*
They believe God ever with them;
They make *the repetition* of God's name their occupation;
They are satisfied and comforted by His sight.
On entering the asylum of the perfect Guru
They become enamoured of God, and their minds and bodies grow happy.
God's lotus feet are the support of their souls.
They behold Him alone and carry out His orders;
They deal in only one thing, they occupy themselves with only one thing;
They think of nothing but the Formless One;
They are free from both joy and sorrow;

They are ever separated from the world, and devoted to religion;
They are seen among the crowd, but are not of it;
They fix their attention on the supreme God.
How can I describe the glory of the saints?
Their wisdom is unfathomable, and cannot be sounded.
O supreme God, have mercy on me,
And bestow on Nanak the dust of Thy saints' feet.

The general prevalence of mammon:

Maya is contained in the rejoicing and mourning diffused throughout the world;

She is contained in heaven, hell, and the incarnations;

She is contained in the rich, the poor, and those who are conspicuous for their splendour;

She is contained in covetousness which is the root of trouble;

She is contained *in the world* in various forms.

O God, the saints live by Thy protection, *and are not subject to Maya.*

Maya is contained in him who is intoxicated with intellectual pride;

She is contained in him who is attached to children and wife;

She is contained in elephants, horses, and other animals;

She is contained in him who is intoxicated with the wine of beauty and youth;

She is contained in kings, in the poor, *and in those addicted to* pleasures;

She is contained in the songs and musical instruments heard at assemblies;

She is contained in couches, in palaces, and their ornaments;

She is contained in the evil passions *which render man* blind;

She is contained in him who performeth religious ceremonies prompted by pride;

She is contained in the family man; she is contained in the anchoret;

She is contained in human occupations and conduct; she is contained in caste;

She is contained in everything except in those who are imbued with God's love.

God hath cut off the entanglements of the saints;
How can she be contained in them?
Saith Nanak, Maya approacheth not those
Who have obtained the dust of the saint's feet.

While the senses are asleep, the deadly sins rob the body:

The eyes sleep while coveting others' property;

The ears sleep on hearing tales of slander;
The tongue sleepeth in the desire for the relish of sweet things;
The mind sleepeth admiring mammon.
In this world few are watchful;
They who are receive their boon whole.
All the senses are intoxicated with their own pleasures,
And take no thought of the body they inhabit;
Wherefore the five plunderers and highway robbers
Fall upon its unguarded citadel to plunder it.
Neither father nor mother can protect man from them;
Neither friend nor brother can protect man from them;
They are not restrained by bride or diplomacy;
They are only controlled by the society of the saints.
Have mercy on me, O God;
Grant me the dust of the saint's feet for all my treasure.
He who meeting the true Guru is awake in the love of God,
O Nanak, hath the capital stock of *his human life* intact.
He is whom God is merciful is awake;
His capital stock, wealth, and property remain whole.
God's praises and glory and the advantages of remembering Him:
There is none besides Him
In whose power are lords and emperors;
In whose power is the whole world;
Who hath created everything.
Address thy supplication to the true Guru,
That he may arrange all thine affairs.
His court is the most exalted of all;
His name is the prop of all the saints.
The Lord whose glory shineth in every heart,
Is contained in everything, and filleth *creation*.
By remembering Him the abode of sorrow is demolished;
By remembering Him Death molesteth us not;
By remembering Him what is withered becometh green;
By remembering Him the sinking stone floateth;
Victory be ever to the society of the saints!
God's name is the support of the lives of His servants.

Saith Nanak, hear, O God, my supplication—
By the favour of the saints, grant me to dwell in Thy name.

The advantages of repeating and writing God's name:

Ever repeat God's praises with thy tongue,
And thou shalt obtain happiness, O my brother and friend.
Write with pen, paper and ink
The ambrosial word of God's name.
Thy hand shall then become pure,
And the entanglements of Maya shall be destroyed.
By thus acting all thy sins shall depart.
By remembering God Death shall not punish thee;
The myrmidons of Dharmraj shall not look at thee;
And even though engaged with the world it shall not fascinate thee.
Thou shalt be saved thyself, and shalt save the world
By repeating the name of the one God.
When God's name hath entered thy heart,
Make use of it thyself and advise others *to do so.*
He on whose forehead the wealth *of the Name*
Hath been written, shall repeat it.
Sing God's praises throughout the day:
Saith Nanak, I am a sacrifice unto Him.
Men act perversely:
What belongeth to another we deem our own;
Our hearts are attached to what ought to be abandoned.
Say how shall the Lord of the earth be found.
We love what is forbidden;
What is false we deem true.
The heart is in no wise attached to what is true.
We go crookedly by the left way;
Leaving the straight way we wend backwards.
God is the Lord of the two worlds—
Nanak, he who meeteth Him shall be saved.

The Guru in his humility feel himself unequal to worthily adoring God:

What form of Thine shall I adore?
By what science of Jog shall I discipline my body?
What art is that by which I can sing Thy praises?

What speech is that, O supreme God, by which I may please Thee?
What worship of Thine shall I perform?
What way is that by which I may cross the terrible ocean?
What is that penance by which I may become penitent?
What is that name by which the filth of pride may be washed away?
Skill, worship, divine knowledge, meditation, *and the fruit* of all his toil
Are obtained by him, O Nanak, whom the compassionate true Guru kindly meeteth.

It is such a man who possesseth excellence; it is he who knoweth God;
And the Giver of comfort granteth his prayers.
The Guru exhorts his soul to practice devotion:
O my soul, desire Him
In whom there is no deficiency:
O my soul, make that beloved God thy friend,
And ever remember Him who is the support of life.
O my soul, serve Him
Who is the primal Being and infinite God.
O my soul, place thy hope in Him
Who is the trusted of every age.
Nanak, on meeting the Guru, singeth the praises of God,
Whose love ever conferreth happiness.

Who are the really great:

They who appear to be very great in this world
Suffer from the malady of anxiety.
Who is great by reason of the greatness of his wealth?
He is great who devoteth his love to God.
Landowners ever strive for land;
Their covetousness is never extinguished; but they must leave their lands and depart.
Saith Nanak, the real thing I consider is,
That without repeating God's name there is no deliverance.

A man without piety is less useful than a beast:

Man eateth many species of food like a beast;
He is bound like a thief by the rope of worldly love;
His mortal body without the company of the saints
Is tortured in the womb by transmigration.

He weareth beautiful clothes of various sorts
Like a scarecrow in the fields to frighten *animals away*.
The bodies of all creatures are of use,
But man's is useless unless he utter the Name.
Saith Nanak, he to whom God is merciful
Uttereth God's name in the company of the saints.

The Guru's mission is accomplished:

The word of the Guru hath dispelled all trouble and affliction;
Transmigration is at an end, and all happiness attained.
By meditating on the Fearless God, fear is extinct.
I have sung the praises of God in the company of His saints.
I have put his lotus feet within my heart.
The Guru hath taken me across the sea of fire:
The perfect Guru extricated me when I was drowning:
The Guru united me *with God*, though separated from Him in various births.
Saith Nanak, I am a sacrifice to that Guru
By meeting whom my salvation hath been accomplished.

The following is repeated by Sikhs over a sick person:

Things which were withered God in a moment maketh green.
His ambrosial glance irrigateth and reviveth them.
The perfect God removeth all affliction.
When He bestoweth His service on His servant,
Anxiety is removed and the heart's desires fulfilled.
When the true Guru, who is an embodiment of good qualities, showeth mercy,
Sorrow fleeth away, and happiness taketh its place—
In this there is no delay—when God giveth the order.
Our desires are fulfilled when the true Guru is found;
Nanak, they *who find Him* bear good fruit.

They who seek God aright have no fear:

The whole world is sunk in fear;
But he who hath the Name for his support hath no fear.
He, O Lord, who taketh Thy protection feareth not:
What pleaseth Thee must be done.
They who mourn and rejoice suffer transmigration,
While they who are pleasing to the Lord obtain comfort.

Maya pervadeth this fiery ocean *of the world:*
They who have found the true Guru have recovered.
O God, the Preserver, preserve me!
Saith Nanak, what a poor creature am I!
Worthless is the body without the Name:
Mouths without the Name are empty
Like husks devoid of grain.
O mortal, ever repeat God's name:
Without it woe to the body, which *shall then become* Death's pray;
Without it the countenance loseth its lustre.
Without her spouse where is the wife?
When through devotion to the pleasures of the world man forgetteth the Name,
His desires are never fulfilled.
Saith Nanak, O God, mercifully grant me the favour
Of repeating Thy name day and night.

Man's sins cannot be concealed from God:

Man doeth evil but pretendeth to do good:
For this he shall be bound *like a thief* in God's court.
He who uttereth the name is *a saint* of God—
Who is equally contained in sea, land, the nether regions, and the firmament—
He who uttereth words of nectar while in his heart is poison,
Shall be bound and punished in Death's city.
The sins which man committeth behind many screens
Shall in a moment be laid bare to the world.
Nanak, God will be merciful to him.
In whose heart is the truth, and who is dyed with the love of the Name.

Man ought to show his gratitude to God by remembering Him:

Why should we show neglect to Him, O mother,
Who hath bestowed on us raiment and food?
He who forgetteth the Lord and attacheth himself to others,
Exchangeth a gem for a kauri.
Man may forsake God, fascinated by other deities;
But who hath honour by saluting a slave *instead of his master?*
Man taketh food and drink tasting like nectar;
But the dog knoweth not Him who gave them.

Saith Nanak, we are ungrateful;
Pardon us, O God, Thou Searcher of hearts.

The advantag of meditation on God:
Meditation in my heart on God's feet
Is for me equal to bathing and ablutions at all places of pilgrimage.
Remember God every day, O my brethren,
And the impurity of millions of births shall be washed away.

Piety is for man's advantage:
Men have made God their friend for their own advantage;
He fulfilleth all their desires and granteth them the dignity of salvation.
Let all so make God their friend
That none may depart in vain.
God removeth the sorrows, pains, and maladies of those
Who for their own objects hold Him in their hearts.
All their desires are fulfilled,
Who practise repetition of God's name with their tongues.
Nanak is many times a sacrifice unto them—
Profitable is a sight of my God.

The advantage of listening to divine instruction:
Hear the story of God in the company of the saints,
And millions of obstacles *to deliverance* shall be removed in a moment.
By drinking the nectareous juice of God's excellences and praises
And adoring His feet, hunger and thirst shall depart.
He in whose heart God dwelleth,
Possesseth the complete treasure of happiness, comfort and peace.
Medicines, charms, and spells are all in vain:
Clasp the Creator to thy heart.
Abandon all doubts, repeat the name of the Supreme Being;
And such religion, saith Nanak, shall be unshaken.

God is omnipotent to save:
The deadly sins like robbers were with me all day long,
But God mercifully dispersed them.
Let every one repeat with love the name of God
Who is full of all resources.

God in a moment causeth man to cross over
The very seething ocean of the world.
Man's many shackles can only be burst
By remembering the Name; thus he obtaineth the reward of salvation.
Man can accomplish nothing by tricks or devices of speech
Saith Nanak, show mercy to me, O God, that I may sing Thy praises.

Meditation on God and obedience to His word are potent for salvation:

The mortal, whether learned or unlearned,
Who meditateth on God, attaineth the supreme State.
In the company of the saints remember God.
Without the Name false is wealth and property.
He who obeyeth the voice of God
Is handsome, clever and wise.
Profitable is his advent into the world
Who recognizeth his Lord in every heart
Saith Nanak, he who is very fortunate
Applieth his mind to God's feet.

Incongruities:

Infidels consort not with God's servants;
The former are sinful; the latter love God.
The association would be as unmeet as if one who cannot ride were put astride a thoroughbred mare;
As if an impotent man were to caress a woman;
As if a spancel were put on an ox to milk him;
As if a man were to mount a cow and chase a lion;
As if one were to worship a sheep instead of the cow
Kamdhen, *which granteth all desires;*
As if one were to pursue trade without capital.
Nanak, repeat God's name in thy heart;
Remember a friend like the Lord God.

This saints' love of God illustrated by familiar examples:

As a wife is delighted on beholding her spouse,
As God's servant liveth by remembering His name,
As a mother reviveth on beholding her son,
So God's servant loveth God who is the warp and woof.
As an avaricious man rejoiceth on acquiring wealth,

So God's servant's heart is attached to His lotus feet.
They who bear such love to God
Enjoy the greatest good fortune: He blendeth them with Himself.
May I not forget Thee even for a moment, Thou beneficent One!
Nanak's God is the support of the soul.

The following was addressed to a hypocritical Brahman:

Thou openest thy waistcloth, and spreadest some of it beneath thee;
Thou loadest thy belly like a donkey;
But without good works, deliverance is not obtained—
The boon of deliverance is granted to meditation on the Name.
Thou performest worship and ablutions, and appliest sacrificial marks *to thy forehead;*
Thou pullest out a knife *to threaten suicide* if alms be not given thee;
Thou recitest the Veds with tuneful voice.
Shrinkest thou not from killing creatures, O mortal?
Saith Nanak, he to whom God showeth mercy
Is pure in heart and meditateth upon Him.

The condition of those who are imbued with God's love:

They who are imbued with God's love burn not in the flames;
They who are imbued with God's love are not deceived by Maya;
They who are imbued with God's love are not drowned in the water;
They who are imbued with God's love bear good fruit:
By God's name all their fear is dispelled;
They meet the society *of the saints,* and sing God's praises.
He who is imbued with God's love is freed from all anxieties;
He who receiveth the Guru's spell becometh attached to God;
He who is imbued with God's love hath no fear of Death;
He who is imbued with God's love hath his desires fullfilled;
He who is imbued with God's love suffereth not misery;
He who is imbued with God's love in watchful night and day;
He who is imbued with God's love abideth in the abode of happiness;
He who is imbued with God's love is preserved from doubts and fears;
He who is imbued with God's love obtaineth the highest wisdom;
He who is imbued with God's love is pure.
Saith Nanak, I am a sacrifice to those
Who forget not my God.

God helps and cherishes His servants:

He himself is His servant's helper.

Like a father and mother He ever cherisheth him.

Every one is saved by entering God's sanctuary.

It is he who acteth and causeth to act; he is omnipresent and true.

The Creator now dwelleth in my heart.

Fear is extinct and my soul hath obtained all happiness.

God mercifully preserveth His servants,

And their sins of many births fall off.

The glory of God cannot be described:

The slave Nanak is ever in His sanctuary.

Helpless man utters his wail to the Almighty:

O strong-armed puissant God, ocean of happiness, I am falling into the pit; take Thou my hand.

Mine cars hear not; mine eyes see not; afflicted and crippled I cry at Thy gate.

Patron of the poor and patronless, full of mercy, friend, father, mother.

Thou who causest Thy saints to cross over the ocean of fear—Nanak holdeth Thy lotus feet within his heart.

Without the Guru man has not wherewithal to recommend him to God.

By what virtue shall I meet the Lord of the soul, O my mother?

I possess no beauty, no understanding, no strength; I am a stranger come from afar.

I have not wealth or the glory of youth; friendless that I am, unite me, O God, with Thee.

Searching and searching I have renounced the world; I wander thirsting for a sight of Thee.

Compassionate to the poor, O merciful God, Nanak prayeth—quench my thirst with the society of the saints.

Instruction and supplication:

Depart, bird of the soul, and make remembrance of God thy pinions;

Meet the saint, embrace his society, put God's perfect jewel into thy heart.

Superstition is a pit, the thirst for pleasure its mire; very entangling is the noose of worldly love.

He who cutteth it is God, the world's Guru; dwell at His lotus feet.

O God, beloved Master, Lord of the poor, mercifully hear my supplication.

O Nanak's Lord, take my hand; the soul and body are all Thy capital.

Though God is in every heart, some men are good and others evil; the reason is known only to God:

O immortal King,

We dwell fearlessly with Thee; whence this fear?

In one person Thou appearest proud, in another lowly;

In one person Thou art haughty, in another humble;

In one person Thou art a pandit and preacher, in another Thou art stupid;

In one person Thou graspest at everything, in another Thou acceptest nothing.

What can man the poor wooden puppet do? He who setteth the puppet in motion knoweth its condition;

It playeth the part for which the Player dressed it.

He hath made various chambers of many descriptions within it, and He Himself guardeth it.

The soul must remain in whatever body it is placed; what can the wretched thing do?

He who made something, *namely,* all the contrivance *of the body,* knoweth its construction.

Nanak, the infinite God knoweth the value of His own work.

Amid the pleasures of sin man thinks not of death:

Abandon, abandon, the pleasures of sin:

O fool and madman, thou art entangled with them, and *shalt be punished* like cattle which fall upon crops.

What thou considerest thine advantage shall not go with thee an inch.

Naked didst thou come, naked shalt thou go: thou shalt become a morsel for Death, and return *to a body* again and again.

Beholding the short-lived sports of the world, thou art absorbed in them, and laughest while they last.

The string *of life* weareth away day and night; thou hast not done aught for thy soul.

Amid vain works old age *hath come upon thee;* thy speech faileth and thy body wasteth away.

Since that fascinating woman bewitched thee, thy love for her hath in no wise diminished.

When the Guru showed me that such was the world, I abandoned pride and entered Thy sanctuary, O God.

The saints showed me the way to God; the slave Nanak hath adopted God's service and praises.

Thanksgiving:

Whom have I but Thee,

My Beloved? Thou art the support of the soul.

Only Thou knowest the state of my heart; Thou art my friend and companion.

I have obtained all happiness from Thee; Thou art in tangible and unequalled.

I cannot describe Thy play, O ocean of merits, Bestower of happiness.

The unapproachable, invisible, and imperishable God is known by means of the perfect Guru.

Since I have destroyed pride, God hath banished my doubts and fears, and made me completely happy.

By showing me the company of the saints Thou hast put an end to my anxiety regarding transmigration.

I wash their feet; I serve the Guru and offer myself a sacrifice a hundred thousand times to him

By whose favour the slave Nanak hath crossed the terrible water and met the Beloved.

The bliss of the holy:

I am a sacrifice to them

Whose sole support is the Name.

How shall their greatness be estimated who are imbued with the love of the supreme Being?

Happiness, peace, and joy are with them; there are no others generous as they.

They who thirst for a sight of God, have come to save the world.

They who have sought their protection have been saved, and all their desires fulfilled in the company of the saints.

If I fall at their feet I shall survive; I am happy in the company of the saints.

O God, be merciful to me that my heart may become the dust of the saints' feet.

Empire, youth, and life—whatever is seen in this world decreaseth.

Nanak hath earned the treasure of the Name which is ever new and pure.

A Jogi came to the Guru and asked him if he had learned the science of Jog. The following was the Guru's reply:

The way of Jog I have heard from my Guru;

The true Guru hath communicated to me the Word.

Every moment I bow before Him who is contained in the nine regions of the earth and in this body.

I have made the Guru's instruction mine earrings, and have set up the one God *in my heart*.

The five pupils collectively I have placed under the control of One.

When the organs of perception and action were obedient, then I became a pure Jogi.

I burnt superstition and applied its ashes to my body; the sight of the one God I made my sect.

I have resignedly and gladly accepted that as the portion which God destined for me.

Where there was no fear, there I assumed my devotional attitude, and the ecstatic sound was was my Jogi's horn.

I have made meditation on God my staff, and love of the Name my rule of life.

The fetters of mammon shall be struck off that fortunate person who meeteth such a Jogi.

Nanak serveth and worshippeth such a person and licketh his feet.

A prayer to the Lord of life:

O Lord of my life, show me compassion and mercy; I helpless have entered Thy sanctuary.

Give me Thy hand, and extricate me from the blind well; I have no device or spell *to assist myself.*

Causer of causes, everything art Thou; Thou art omnipotent; there is none beside Thee.

Only Thou Thyself knowest Thine own state and condition; they who are so destined become Thy worshippers.

Thou, O God, lovest Thy worshippers: Thou art contained in them as the warp and woof.

They long for Thy very beloved name and a sight of Thee, as the chakor longeth for the moon.

There is no difference between God and His saints; but out of hundreds of thousands and millions there is only one real servant of God.

He in whose heart God is manifested repeateth His praises night and day.

O God, Thou art omnipotent, infinite, the Most High, the Giver of comfort and the Prop of life.

O God, mercifully grant Nanak the companionship of the saints.

Relations and worldly wealth avail not without devotion to God:

There is no happiness without devotion to God;

Win for thyself the priceless jewel of human life by repeating His name even for one moment in the company of saints.

Several people have left

Sons, wealth, wives, and pleasures after enjoying them.

Fools have departed naked leaving behind them

Excellent horses and elephants, and even the pomp of empire.

The bodies which were perfumed with distilled aloe wood and sandal,

Have been blended with the dust.

Infatuated by worldly love they deemed God distant,

But, saith Nanak, He is ever present.

Contempt for the body:

O body, great thy pride from such an origin.

Transitory art thou, however much thou grasp at worldly things.

Thou lovest those things which learned saints have forbidden thee.

As a gambler who while losing remaineth attached to play, so thy senses conquer and hold thee in bondage.

Thou art not imbued with love for the lotus feet of Him who destroyeth and createth all things.

The Treasure of mercy gave me, Nanak, the company of the saints by which I am saved.

Man, groping in the darkness of worldly love, desires the light of divine knowledge to dawn for him:

Is there any one who will dispel man's pride,

And turn his heart away from sweet mammon?

Man hath become spiritually ignorant; he desireth what existeth not.

His night is dark and gloomy; how can morning dawn for him?

I have grown weary wandering and searching in every way;

But *at last* God hath been merciful, *and I have obtained* the treasure of the company of the saints.

Man should think of his soul, not of his short-lived body:

O my soul, seek God's protection, and thou shalt be happy.

The days in which the Giver of life and happiness is forgotten, pass away in vain.

Thou hast come as the guest of one night, yet thou extendest the hope *of living* for many ages.

Houses, palaces, wealth, *everything* that is seen is like the shadow of a tree.

This body of mine, my entire wealth, gardens, and property shall all pass away.

Thou hast forgotten God, the Giver; in one moment these things shall become another's.

Thou bathest and puttest on clean clothes, and perfumest thyself with distilled aloe wood and sandal.

Thou thinkest not of the Fearless, the Formless One; thou art as an elephant *which throweth dust on itself after being* bathed.

When God is merciful, He will cause thee to meet the true Guru; all happiness abideth in God's name.

Nanak, by singing Gods' praises the Guru shall unlock thy fetters, and thou shalt be freed.

The following was written by the Guru on hearing that a raja was preparing an expedition to seize another raja's territory:

The thirst of only a few is slaked.

Man amasseth thousands and millions but restraineth not his mind;

He is burning for more and more.

Though possessing beautiful women of many races, he committeth adultery in other men's houses.

He distinguisheth not between bad and good.

Under the many bonds of mammon he wandereth and singeth not the praises of the Treasury of excellences;

His mind is absorbed in worldly affairs.

He to whom God is merciful is dead while alive, and in the company of the saints crosseth over *the ocean* of the world:

Nanak, that man shall be acceptable in God's court.

To man God should be the dearest of all:

God is the darling object of all men.

Some love contemplation, some pleasure, some divine knowledge, some meditation,

And some a hermit's life.

Some love lip-worship, some austerities, some adoration, burnt offerings, and daily ceremonies;

And some a wandering existence.

Some love the shore, some the sea, some the study of the Veds,

But to Nanak *only* God's service is dear.

God to the Guru is everything that is precious:

The celebration of Thy praises is my treasure.

Thou art my delight, Thou art my glory; Thou art my beauty, Thou art my love;

Thou, O God, art my Hope and my Shelter;

Thou art my pride, Thou art my wealth, Thou art mine honour, Thou art my life,

The Guru hath united me with Thee from whom I had parted.

Thou art my home, Thou art my forest, Thou art my village, Thou art my desert;

Saith Nanak, Thou art to me the nearest *and dearest* of all.

The Guru gives the opinion of holy men as to the means of salvation:

They who dwell under the sovereign Lord's protection shall be saved:

All others fall to the ground from the lofty heights of mammon.

Great men after the study of the Shastras, the Simritis, and the Veds, have thus expressed themselves—

'There is no salvation, nor hath any one found comfort without the repetition of God's name.'

Man may have amassed the wealth of the three worlds, yet his avarice will not *otherwise* be slaked.

Without repeating God's name can stableness be obtained? *No*; man shall transmigrate again and again.

Man engageth in various fascinating recreations, yet his desires are never satisfied.

They ever burn and are never quenched; without the Name all things are vain.

Repeat God's name, O my friend; this is the essence of perfect happiness.

In the company of the saints and by becoming the dust of their feet, Nanak hath freed himself from transmigration.

The Guru gives a compendium of his teaching:

Without God all works are vain.

By works of *hypocritical* devotion, penance, and austerities man is plundered on this side.

He who abideth in fasting, insincere ceremonies, and austerities shall not obtain an eighth of a paisa.

In the next world the coin is different, my brother; this coin will be of no use there.

He who batheth at a place of pilgrimage and wandereth over the earth, shall find no abiding place hereafter.

Such things shall avail him not; he merely pleaseth people thereby.

Man shall not hereafter find a place in God's court by reciting the four Veds.

He who knoweth not the Pure and Imperishable One, uttereth sheer nonsense.

Nanak hath expressed this opinion; he who acteth on it shall be saved.

Serve the Guru, meditate on God's name, and dismiss pride from thy heart.

The Guru addresses God with great fervour:

Come, my beloved God,

Night and day, at every breath let me meditate on Thee.

O saints, give God this message, 'I fall at Thy feet;

Without Thee how shall I be saved?

With Thee I rejoice;

Thou art in the forest, in the glades, in the three worlds;

Thou conferrest supreme happiness and joy.

My couch is pleasant, my soul expandeth *towards Thee*. On beholding Thee happiness shall be mine.

I will wash Thy feet, and continually perform Thy service.

I will worship Thee, make Thee offerings, and do Thee homage;

Thy slave of slaves will repeat Thy name.'

Repeat, O saints, this my supplication to God;

So shall my desires be fulfilled and my soul and body revive.

On beholding God all my griefs shall be dispelled.

By continually repeating God's name Nanak shall be saved,

And obtain unfading happiness.

Sing God's praises received from a saint and pray for God as your alms:

O my soul, sing God's delicious praises; sing God's delicious praises.

Attached to the True One, the homeless obtain a home.

All other relishes are insipid and render body and soul insipid.

Accursed is his life who doeth aught contrary to God's will.

Grasp the saint's skirt and thou shalt cross over the ocean.

Adore the supreme God, and all thy family shall be saved.

He who putteth God's name into my heart is my saint, my kinsman, my friend;

He bestoweth on me the favour of blotting out all my demerits.

My property, my treasure, and my home may go to ruin; my wealth is in God's feet.

Nanak begging at Thy gate, O God, craveth for Thee as his alms.

Gauri Ashtapadi

It is said that one Raj Chand went to the Guru and asked him how happiness could be obtained and unhappiness avoided. The following was the Guru's reply:

When man harboureth pride in his heart,

He wandereth about mad and estranged from God.

When man becometh the dust of all men's feet,

He on that account beholdeth God in every heart.

The fruit of humility is naturally pleasant:

This gift my true Guru gave me.

When men deemeth others bad,

All weave plots against him.

When he hath ceased to speak of things as his own,
No one beareth him enmity.
When man holdeth things as his own,
He suffereth serious trouble.
When man recognizeth the Creator,
His sufferings are at an end.
When man entangleth himself with worldly love,
He suffereth transmigration and falleth under Death's continual ken.
When man's doubts are removed,
There is no difference between him and the Supreme.
From the moment that man recognizeth a difference,
He suffereth pain, punishment and affliction.
From the moment that man knoweth the one God,
He hath obtained all knowledge.
When man runneth after mammon,
He findeth it not, nor doth his thirst depart.
When man fleeth from mammon,
She proceedeth to pursue him.
When the true Guru is found by his own mercy,
The lamp is lit in the temple of one's heart.
When man considereth his gain and loss,
He realizeth the value of this temple.
The one God doth everything and causeth everything to be done.
He Himself is wisdom, reflection and discrimination.
He is not distant, He is near and with all.
Nanak, praise the true God with love.

All must perish save God who has no end or limit:
In the first place, man issueth from his dwelling in the womb;
He afterwards attacheth himself to his children, wife and family.
Thy dishes of many sorts and thy varied dresses,
O wretched man, shall assuredly pass away.
What place is that which shall ever be permanent?
What word is that by which evil inclinations shall be removed?
Even the realm of Indar must assuredly perish;
Even the realm of Brahma remaineth not permanent;
And even the realm of Shiv shall dissolve.

Maya with the three qualities and the demons shall perish.
Mountains, trees, the earth, the firmament, and the stars
The sun, the moon, wind, fire and water,
The laws and alternations of day and night,
The Shastras, the Simritis, and the Veds,
Places of pilgrimage, demigods, temples, and books,
Rosaries, frontal marks, purely cooked victuals,
Loin cloths, prostrations, raiment, food,
Shall pass away with all men.
Race, caste, Musalmans, Hindus,
Beasts, birds, animals of different species,
All the visible creation,
And all forms of existence shall perish.
By praising and serving God real divine knowledge is *obtained,*
Which ever conferreth happiness and the permanent and true abode.
Where the congregation of the saints are absorbed in God's praises,
And dwell for ever in the fearless city,
There is no fear, no doubt, no mourning, no anxiety,
No transmigration, no death, no birth.
There is for ever joy and the theatre of spontaneous music.
The saints dwell there, singing God's praises is their sustenance.
The supreme Being hath no end or limit.
Who can describe Him?
Saith Nanak, he to whom *God* is merciful
Shall reach the imperishable place in the company of the saints.

He who divests himself of love of mammon shall attain all perfection:

He who divesteth himself of the love of mammon, is a hero;
He who so divesteth himself, is perfect;
He who so divesteth himself, shall obtain greatness;
He who so divesteth himself, shall be free from suffering.
If there is any one who so divesteth himself,
And banisheth his love of mammon, he accomplisheth raj jog.
He who so divesteth himself, shall have no fear;
He who so divesteth himself, shall be absorbed in the Name
He who so divesteth himself, shall have his thirst extinguished;
He who so divesteth himself, shall be acceptable in God's court:

He who so divesteth himself, shall become wealthy;
He who so divesteth himself, shall be honoured;
He who so divesteth himself, shall become continent;
He who so divesteth himself, shall obtain deliverance—
The advent of him who so divesteth himself, is profitable—
He who so divesteth himself, shall be stable and opulent;
He who so divesteth himself, shall be very fortunate;
He who so divesteth himself, shall be watchful night and day;
He who so divesteth himself, shall obtain salvation while alive;
He who so divesteth himself, shall lead a pure life;
He who so divesteth himself, shall be thoroughly versed in divine knowledge;
He who so divesteth himself, shall meditate on God—
Without so divesting himself man shall not be acceptable,
Even though he perform millions of *superstitious* ceremonies and forms of worship—
Without so divesting himself he shall be born again;
Without so divesting himself he shall not escape from Death;
Without so divesting himself he shall not obtain divine knowledge;
Without so divesting himself his impurity shall not be washed away;
Without so divesting himself everything is defilement;
Without so divesting himself everything is an entanglement.
He to whom the Ocean of mercy is merciful,
Shall be freed and shall obtain all perfection.
He whose love of mammon is removed by the Guru,
Shall, saith Nanak, meditate on God.

He who embraces a holy life shall obtain everything that is prized:

He who attacheth himself to God findeth a friend in everybody;
He who attacheth himself to God hath a stable mind;
He who attacheth himself to God feeleth no anxiety;
He who attacheth himself to God shall be saved.
O my soul, unite thyself with God;
Naught else shall avail thee.
Great worldly people *who think not of God,*
Are useless and ignorant.
Although God's slave be accounted of lowly birth,
Yet in his company men shall be at once saved.
Hearing God's name is equal to millions of ablutions;

Meditating on Him is equal to millions of adorations;
Hearing His praises is equal to millions of alms-deeds;
Knowing His ways from the Guru bringeth millions of rewards.
Think again and again *upon God* in thy heart,
And thy love for mammon shall depart.
The immortal God is with thee;
O man, be absorbed in thy love for Him,
Specially perform the service of Him
By serving whom all thine avarice shall depart;
By serving whom the myrmidons of Death will not look at thee;
By serving whom thou shalt obtain great honour;
By serving whom thou shalt be immortal;
Whose servant shall not be punished;
Whose servant shall not be *even* bound;
And in whose office thine account shall not be called for
O man, perform the service of Him
Who is in need of nothing,
Who is one though of various forms,
And at whose sight thou art ever happy.

Without remembering God man is on a level with everything that is low and base:

He who remembereth not God, leadeth the life of a snake;
So liveth the infidel who forgetteth the Name.
He who liveth remembering God even for a moment,
Shall live for millions of days, yea, for ever.
Cursed be the acts done without remembering God!
The infidel like a crow's beak dwelleth in filth:
Without remembering the name his desires are those of a dog.
The infidel is nameless like a prostitute's son;
Without remembering the Name he is like a ram's horn.
The infidel uttereth falsehood and his face is blackened;
Without remembering God's name he is like a donkey
Which wandereth about in foul places.
Without remembering the Name he is as a mad dog.
The covetous infidel falleth into entanglements;
Without remembering the Name he committeth suicide.
The infidel is low; he hath neither family nor caste.

The Guru causeth him to whom he is merciful to meet the society of saints,
And, O Nanak, to cross over *the ocean of* the world.

The evil fate of him who forgets the Name:

Come to me, O my God, bestow on me Thy name;
Totally accursed be the love which is without the Name!
He who dresseth himself or eateth without invoking the Name,
Is like a dog fallen on garbage.
Business performed without the Name
Is futile as the decorations of a corpse.
He who enjoyeth pleasures in forgetfulness of the Name,
Hath no happiness even in his dreams; nay, his body becometh diseased.
If man abandon the Name for any other occupation,
The whole of false gilding shall fall off.
He who loveth not heartily the Name,
Shall go to hell even though he perform millions of ceremonies.
He who remembereth not God's name in his heart,
Shall be bound like a thief in the realm of Death.
There might be hundreds of thousands of displays and great profusion,
Yet without the Name they would all be vain ostentation.
That man repeateth God's name
To whom, O Nanak, He mercifully granteth it.

What God the Friend does for man:

My soul longeth for that Friend,
Who forsaketh me not at the beginning, middle, or end of my undertakings.
God's love ever accompanieth us;
He is the Compassionate and omnipresent Cherisher.
He perisheth not, neither doth He abandon *His servant*.
Wherever I gaze, there is He contained.
He is beautiful, skilful clever, the Giver of life;
He is brother, son, father and mother;
He is the support of my life and soul; He is my capital.
Dwelling in my heart He hath made me love Him.
He hath cut off mammon's chains,
And, beholding me with a favourable eye, made me His own.
By ever remembering God all diseases are healed,
And by meditating on His feet all happiness enjoyed.

The all-pervading Being is ever fresh and youthful;

He is the companion and protector of man whether at home or abroad.

Saith Nanak, the saint who knoweth God's dignity

Hath obtained from Him the Name for all his *wealth*.

The man who knows not God passes his life in pleasures, worldly love, and pride, and cannot obtain salvation:

Through pleasures, social gatherings, and the gratification of evil passions, man, blind that he is, knoweth not God.

His whole life passeth away saying, 'I hoard, I earn;

I am a hero, I am distinguished; no one is equal to me;

I am young, religious, of good family'; thus pride entereth his heart,

And he forgetteth it not until death, so entangled is he in his boastful intellect.

He resigneth *his wealth* to his brothers, friends, kinsmen, and companions who survive him.

The desire to which the mind is attached becometh supreme at the last hour.

If man perform purifications through pride, he becometh bound by such entanglements.

O merciful God, show mercy that Nanak may become the slave of Thy slaves.

Gauri Chhant

Man should consider how to obtain God's favours:

Hear, my companions, let us join and make efforts to please God the Bridegroom;

Through the saint's spell let us abandon pride and through the philtre of devotion fascinate our Spouse.

O my companions, once He cometh into our power, He will not again forsake us; this is a good custom of the Lord;

Nanak, God will make us pure and dispel the fear of old age, death and hell.

Hear, my companions, this is a good course; let us adopt it.

Having withdrawn from worldly cares let us sing God's praises with composure and devotion.

Our troubles and difficulties shall depart, our doubts be dispelled, and we shall obtain the reward our hearts desire.

Nanak, let us meditate on the name of the supreme and omnipresent God.

O My companions, I have ever desired to devote myself to God; may He grant my desires!

Having renounced the world I thirst for a sight of His feet; I look for them everywhere.

To find the omnipresent Being I will trace His tracks in the company of the saints.

Nanak, the holy men who have found the Giver of comfort are very fortunate.

O my companions, I now dwell with my beloved Spouse; and my soul and body have become attached to Him.

Here me, O my companions, I sleep well since I have found my Beloved.

I have lost my doubts, I have obtained peace and rest; the Lord hath appeared unto me, and the lotus of my heart hath blossomed.

I have found my Husband, the Lord, the Searcher of hearts; O Nanak, my married state shall never cease.

The Bawan Akhari

Or Acrostic

The divine Guru is my mother, the divine Guru is my father, the divine Guru is my lord and Supreme God;

The divine Guru is my companion and dispeller of spiritual ignorance, the divine Guru is my relation and my brother;

The divine Guru is the giver and the teacher of God's name, the divine Guru hath the spell that cannot be counteracted;

The divine Guru is peace, truth, the image of wisdom; the divine Guru is a philosopher's stone by touching which man is saved;

The divine Guru is a place of pilgrimage, his divine knowledge a lake of nectar, by bathing in which the Illimitable is obtained;

The divine Guru is the Creator, the remover of all sin, the divine Guru is the purifier of the impure;

The divine Guru is from the beginning, from the beginning of time, and in every age; the divine Guru is the speil of God's *name* by the utterance of which man is saved.

O God, mercifully bring me—foolish and sinner that I am—into the company of the Guru, so that by clinging to him I may be saved.

Nanak boweth to the divine Guru, the true Guru, the Supreme Brahm, the Supreme God.

Slok I

God himself created and caused *men* to act; He himself is capable of acting.

Nanak, there is one pervading God; there neither was nor shall be another.

Pauri I

O A M. I bow to the one God, and to the saint the true Guru.

The Formless One is the beginning, the middle , and the end.

He Himself is rest, He Himself hath His seat in bliss;

He Himself heareth His praises;

He himself created Himself;

He is His own father, His own mother;

He Himself is small, He Himself is large—

Nanak, His play cannot be understood.

O God, compassionate to the poor, be merciful,

That my heart may become the dust of the saints' feet.

Slok II

The one God is without form and yet with form; He is without qualities and yet possesseth all qualities.

Define the one God as one, Nanak, and the one God as manifold.

Slok III

O A M. The one God, the great Guru, created all things;

He hath strung them all on one string.

The three qualities are separately diffused.

Instead of possessing no attributes God now appeareth possessing all attributes.

He made creation of all forms;

From the increase of mental desires resulteth transmigration;

He himself is free from both birth and death.

Nanak, He hath no end or limit.

Slok III

They are rich and fortunate who possess the hoard of the truth and the stock-in-trade *of God's name.*

Nanak, the true and pure *Name* is obtained from the saints.

Slok III

S. True, true, true is He;

There is nothing separate from the True Being.

It is he whom He putteth into his asylum who obtaineth *His protection,*

Remembereth Him, singeth His praises, and causeth others to hear them:

Doubt and error in no way enter him;

His glory appeareth manifest.

Nanak is ever a sacrifice unto the holy man

Who attaineth to this distinction.

Slok IV

Why art thou crying out for wealth? All worldly love is false.

All they who are without the Name, Nanak, are as dust.

Pauri IV

D.H. The dust of Thy servant's feet is pure, *O God;*

Blest are they whose souls desire it;

They want not wealth, they desire not even paradise;

They are fascinated with the love of the very Dear One, and the dust of the saint's *feet.*

Why should worldly affairs affect those

Who forsake not the one God or go elsewhere *to worship?*

He in whose heart God hath put the Name,

O Nanak, is a perfect saint of God.

Slok V

It is not by *adopting* various religious garbs or by knowledge or meditation, or by obstinacy that God is obtained by any one:

Saith Nanak, he to whom God is merciful is a saint and possessor of divine knowledge.

Pauri V

N G. Divine knowledge consisteth not in words uttered by the mouth,

Nor *in extracting* different species of arguments from the Shastras.

He possesseth divine knowledge in whose heart God is firmly fixed;

It is not by discussion be becometh capable.

He who is strict in his obedience to God's order possesseth divine knowledge;

Heat and cold are all the same to him.

The possessor of divine knowledge, to whom God extendeth mercy,

Meditateth on God, O Nanak, under the Guru's instruction.

Slok VI

Men come into the world, but without knowing God they are as beasts and cattle.

Nanak, the holy man, on whose forehead such destiny hath been written, knoweth God.

Pauri VI

The foetus reversed in the pit of the womb performeth penance,

And continueth to remember God at every breath.

Man then cometh into this world to meet the one God,
But fascinating Maya fascinateth him at his birth.
He becometh entangled with what he must abandon,
And in his soul forgetteth the Giver.
He to whom Thou showest favour, O Lord of the earth,
Will not forget Thee, *saith* Nanak, either here or there.

Slok VII

Man is born by God's order, he dieth by God's order, no one is exempt from His order;

Transmigration is at an end for him, Nanak, in whose heart God abideth.

Pauri VII

This soul hath dwelt in many wombs;
Immersed in sweet illusion it was entangled in them;
This illusion hath reduced the world to subjection,
And infused a love for itself into every heart:
O my friend, tell us of some device
By which we may escape this dangerous illusion.
Maya approacheth not him,
O Nanak, whom God mercifully associateth with the saints.

Slok VIII

God Himself hath appointed good and bad acts for man to perform;
But man the brute indulgeth in pride; Nanak, what can he do without God?

Pauri VIII

It is God alone who causeth *man* to act;

It is He Himself who diffuseth demerits and merits.

Man performeth the duties *of the station* in which God hath placed him in this world,

And receiveth what God conferreth upon him.

No one knoweth God's limit;

It is only what He doeth that occurreth.

It is from Him alone the whole creation hath proceeded. Nanak, He himself is the arranger.

Slok IX

Man continueth to love women, pleasures, and the tumult of the passions, *Things fleeting* as the dye of the safflower.

Nanak, take God's protection and thy selfishness shall depart.

Pauri IX

O my soul, the more thou lovest anything except God, the greater thine entanglements.

The apostates do the very things which in every way hinder their emancipation.

They who while practising pride continue to perform ceremonial works, bear a crushing load:

When there is not love for the Name such works are sinful.

They who are in love with delicious Maya are bound by death's rope;

Deluded by error they know not that God is ever with them;

They shall not be acquitted when their accounts are examined: a mud wall can never be clean.

He to whom God giveth knowledge, O Nanak, becometh holy and his understanding pure.

Slok X

They who associate with the saints and who are dyed with the deep dye of the one God's love,

O Nanak, shall have their fetters cut off.

Pauri X

R. Dye this heart of thine *with God's love;*

Repeat God's name with thy tongue,

So shall no one address thee rudely in God's court:

Every one shall honour thee, saying, 'Come, sit down.'

In that palace thou shalt obtain thy dwelling

Where there is no transmigration or destruction.

God's wealth is in the house of him,

Nanak, on whose forehead such destiny was recorded in the beginning.

Slok XI

The sins of covetousness, falsehood, and worldly love are committed by the foolish and the blind;

Slaves of Maya, O Nanak, They love an offensive small.

Pauri XI

L. They are entangled and steeped in the juice of evil passions;

They are intoxicated with the wine of mental pride and worldly love;

And from this worldly love resulteth transmigration.

As God ordereth so man acteth.

There is no one imperfect and no one perfect;
There is no one wise and no one foolish.
Where God appointed men there they perform their duties.
Nanak, the Lord is always unaffected by *mundane affairs*.

Slok XII

My darling God, the Lord of the earth, is deep, profound, and unfathomable;
Nanak, there is none like unto Him, He is unconcerned.

Pauri XII

L. There is none equal to Him;
He Himself is the only one, there shall be none other;
He is now and ever hath been;
No one hath found His limit;
He is contained as fully in an ant as in an elephant;
He is famous, known everywhere:
He to whom He hath given His love
Repeateth His name, O Nanak, under the Guru's instruction.

Slok XIII

He who hath tasted the savour of God naturally enjoyeth He love.
Nanak, blessed is the advent of such into the world; he is acceptable *to God*.

Pauri XIII

Deem fortunate the birth of him
Whose tongue repeateth God's praises;
He goeth and sitteth with the saints,
And night and day meditateth on the Name with love.
He to whom God showeth compassion and mercy,
Is at his birth endued with the Name;
He has been born once, but shall not again enter the womb;
Nanak, he shall be absorbed in the sight of God.

Slok XIV

Nanak, be absorbed in the Name by the repetition of which the heart becometh happy, worldly love is erased,
And there is an end to pain, sorrow, and longing for earthly pleasures.

Pauri XIV

Y. Rid thyself of evil inclinations and duality;

Relinquishing them sleep in peace and composure.

Y. Go and take the protection of the saints,

By whose assistance thou shalt cross *this* terrible ocean.

Y. He who taketh the one Name and stringeth it in his heart,

Shall not be born again.

Y. By the support of the Guru thou shalt not lose thy *human* birth.

Nanak, he in whose heart the one God dwelleth hath obtained happiness.

Slok XV

He who is our friend in this world and the next, dwelleth within our souls and bodies.

The perfect Guru teacheth us, O Nanak, to utter God's Name continually.

Pauri XV

Night and day remember Him who will in the end be thy helper.

These worldly pleasures only last for a few days; every one must leave them and depart.

Who hath a mother, father, son, daughter,

Home, or wife? Though canst take none of them with thee.

Amass such things as are not perishable,

So shalt thou depart to thine own home with honour.

They who in this Kal age sing God's praises in the company of the saints,

O Nanak, shall not come again *into the world*.

Slok XVI

Though one be very beautiful, of high birth, wise, a divine in words and wealthy,

Yet shall he be deemed as dead, O Nanak, if he have no love for God.

Pauri XVI

N.G. Even though man be versed in the six Shastra systems,

And perform the exercises of purak, kumbhak and rechak;

Even though he practise divine knowledge, meditation, pilgrimages and ablutions,

Only eat food cooked by himself, live apart from human contact and dwell in the forest;

Yet if he feel no love for God's name in his heart,

Every act of his shall only be brief.

Superior to him deem thou the pariah,

O Nanak, in whose heart God dwelleth.

Slok XVII

Man wandereth about in the four quarters and the ten directions of the world bearing the mark of deeds done.

Weal and woe, deliverance and transmigration, Nanak, are according to man's written record.

Pauri XVII

K. God is the Creator and cause of everything;

No one can efface that written record;

What God once doeth cannot be altered;

The Creator erreth not.

To one He Himself pointeth out the right way;

Another He causeth to wander sorrowfully in the wilderness;

He playeth His own play.

Whatever He giveth, Nanak, man receiveth.

Slok XVIII

Various and countless people, O Nanak, repeat God's name.

Men eat, spend, and enjoy themselves, but God's storehouses fail not *them*.

Pauri XVIII

K.H. With that all-powerful One there is no stint;

He continueth to give what *He deemeth right* to give, wheresoever man may go.

The wealth of the Name is the treasure from which the saints spend; it is their capital.

With patience, humility, joy, and composure they continue to repeat God's praises.

They to whom God is merciful sport and enjoy themselves.

They who have God's name for their wealth in their homes are ever wealthy and of good report.

They on whom God looketh with favour suffer not trouble, or pain, or torture;

Nanak, they who are pleasing to God are successful.

Slok XIX

Calculate and consider in thy mind that men must assuredly depart.

The desire for transitory things is effaced by the Guru's instruction; only in the Name is there health.

Pauri XIX

G. Sing God's praises at every breath and ever repeat His name.

Why repose confidence in thy body? Delay not, my friend;

There is no reliance on childhood, youth, or old age:

The time is not known when the noose of Death will fall upon thee.

Behold the wise, the meditative, and the clever; *even* they remain not here.

The fool clingeth to the things which the rest of the world leaveth behind.

He on whose forehead such destiny hath been written, continueth to remember God by the Guru's favour.

Nanak, fortunate is her advent who is the spouse of the Beloved.

Slok XX

I have searched all the Shastras and Veds; they tell of nothing save this,

That the one God was in the beginning, in the beginning of time, is now, Nanak, and ever shall be.

Pauri XX

G.H. Put this into thy heart that there is none but God;

There was none and there shall be none: He is everywhere contained.

Thou shalt be absorbed in Him, O man, when thou enterest His asylum.

In the Kal age the Name is the real atonement for sins.

After toiling and moiling in superstitious exercises many regret it;

Without devotion to God how can stability be obtained?

He to whom the divine Guru gave the great nectareous essence,

Hath stirred it up, O Nanak, and drunk it.

Slok XXI

God has counted and fixed for man all his days and breathings; these cannot be increased or diminished the length of a sesame seed;

Nanak, they who desire to live on in error and worldly love are fools.

Pauri XXI

N.G. Death shall seize him who hath fallen away from God.

He seeth not God who dwelleth in his heart, and he shall suffer many transmigrations.

Divine knowledge and meditation shall come to him

To whom God mercifully granteth them.

No one shall be emancipated by making calculations;

The frail pitcher shall burst at last.

Only they who utter God's name their lives long really live;

The become distinguished, Nanak, and not obscure.

Slok XXII

In thy heart meditate on God's lotus feet, and its inverted lotus shall bloom.

God Himself will appear, O Nanak, under the saints' instruction.

Pauri XXII

C.H. Blest blest that day and auspicious that conjuncture
When I cling to the Guru's lotus feet.
After wandering in the four corners and the ten directions *of the globe,*
I through the favour of God obtained a sight of him.
Through excellence meditation all duality is removed;
My mind hath become pure by association with the saints.
Nanak, he to whose eyes the salve of divine knowledge hath been applied,
Shall forget his anxieties and behond the one God.

Slok XXIII

The breast becometh cool and the heart happy by singing the chant of God's praises;

Show such mercy, O God, that Nanak may become Thy slave of slaves.

Pauri XXIII

C H H. We are Thy slave-boys.
Yea, we are the water carriers of the slave of Thy slaves.
C H H. We are the dust of Thy saints' feet :
Show us Thy mercy, O God.
We have abandoned all devices and stratagems,
And propped up our souls with the prop of the saints.
The puppet of ashes whom the saints assist
Shall, Nanak, obtain the supreme state.

Slok XXIV

Man is greatly elated by his strength and power, and thereby diseaseth his frail body;

Through his pride he is entangled, Nanak, but the Name will released him.

Pauri XXIV

J. When a man thinketh something of himself,
He is caught like a parrot in a trap;
When he thinketh he is a saint and possessed of divine knowledge,
God will show him no respect whatever in the next world;

When he thinketh he is a preacher,

He *merely* roameth over the earth like a trader.

He who removeth his pride by association with the saints

O Nanak, meeteth God.

Slok XXV

Rise at dawn, utter the Name, *yea,* night and day worship *God;*

Thus shalt thou feel no anxiety, Nanak, and all thy troubles shall vanish.

Pauri XXV

J.H. By occupying thyself with God's name

All thy griefs shall be effaced.

The perverse man whose heart feeleth worldly love

Shall die in excessive grief.

O my soul, when thou hearest the ambrosial word in the company of saints,

Thine impurities and sins shall depart.

Nanak, from him to whom God is merciful,

Lust, wrath, and other evil passions shall depart.

Slok XXVI

Though you make efforts of various kinds, you shall not have eternal life, my friends.

You shall have eternal life, *saith* Nanak, if you repeat God's name with love.

Pauri XXVI

N.Y. Know for a certainty that *these bodies of yours* which you love shall perish.

Even though you make calculations, you cannot count how many have departed.

Whatever you behold shall perish; to what shall you attach yourselves?

Know this in your hearts as certain that love of the world is false.

He who knoweth this is a saint and removed from error.

Him with whom God is pleased, He extricateth from the blind well.

He whose arm is omnipotent is able to create the world—

Nanak, praise him who uniteth the *soul with Himself.*

Slok XXVII

By serving the saints the bonds of transmigration are broken, and man obtaineth rest:

Nanak, may I never forget the sovereign God, the treasury of excellences!

Pauri XXVII

Serve the one God to whom no one appealeth in vain;

If He dwell in thy soul, body, mouth, and heart, thou shalt obtain whatever thou desirest.

He to whom the holy man is kind, shall obtain the service *by which God's court shall be won*.

If God be compassionate thou shalt abide in the company of the saints—

I have searched in many lands, but *found* no happiness without the Name.

The ministers of Death shall recede from him who joineth

The society of the saints;

Again and again I sacrifice myself to the saints,

Through whom, O Nanak, the sins of old are blotted out.

Slok XXVIII

They with whom God is pleased are not stopped at His gate;

Supremely blest are they, Nanak, whom God hath made His own.

Pauri XXVIII

T.H. He who having abandoned all else attacheth himself to the one God,

Afflicteth no one's heart.

They who are buffeted by worldly love are dead,

And find nowhere comfort.

They who abide in the company of the saints are refreshed;

The ambrosial Name is sweet to their souls.

The soul of the man who pleaseth his Lord,

O Nanak, becometh refreshed.

Slok XXVIX

Prostrations and obeisance many times to Thee, *O God,* who possessest all contrivances and art omnipotent!

Reach me Thy hand, O God, *saith* Nanak, and save me from wavering.

Pauri XXIX

D.O. my soul, this is not thy dwelling; know that Place where thy dwelling is;

Learn from the Guru's instruction the way to that dwelling.

Man undergoeth toil to erect of dwelling here

Which will not go an inch with him.

He on whom the omnipotent God looketh with favour,

Knoweth the way to that dwelling.

That dwelling is permanent and true, and is obtained in the company of the saints.

Nanak, they who find it waver not.

Slok XXX

When Dharmraj beginneth to smite, none can restrain him:

Nanak, they who repeat God's name in association with the saints shall be saved.

Pauri XXX

D.H. Why goest thou about searching? Search in thine own heart.

God dwelleth with thee; why wanderest thou from forest to forest?

Throw down thy heap of terrible pride in the company of the saints;

So shalt thou find rest, abide in peace, and be blest with the sight of God:

He in whom that heap is, shall be born and die, and suffer the pain of the womb;

He who is steeped in worldly love and entangled with egotism shall come and go.

I have now gradually fallen under the protection of the saints;

God hath cut the meshes of sorrow, Nanak, and united me with Himself.

Slok XXXI

Where the saints ever repeat God's name and praises—

Dharmraj saith, 'Approach not there, O my ministers: *if you do,* neither you nor I shall escape.'

Pauri XXXI

N. He who conquereth his own heart is victorious in the battle;

He who dieth fighting with his pride and worldly love is blest;

He who effaceth his pride shall under the perfect Guru's instruction be dead while alive;

He shall conquer his heart, meet God, and obtain a robe of honour for his bravery;

He shall consider nothing his own; the one God shall be his prop and support;

He shall continue night and day to remember the supreme and infinite God;

He shall so act as to make his heart the dust of all men's feet;

He shall understand God's order, be ever happy, Nanak, and obtain what was destined for him.

Slok XXXII

I will devote my body, soul, and wealth to him who causeth me to meet God;

Nanak, my doubts and fears shall then be dispelled, and Death shall no longer look for me.

Pauri XXXII

T. Love Him who is the treasury of excellences, the sovereign God;

Thou shalt then obtain the fruit thy heart desireth, and thy yearning shall depart.

He in whose heart the Name dwelleth, shall have no fear on the road to death;

His understanding shall become enlightened; he shall obtain salvation and a place in God's court.

Nor wealth, nor mansion, nor youth, nor empire shall depart with thee.

In the company of the saints continue to remember *God's name;* it is this that shall avail thee.

There shall be no more burning when God Himself removeth thy fever;

Nanak, God Himself protecteth us; He is our mother and father.

Slok XXXIII

The perverse have grown weary of their various toils, *yet* they are not satisfied and their thirst is not allayed;

They shall die in the midst of their hoarding, Nanak, and their wealth *shall* not *depart* with them.

Pauri XXXIII

T.H. None is permanent; who stretchest thou thy feet forward?

In thine efforts after wealth alone thou committest great fraud and deceit;

Thou toilest to fill thy purse, O fool, and then fallest down weary:

At the last moment that shall not avail thy soul.

Thou shalt obtain permanence by worshipping God and accepting the saints' instruction.

Ever love the one God—that is the true love.

He is the cause of causes; all contrivances are in His hand alone.

We remain at the posts to which Thou, *O God,* hast appointed us; *saith* Nanak, the creature is helpless.

Slok XXXIV

His slaves have seen the one God who giveth everything;

They continue to remember Him at every breath; Nanak, a sight of Him is their support.

Pauri XXXIV

D. The Giver is one; He giveth to all;

In His giving their is no stint; innumerable are His full storehouses.

The Giver liveth for ever.

O my foolish mind, why forgettest thou Him?

No man is at fault, my friend;

It is God who forged the fetters of Maya's illusion.

The holy men whose pain He Himself removeth

Shall, O Nanak, be satisfied.

Slok XXXV

O my soul, grasp the prop of the one God, lay aside thy hopes in others;

Ponder on the Name, and thine affairs shall succeed.

Pauri XXXV

D.H. If thou abide with the saints the wanderings of thy heart shall then cease;

If God Himself bestow mercy from the beginning, the mind shall become enlightened,

They have the true capital and are the true traders,

Whose stock-in-take is the Name and who deal in God.

Patience, glory, and honour are for him

Who attentively heareth God's name.

The holy man in whose heart *God* is contained

Shall, O Nanak, obtain greatness.

Slok XXXVI

Nanak, the perfect Guru hath taught that for him who, in the company of the saints,

Repeateth the Name with his tongue and with love in his heart, there is no hell.

Pauri XXXVI

N. They in whose souls and bodies the Name abideth

Shall not fall into hell.

They who under the Guru's instruction repeat the Name, which is a treasure,

Shall not perish by the poison of mammon.

No refusal awaiteth him

To whom the Guru hath given the spell of the Name.

God's *name* which is full of nectar is the treasury of wealth:

Nanak, unbeaten musical instruments sound for him *who repeateth it*.

Slok XXXVII

When I abandoned deceit, worldly love, and sin, the great Supreme Being preserved mine honour:

Nanak, adore Him who hath no end or limit.

Pauri XXXVII

P. The sovereign God is beyond estimate; His limit cannot be ascertained;

He is the purifier of sinners, and inaccessible.

Millions of sinners who meet the saints

And repeat the ambrosial Name become pure.

He whom Thou Thyself preservest, O Lord of the earth,

Loseth all deception, fraud, and worldly love.

God is emperor; He alone *is entitled to* the umbrella over His head:

Nanak, there is no other sovereign.

Slok XXXVIII

By restraining the mind *Death's* nooses are cut, transmigration is at an end, and victory obtained.

Nanak, permanence is obtained from the Guru and transmigration effaced for ever and ever.

Pauri XXXVIII

P H. O soul, thou hast returned after long wanderings;

In this Kal age thou hast obtained a *human* body so difficult to obtain;

Thou shalt not again have the present opportunity.

Repeat God's name, then *Death's* noose shall be cut away,

And there shall be no transmigration for thee.

Utter *the name of the* one God; that is the real utterance.

Have mercy, O God the Creator,

And unite poor Nanak with Thyself.

Slok XXXIX

Hear Thou my supplication, Supreme Being, compassionate to the poor and Lord of the earth—

Nanak, the dust of the saints' feet is to me comfort, wealth, great enjoyment and pleasure.

Pauri XXXIX

B. It is he who knoweth God who is a Brahman;

He is a Vaishnav who is pious, and accepteth the pure religion.

He is a hero who effaceth his wickedness;

Nothing evil may approach him.

Man is bound by the fetters of his own pride,

And yet, blind that he is, he imputeth blame to others.

Discussion and subterfuges are all of no avail.

O God, he whom Thou causest to know Thee, *saith* Nanak, knoweth Thee.

Slok XL

Heartily worship God who is the destroyer of fear and the remover of sin and sorrow;

He in whose heart he dwelleth through the companionship of the saints shall never again, O Nanak, wander *in transmigration*.

Pauri XL

B H. Dispel thine errors;

This world is all a dream.

In error are demigods, goddesses and Gods;

In error are Sidhs, Strivers, and so is Brahma;

In mazes of error man is ruined.

This world is difficult to cross and very dangerous.

The pious who have effaced error, fear, and worldly love,

Shall, Nanak, obtain supreme happiness.

Slok XLI

Through wealth the mind wavereth in many ways and becometh entangled;

He whom Thou, O God, preservest from asking for it, *saith* Nanak, loveth the Name.

Pauri XLI

M. He who asketh is silly;

The Bestower who is wise continueth to bestow:

What God giveth *He giveth* once for all.

O foolish man, why callest thou aloud?

When thou prayest, thou prayest for worldly things,

From which happiness resulteth to no one.

If thou pray for anything, then pray for the one God,

By whom, *saith* Nanak, thou shalt be saved.

Slok XLII

Their wisdom is perfect and they are distinguished in whose hearts is the perfect Guru's instruction;

Nanak, they who know their God are fortunate.

Pauri XLII

M. He who knoweth *God's* secret

Is satisfied on meeting the company of the saints;

He deemeth woe and weal as the same;

He is exempted from entering hell or heaven;

The man who knoweth God's secret dwelleth in the world, *and yet* is apart from it;

He is, *as it were,* the eminent being who filleth every heart.

He who is not entangled by mammon,

Nanak, hath found happiness in God's love.

Slok XLIII

O my friends, allies, and adherents, hear me—there is no emancipation without God:

Nanak, he who falleth at the Guru's feet hath all his fetters cut away.

Pauri XLIII

Y. Though man make efforts of many kinds,

How far can he succeed without the one Name?

The efforts by which emancipation is obtained,

Are made in the company of the saints.

The salvation which every one holdeth to,

Cannot be obtained without the repetition of God's name;

God is capable of giving salvation.

O Master, preserve us men without merits.

Nanak, that man's intellect becometh enlightened,

Whom *God* Himself instructeth in thought, word and deed.

Slok XLIV

Think of thyself; be angry with no one;

Abide humble in the world, Nanak, and through God's favour thou shalt be saved.

Pauri XLIV

R. Become the dust of every one's feet;

Abandon pride, and *The sins* to thy debit shall be blotted out.

Thou *shalt be victorious* in the struggle, O brother, and acceptable in *God's* court,

If under the Guru's instruction thou fix thine attention on God's name,

Thy sins shall gradually be blotted out
By the perfect Guru's peerless word.
Nanak, they on whom God and the Guru have conferred favours,
Are dyed with the love of *God's* name and intoxicated with its savour.

Slok XLV

The diseases of covetousness, falsehood, and the other deadly sins infest this body;

But the pious who drink *the medicine* of God's nectar,
O Nanak, shall be healed.

Pauri XLV

L. He, *O God,* to whom Thou administerest medicine,
Is at once cured of his sorrows and pains.
That medicine is the Name; whosoever heartily loveth it
Shall not even dream of disease.
The medicine of God's *name* is in every heart, my brethren.
Except the perfect Guru no one knoweth how to prepare it.
He whose way of life the perfect Guru hath appointed,
O Nanak, shall never again sicken.

Slok XLVI

God is everywhere, there is no place without Him;

He is with thee, Nanak, whether thou art at home or abroad; what concealest thou from Him?

Pauri XLVI

W. Bear not enmity to any one—
God is contained in every heart;
He is contained in sea and land;
By the favour of the Guru some rare person singeth *His praises.*
Enmity and jealousy shall depart from the heart of him
Who under the Guru's instruction heareth God's praises.
Nanak, he who under the Guru's instruction repeateth
God's name,

Shall be released from all caste and *caste* marks.

Slok XLVII

The stupid and ignorant infidel passeth his life in egoism;
In agony he dieth as one thirsty, O Nanak, and *thus* obtaineth his deserts.

Pauri XLVII

R. He who by association with the saints worshippeth the Name,
Which is the essence of religious acts, shall not engage in strife.
He in whose heart the Beautiful One dwelleth,
Shall have his strife erased and ended.
It is the ignorant perverse man, in whose heart
The sin of pride dwelleth, who harboureth strife.
Nanak, when the holy man instructeth,
All strife ceaseth in a moment.

Slok XLVII

O my soul, grasp the protection of the holy man; lay aside thy phrases and devices:

The Guru's instruction, Nanak, dwelleth in the heart of him on whose forehead good fortune *was written*.

Pauri XLVII

S.H. Weary of repeating the Shastras, the Simritis, and the Veds,
We have now, *O God,* entered Thine asylum.
In my researches I have come to this conclusion,
That without worshipping God there is no deliverance.
We constantly make mistakes;
Thou art omnipotent, infinite and illimitable.
O Compassionate One, protect us who have fallen under Thy protection!
Saith Nanak, O God, we are Thy children.

Slok XLIX

When pride is erased, happiness resulteth, the mind and body are healed,
Nanak, and He who is worthy of praise becometh manifest.

Pauri XLIX

K H. Thoroughly praise God
Who in an instant can fill to the brim what is empty.
When a mortal is thoroughly humble,
He night and day repeateth *the name* of the eternal God.
The Lord giveth happiness to those who please Him
The infinite supreme Being is so potent,
That He can in a moment pardon numberless sins:
Nanak, the Lord is merciful.

Slok L

Verily I say unto thee, hear me, O my soul, fall under the sovereign God's protection;

Cast aside all thy phrases and devices, Nanak, and *God* will unite thee with Himself.

Pauri L

S. O silly man, lay aside devices:

The Lord is not pleased with tricks and orders.

Even though thou practise a thousand forms of cleverness,

Not one shall avail thee.

Day and night repeat His *name,*

O my soul, which will go with thee.

He whom *God* Himself applieth to the saint's service,

Nanak, shall never feel unhappy.

Slok LI

Happiness resulteth from uttering God's name and keeping it in mind.

Nanak, God provideth all things, and is everywhere equally contained.

Pauri LI

Lo! God filleth the hearts of all—

Men are continually born, but the Guru's wisdom destroyeth their pain.

He is happy who hath escaped from pride; where there is no pride there is God.

By the power of the company of the saints the pain of birth and death is removed.

God becometh merciful to those who, by association with the saints,

Lovingly fix the name of the compassionate One *in their hearts.*

Nanak, everything hath proceeded from God;

Without Him no one hath accomplished anything.

Slok LII

Looking to his account man shall never be released *since* he erreth every moment.

Saith Nanak, O Thou Pardoner, Pardon us and save us.

Pauri LII

Man is disloyal and a sinner; he is a stranger *to God* and of little wisdom;

He knoweth not the Essence *of all things,* who gave him soul, body and happiness.

For the sake of worldly gain he goeth searching in every direction;

God, the Giver, the Bestower, he treasureth not in his heart for an instant.

Greed, falsehood, sin, worldly love, these things he harboureth in his heart.

He passeth *his life* with great adulterers, thieves and slanderers.

If pleasing to Thee, *O God,* pardon the counterfeit along with the genuine.

Saith Nanak, O supreme God, if it please Thee, stones shall float on water.

Slok LIII

Eating, drinking, playing, and laughing have we wandered in many births;

O God, rescue us from the terrible ocean, *prayeth* Nanak; we rely on Thee.

Pauri LIII

Having both enjoyed and suffered the pain of many births, we have returned *as human beings.*

Troubles are removed by meeting the holy man, and being absorbed in the true Guru's instruction.

Man adopting contentment amasseth truth, and liveth upon the ambrosia of the Name.

Genuine is the mercy of God; I have found my haven in joy and happiness.

My cargo hath safely arrived; *I have had great* profit, and I return home with honour.

Genuine is the consolation the Guru gave me; I have met God on my return.

God Himself acted and acteth; *He was* in the beginning and *shall be* in the end.

Nanak, praise Him who is contained in every heart.

Slok LIV

O Ocean of mercy, compassionate God, we have entered Thine asylum.

Nanak is happy in giving the one word God a place in his heart.

Pauri LIV

God holdeth the three worlds by letters;

Through letters the Veds are studied;

Through letters the Shastras, the Simritis, and the Purans;

Through letters hymns, discourses and sermons;

Through letters is the way of escape from fear and error;

Through letters religious and worldly acts are performed and pure faith obtained.

The whole visible world is contained in letters;

But, Nanak, the Supreme Being is beyond letters.

Slok LV

O inaccessible One, Thy hand holdeth the pen which writeth *men's destiny* on his forehead.

Thou of incomparable form art contained in all things;

Man's tongue cannot describe Thy praises;

Nanak on beholding Three is fascinated, and devoted unto Thee.

Pauri LV

O eternal, supreme God indestructible, Destroyer of sin,

O All-prevading, contained in everything Destroyer of grief, Lord of excellences,

Formless one, O man's companion, O Thou without the three *human* attributes, Prop of all,

Supporter of the earth, O Ocean of excellences who hast ever discrimination,

O God, most remote Thou art, wast, and shalt be.

O Thou, constant Companion of the saints, Support of the supportless,

I am Thy slave, I am without merits, no merit is mine.

Saith Nanak, grant me the gift of Thy name that I may string it and keep it in my heart.

Slok

The divine Guru is my mother, the divine Guru is my father, the divine Guru is my Lord and supreme God;

The divine Guru is my companion and dispeller of spiritual ignorance, the divine Guru is my relation and my brother;

The divine Guru is the giver and the teacher of God's name, the divine Guru hath the spell that cannot be counteracted;

The divine Guru is peace, truth, and the image of wisdom; the divine Guru is a philosopher's stone by whose touch man is saved;

The divine Guru is a place of pilgrimage, his divine knowledge a lake of nectar, by bathing in which the Illimitable is obtained;

The divine Guru is the creator, the remover of all sin, the divine Guru is the purifier of the impure;

The divine Guru is from the beginning, from the beginning of time and in every age; the divine Guru is the spell of God's *name,* by whose utterance man is saved.

O God, mercifully bring me—foolish and sinner that I am—into the company of the Guru, so that by clinging to him I may be saved.

Nanak boweth to the divine Guru, the true Guru, the supreme Brahm, the supreme God.

5

Sukhmani

Slok I

I bow to the primal Guru;
I bow to the Guru of the primal age;
I bow to the true Guru;
I bow to the holy divine Guru.

ASHTAPADI I

1

Remember, remember God; by remembering Him you shall obtain happiness,
And erase from your hearts trouble and affliction.
Remember the praises of the one all-supporting God.
Numberless persons utter God's various names.
Investigating the Veds, the Purans, and the Simritis,
Men have made out the one word which is God's name.
His praises cannot be recounted,
Who treasureth *God's name* in his heart even for a moment.
Saith Nanak, save me, *O Lord,* with those who are desirous of one glance of Thee.
In this Sukhmani is the name of God *which like* ambrosia *bestoweth* heppiness.
And giveth peace to the hearts of the saints.

2

By remembering God man doth not *again* enter the womb;
By remembering God the tortures of Death disappear;
By remembering God death is removed;
By remembering God enemies retreat;
By remembering God no obstacles are met;
By remembering God we are watchful night and day;
By remembering God fear is not felt;

By remembering God sorrow troubleth not :
Men remember God in the company of the saints—
Nanak, by the love of God all wealth is obtained.

3

By remembering God we obtain wealth, supernatural power, and the nine treasures;

By remembering God we obtain divine knowledge, meditation, and the essence of wisdom;

Remembrance of God is the *real* devotion, penance, and worship;

By remembering God *the conception of* duality is dispelled;

By remembering God we obtain *the advantages* of bathing at places of pilgrimage;

By remembering God we are honoured at His court;
By remembering God we become reconciled to His will;
By remembering God men's *lives* are very profitable;
They whom He hath caused to do so remember Him—
Nanak, touch the feet of such persons.

4

To remember God is the most exalted of all duties.
By remembering God many are saved;
By remembering God thirst is quenched;
By remembering God man knoweth all things;
By remembering God there is no fear of death;
By remembering God our desires are fulfilled;
By remembering God mental impurity is removed,
And the ambrosical filleth the heart.
God abideth on the tongue of the saint
Whose humble slave Nanak is.

5

They who remember God are wealthy.
They who remember God are honoured;
They who remember God are acceptable;
They who remember God are distinguished;
They who remember God feel not want;
They who remember God rule the world;

They who remember God dwell in happiness;
They who remember God live for ever;
They to whom God showeth mercy ever remember Him—
Nanak prayeth for the dust of such men's feet.

6

They who remember God are philanthropic;
I am ever devoted to those who remember God.
The faces of those who remember God look bright;
They who remember God pass their lives in bliss;
They who remember God chasten their hearts;
The ways of those who remember God are holy;
They who remember God feel extreme joy;
They who remember God dwell near Him,
And by the favour of the saints are watchfull night and day—
Nanak, meditation on God is obtained by complete good fortune.

7

By remembering God everything is accomplished;
By remembering God man never grieveth;
By remembering God man uttereth His praises;
By remembering God man is easily absorbed in Him;
By remembering God man findeth an immovable seat;
By remembering God the lotus of *man's heart* bloometh;
By remembering God man *heareth* the unbeaten melody;
The happiness which is obtained by remembering God hath no end or limit

They to whom God is merciful remember Him;
Nanak seeketh the protection of such men.

8

By remembering God His saints have become distinguished;
By remembering God the Veds were composed;
By remembering God men have obtained supernatural power, continence and generosity;
By remembering God even the lowly are known in every direction;
By remembering God the whole earth is supported;
Remember, remember God the Cause of causes—

For the remembrance of God He created the whole world:
Where God is remembered there is God Himself:
Nanak, the pious whom God hath mercifully instructed,
Have obtained the boon on remembering Him.

Slok II

O Thou Destroyer of the pain and grief of the distressed, Lord of every heart, Thyself without a lord,

I have come under Thy protection; O God, be with Nanak!

ASHTAPADI II

1

Where man hath neither mother, nor father, nor son, nor friend, nor brother,
There, O my soul, God's name shall be with thee and assist thee.
Where the very terrible ministers of Death crush thee,
There the name of God alone shall go with thee,
There the name of God alone shall go with thee.
Where there are very great obstacles,
The name of God will remove them in a moment.
Thou shalt not be saved *even* by many expiations;
It is the name of God which removeth millions of sins.
O my soul, utter, the name of God under the Guru's instruction;
Thus shalt thou, *saith* Nanak, have manifold joys.

2

The king of the whole world is miserable;
Only he is happy who uttereth God's name.
Even though there be millions of entanglements,
By uttering the name of God, we shall be freed from them all.
The various pleasures of the world allay not our thirst,
Buy by pondering on God's name it is quenched.
On the road on which man goeth alone,
The name of God is with him to cheer him.
Ever ponder on such a Name in thy heart,
And under the Guru's instruction, Nanak, thou shalt obtain the supreme state.

3

Even though thou have millions of arms, thou shalt not be saved;

But, if thou utter Name, thou shalt be saved.
When many obstacles harass thee,
The name of God will at once save thee.
Man dieth and is born in many births,
But he shall obtain rest by uttering the Name.
The soul is defiled by filthy pride—filth which is never washed away;
But the name of God cleanseth all impurity:
Repeat such a Name, O my soul, with love:
Nanak, it is obtained in the company of the saints.

4

On the way where the miles cannot be counted,
The name of God shall there by thy provision;
On the way where there is pitch darkness,
The name of God shall accompany and light thee;
On the way where nobody knoweth thee,
The name of God shall be there to recognize thee;
Where there is very terrible heat and great sunshine,
There the name of God shall be a shadow over thee.
O man, where thirst tormenth thee,
There, *saith* Nanak, *the name of* God shall rain nectar on thee.

5

Uttering the Name is the business of the pious;
It giveth peace to the hearts of the saints;
God's name is the shelter of His servants;
By God's name millions have been saved.
The saints day and night praise God:
The pious use God's name as their medicine.
The name of God is the treasure of the holy;
The Supreme Being gave this gift to man.
Nanak, *the pursuit* of divine knowledge is the rule of the holy,
Whose souls and bodies are dyed with the love of the one *God*.

6

The name of God is the way of salvation of His servant;
The food of God's name satisfieth His servant;
The name of God is His servant's beauty and delight;

By uttering God's name harm never befalleth one;
God's name is His servant's glory;
From God's name man obtaineth lustre;
God's name is injoyment and salvation to His servant;
By uttering God's name man is never separated *from Him.*
Nanak, every demigod worshippeth him
Who is dyed with worship of God's name.

7

God's name is wealth and treasure to His servants;
God Himself gave His name as a boon to man;
God's name is to His servant a powerful stronghold;
God's servant knoweth naught but God's glory.
The man of God who is the wrap and the woof, is dyed with God's love;
In deep meditation man is intoxicated with the essence of the Name;
During the eight watches of the day the man of God repreateth His name.
The saints of God are distinguished and not obscure;
The worship of God conferreth salvation upon many—
Nanak, how many shall be saved with holy men?

8

This name of God is as the tree which groweth in heaven;
The singing of God's praises is *as the gifts of* Kamdhen;
Speaking of God is the best of all utterances;
By hearing the Name pain and sorrow are removed:
The praise of the Name dwelleth in the hearts of the pious;
By their influence all sins depart.
It is by great good fortune association with the pious is obtained;
It is by serving them man meditateth on God's name:
There is nothing equal to God's name—
Nanak, a few men obtain it by the Guru's instruction.

Slok III

I have seen many Shastras, many Simritis, and searched them all—
They are, Nanak, not equal to God's priceless name.

ASHTAPADI III

1

Muttering spells, doing penance, *pretended* knowledge, all meditation,
The exposition of the six Shastras and of the Simritis,
The practice of Jog, the performance of *vain* religious ceremonies,
The abandonment of everything, wandering in the forest,
Superstitious efforts of various descriptions,
Almsgiving, the sacrifice of hom, *the bestowal* of many jewels,
Cutting pieces off one's body and making them a burnt offering,
The performance of fasting and vows of many kinds—
All are not equal to the contemplation of God's name,
Nanak, even if it be only once repeated as directed by the Guru.

2

Were one to wander through the nine continents of the earth, live for a long time,
And become a great anchoret and penitent;
Where one to burn oneself in the fire,
Make gifts of gold, excellent horses, and lands,
Perform the niwali feat, adopt many *Jogi* attitudes,
Adopt the Jain mortifications, make great *spiritual* efforts,
And cut one's body into pieces—
Even then the filth of pride would not depart.
There is nothing equal to God's name:
Nanak, by the utterance of the Name under the Guru man obtaineth salvation.

3

Even though the soul leave the body at a place of pilgrimage; yet if it retain worldly desires,
Pride and arrogance will not depart from it.
Even though one practice purification day and night,
The filth of the heart will not leave the body.
Even though man subject his body to much mortification,
Evil passions will never abandon his heart.
Even though we wash this temporary body with much water,
How can a wall of mud become clean?

O my soul, exalted is the name of God.
Nanak, the worst sinners have been saved by the Name.

4

By too much cleverness man shall feel the fear of Death:
Even by various efforts his thirst shall not be satisfied;
Even by adopting various *religious* garbs the fire of his *worldly love* is not quenched;
Even by millions of *other religious* efforts man is not acceptable in God's court.
He over whom worldly love hath spread its net,
Shall not escape in heaven or hell.
Death heedeth naught but the praises of God;
He punisheth all other works of man.
By repeating God's name grief is dispelled:
Nanak uttereth the *Name* without effort.

5

Let him who prayeth for the four boons,
Apply himself to the service of holy men.
Let him who *desireth* to remove his troubles,
Continually sing the name of Good in his heart.
Let him who desireth honour for himself,
Renounce pride by association with holy men.
Let him who feareth transmigration,
Come under the protection of holy men.
Nanak is a sacrifice, a sacrifice
Unto those who thirst for the sight of God.

6

Among all men foremost is he
Who by association with the pious effaceth pride.
He who deemeth himself lowly,
Shall be deemed the most exalted of all.
They whose minds are the dust of all men's feet,
Shall see God's name in their inmost hearts.
They who expel evil from their hearts,
Shall regard the whole world as their friends.

The holy man who looketh upon weal and woe as the same,
Shall not, Nanak, be affected by evil or good.

7

To him who hath no wealth, O God, Thy name is wealth;
To him who hath no home, thy name is a home;
To him who hath no honour, Thy *name* is an honour:
Thou givest gifts to all persons.
Thou, O Lord, actest and causest to act.
It is *only* Thou, who hast the secrets of all hearts,
Who knowest Thine own condition and limit.
Thou art, O God, Thine own beloved;
It is Thou alone who canst praise Thyself.
Saith Nanak, no one else knoweth Thy praises.

8

Of all devotion, the best devotion is
To utter the name of God and do pious works;
Of all rites, the best rite is
To remove the filth of evil inclinations by association with saints;
Of all efforts, the best effort is
Ever heartily to repeat God's name;
Of all speech, the divine speech is
To utter with the tongue God's praises heard *from the Guru;*
Of all places, that is the best place
Nanak, where God's name dwelleth in the heart.

Slok IV

O unworthy and foolish man, ever remember God.
Fix thy heart upon Him, Nanak, who made thee; this will avail thee in the end.

ASHTAPADI IV

1

Mortal, think upon the goodness of God,
What thine origin is, and what thou appearest now—
That God who made thee, fashioned thee, and adorned thee,
Who preserved thee in the fire of the womb,

Who in thine infancy gave thee milk to drink,
In thy youth food, comfort, and intelligence,
In thine old age relations to watch over thee,
And who put food into thy mouth as thou wast seated.
Unworthy man, however, value not these favours.
If Thou, O God, pardon him, then, O Nanak, he shall be acceptable.

2

Thou feelest an affection for others, and abandonest Him
By whose favour thou dwellest in comfort on the earth,
And rejoicest with children, brothers, friends and wives;
By whose favour thou drinkest cool water,
And the pleasant winds and the priceless fire *are at thy service;*
By whose favour thou enjoyest all pleasures,
And livest with all the necessaries *of life;*
Who gave thee hands, feet, ears, eyes, and a tongue—
Such sins *of ingratitude* attach to blind and foolish man:
Nanak *prayeth,* save us, O Lord, *from such sins.*

3

The ignorant man loveth not Him
Who protecteth him in the beginning and the end;
The fool fixeth not his heart on Him
By service to whom the wealth of the world is obtained;
The Lord who is ever and ever present
Is thought by the blind to be far away;
The stupid and foolish forget Him
By service to whom honour is obtained at His court.
Man erreth ever and ever:
Nanak, the Infinite One is the *only* Preserver.

4

Man abandoneth a jewel and loveth a kauri;
He renounceth truth and occupieth himself with falsehood;
What he shall have to part with he deemeth enduring;
The thought of death which is to happen he putteth away from him;
He troubleth himself about what he must part with;
He spurneth the Succourer who abideth with him;

He washeth away and removeth the coating of sandal,
And like a donkey conceiveth a love for ashes to *roll in*.
Man hath fallen into a terrible blind well:
Saith Nanak, O Merciful God, extricate him:

5

He is only man in appearance; he acts are those of a brute;
He beguileth people day and night;
He weareth a religious dress, but within him is the filth of worldly love;
However much he try, he cannot conceal *his sins;*
Before the world he *practiseth* contemplation, meditation and ablution,
While in his heart he hath the greed of a dog;
In his heart is the fire of *avarice* while he applieth aslies to his body;
There is a stone *tied to* his neck; how shall he cross over the bottomless *ocean?*
He in whose heart God Himself dwelleth,
Shall, O Nanak, be easily absorbed in Him.

6

How shall a blind man find the road even though he hear *where it is?*
Take his hand and he shall reach the goal.
How can a deaf man understand riddles?
Talk to him of the night, and he will think *you are talking of* the dawn;
How can a dumb man sing a stave
When, though he try, it would break his voice,
How can a cripple roam on a mountain?
He could never reach there.
O merciful creator, Nanak humbly supplicateth Thee,
That by Thy favour he may be saved.

7

Man thinketh not upon the Succourer who abideth with him;
He loveth what is hostile to him;
He dwelleth within a house of sand,
And indulgeth in joy, and sports, and the pleasures of the world:
He is certain in his heart that they shall last for ever.
Attached to the sins of revenge, enmity, lust, wrath, worldly love,
Falsehood, excessive avarice and deceit,
The thought of death never entereth his foolish heart.

In this way he hath passed several lives;
Nanak *prayeth, O God,* save him by Thy favour.

8

Thou art the Lord; I make this supplication unto Thee.
Soul and body are all Thy property;
Thou art mother and father, we are Thy children.
By Thy favour we obtain many comforts:
Nobody knoweth Thy limit.
O God, Thou art the most exalted of the exalted.
All things are strung on Thy string,
And must obey the orders Thou issuest.
It is only Thou Thyself who knowest Thine own condition and limit:
Nanak, Thy slave, is ever a sacrifice unto Thee.

Slok V

They who leave God and Giver and attach themselves to other pleasures,

Shall never be acceptable; O Nanak, without the Name their honour shall depart.

ASHTAPADI V

1

If man obtain ten things and lay them by,
Shall he basely forfeit his faith for the sake of one thing?
If God give not even one thing and take away the ten things,
Say what can foolish man do?
Ever bow down to that Lord
With whom force is of no avail.
All happiness abideth in him
To whose heart God is dear.
The man whom God hath caused to obey His order,
Hath, Nanak, obtained all things.

2

The Banker giveth countless capital to man:
He eateth, and drinketh, and useth it with pleasure and joy;
But if God the Banker take back some of what He hath entrusted to man,
The fool becometh angry.

He by his own act forfeiteth confidence,
And God will not *again* trust him.
If thou place the things before their Owner,
And obey God's order with all thy might,
He will make thee fourfold happy.
Nanak, the Lord is ever compassionate.

3

Man is enamoured of the various forms of mammon,
But it is temporary; know this for a certainty.
Man falleth in love with the shadow of a tree:
When that vanisheth he mourneth in his heart.
Everything we see is transitory;
Yet man, thoroughly blind that he is, is attached to it.
He who giveth his love to a passing visitor,
Shall gain nothing thereby.
O my soul, the love of God's name is comfortable.
Nanak, God attacheth to Himself those to whom He showeth mercy.

4

Perishable are body, wealth and family;
Perishable are pride, egoism, and worldly love;
Perishable are dominion, youth, wealth, and property;
Perishable are lust and direful wrath;
Perishable are carriages, elephants, horses, and raiment;
Perishable the love of worldly things, a sight of which causeth man to rejoice;
Perishable are deceit, worldly love, and pride;
Perishable is self-conceit;
Imperishable the worship performed under the protection of holy men—
Nanak liveth by meditating on God's feet—

5

Perishable the ears which listen to slander of others;
Perishable the hands which steal the property of others;
perishable the eyes which behold the beauty and other charms of another's wife;
Perishable the tongue which tasteth *dainty* food and other savours;
Perishable the feet which run after evil;

Perishable the heart which coveteth another's goods;
Perishable the body which benefiteth not others;
Perishable *the nose* which *delighteth in the* smell of evil;
Without understanding *God* everything is perishable.
Fruitful is the body, Nanak, which taketh the name of God.

6

Vain is the life of the infidel.
How can man be pure without truth?
Vain are the spiritually blind without God's name;
Foul breath issueth from their mouths:
Without remembering the Name their days and nights pass away in vain.
As the crop perisheth without rain,
As the money of the miser is worthless,
So everything is vain without repeating God's name.
They are to be highly congratulated in whose hearts the name of God abideth:
Nanak is a sacrifice, a sacrifice unto them.

7

He who professeth one thing and doeth another,
In whose heart there is no love, but who attacheth men to him by his words,
Shall be tried by the Lord, who is wise, who knoweth everything,
And is not pleased *simply* by outward appearances.
He who practiseth not what he preacheth,
Shall come and go, shall be born and die.
The world shall be saved by his teaching
In whose heart the Formless One dwelleth.
Only they who are pleasing to Thee, O God, can know Thee:
Nanak falleth at the feet of such men.

8

Supplicate the Supreme Being who knoweth all things. God accepteth *the prayers* of His creatures:
He Himself and by Himself decideth:
To one man He showeth himself afar, and to another near.
He Himself is free from all stratagems and wiles;
He thoroughly knoweth the ways of man's heart;
The man who is pleasing to Him He attacheth to His skirt—

He is contained in every place—

He to whom He showeth favour is His servant.
Nanak, every moment repeat God's name.

Slok VI

Nanak hath taken Thy protection, O Divine Guru; mercifully grant
That his lust, wrath, avarice, worldly love, and pride may depart.

ASHTAPADI VI

1

Bear that God in thy mind
By whose favour thou eatest of the thirty-six dishes.
Thou shalt obtain salvation by remembering Him
By whose favour thou appliest perfume to thy body.
Meditate on Him continually in the heart
By whose favour thou dwellest comfortably at home.
Repeat His name with thy tongue for the eight watches
By whose favour thou dwellest in comfort with thy family.
Nanak ever meditateth on Him
By whose favour thou enjoyest mental and bodily pleasure; He is worthy of meditation.

2

Why shouldest thou be enamoured of others and forsake Him
By whose favour thou wearest silks and satins?
O Man, sing His praises for the eight watches
By whose favour thou sleepest in comfort on thy bed.
Repeat His praises with thy mouth and with thy tongue
By whose favour every one honoureth thee.
O man, ever think upon the Supreme Being alone
By whose favour thy faith is preserved.
By uttering the name of God thou shalt obtain honour at His court,
O Nanak, and go home with honour.

3

Fix thine attention on that lovable God
By whose favour thy beautiful body remaineth healthy.

O man, thou shalt obtain happiness by uttering God's praises,
By whose favour thy honour is preserved.
O man, take shelter in that Lord God
By whose favour all thy defects are concealed.
O man, at every breath remember the Most High
By whose favour none can equal thee.
Nanak, perform His service
By whose favour thou obtainest a human body so difficult to obtain.

4

O man, why art thou slow in remembering Him
By whose favour thou wearest jewels?
O man, never forget thy God
By whose favour thou ridest on horses and elephants.
String and keep God in thy heart
By whose favour thou hast gardens, and property and wealth.
Standing or sitting, O man, ever meditate upon Him
Who made the framework of thy body.
Meditate upon Him who is the Invisible One,
And he will preserve thee, Nanak, in this world and the next.

5

Meditate upon Him during the eight watches of the day
By whose favour thou bestowest much in charity.
remember that God at every breath
By whose favour thou performest they religious and worldly duties.
Remember that God ever incomparable
By whose favour thy form is beautiful.
Meditate on that God day and night
By whose favour thou hast obtained the superior state.
By the Guru's favour, Nanak, repeat His praises
By whose favour thine honour is preserved.

6

Why attach thyself to any other and forsake Him
By whose favour thine ears hear melody,
By whose favour thou beholdest wonders,

By whose favour thou utterest ambrosial words,
By whose favour thou abidest in ease and comfort,
By whose favour thy hands move to discharge *their duties,*
By whose favour thou art completely successful,
By whose favour thou obtainest supreme bliss,
By whose favour thou shalt be filled with happiness and comfort?
Awaken thy heart, Nanak, by the Guru's favour.

7

Never at all forget that God in thy heart
By whose favour thou art distinguished in the world.
O foolish man, repeat His name
By whose favour thou obtainest glory.
Know in thy heart that He is ever present
By whose favour thine affairs are completed.
O my soul, attach thyself to Him
By whose favour thou obtainest the truth.
Nanak, utter the name of Him
By whose favour all are saved.

8

He uttereth God's name whom He causeth to utter it;
He singeth God's praises whom He causeth to sing them.
Through God's mercy man becometh enlightened;
Through God's compassion the lotus of *the heart* bloometh.
If God be pleased, He abideth in man's heart.
By God's compassion man's intellect is superior to that of others.
All wealth is obtained, O God, by Thy kindness;
No one obtaineth anything by himself.
We apply ourselves to the duties to which Thou hast appointed us, O Master:
Nanak, we have no power in ourselves.

Slok VII

The supreme Being is inaccessible and unfathomable;
He who repeateth His name shall be saved.
Hear, O my friends, Nanak's representation
And the wonderful story of the saints:

ASHTAPADI VII

1

By association with saints the face becometh bright,
By association with saints all filth is removed,
By association with saints pride is effaced,
By association with saints divine knowledge is revealed,
By association with saints God is known to be near,
By association with saints everything is decided,
By association with saints the jewel of the Name is obtained,
By association with saints we should strive for the one God—
What mortal can express saints' praises?
Nanak, the glory of saints is merged in that of God.

2

By association with saints the Unseen is obtained,
By association with saints man ever flourisheth,
By association with saints the five evil passions are restrained,
By association with saints man partaketh of the ambrosial essence of the Name,
By association with saints man becometh the dust of all *man's feet,*
In the association of saints is fascinating converse,
By association with saints, the mind wandereth not in any direction,
By association with saints it becometh stable,
By association with saints the mind is free from illusion—
Nanak, by association with saints, God is well pleased.

3

By association with saints all enemies become friends,
By association with saints man becometh very pure,
By association with saints man feeleth not enmity for any one,
By association with saints man's feet *walk* not awry—
A man cannot be evil who associateth with saints—
By association with saints man knoweth the Supreme Joy,
By association with saints there is no fever of pride,
By association with saints man abandoneth all self-conceit.
Only God knoweth His saints' greatness—
Nanak, there is an understanding between God and His saints—

4

By association with saints *the mind* never wandereth,
By association with saints happiness is ever obtained,
By association with saints man obtaineth what is unseen,
By association with saints man beareth intolerable things,
By association with saints man dwelleth in an exalted position,
By association with saints man shall reach *Good's* palace,
By association with saints man's faith is completely established,
In the association of saints the Supreme Being alone *is mentioned,*
By association with saints man obtaineth the treasure of the Name—
Nanak is a sacrifice to the saints—

5

By association with saints all one's family is saved,
By association with saints acquaintances, friends, and family are saved,
By association with saints that wealth is obtained
From which every one gaineth advantage—
Dharmraj performeth service for those who associate with saints—
By association with saints the king of the demigods singeth man's praises.
By association with saints sins flee away,
By association with saints man singeth the praises of the ambrosial *Name,*
By association with saints man reacheth every place,
Nanak, by association with saints man's birth is profitable.

6

By association with saints man hath no travail—
On beholding and meeting them man becometh happy—
By association with saints blemishes are removed,
By association with saints hell is avoided,
By association with saints man shall be happy in this world and the next,
By association with saints they who are separated from God shall meet Him,
By association with saints man departeth not empty,
But obtaineth the fruit he desireth.
The Supreme Being dwelleth in the hearts of saints;
Nanak, man hearing God's delicious *name* from saints shall be saved.

7

In the association of saints hear God's name,

In the association of saints sing God's praises,
In the association of saints God is not forgotten,
In the association of saints man shall assuredly by saved—
To the association of saints God is dear—
By association with saints He is seen in every heart,
By association with saints man becometh obedient,
By association with saints I have been saved,
By association with saints all maladies are healed.
Nanak, association with saints is obtained by good fortune.

8

Even the Veds know not the greatness of saints;
They described them as far as they had heard of them.
The greatness of saints is beyond the three qualities,
The greatness of saints pervadeth every place;
There is no end to the glory of saints;
The glory of saints is ever endless,
The glory of saints is the highest of the high,
The glory of saints is the greatest of the great,
The glory of saints appertaineth to them alone;
Saith Nanak, me brethren, there is no difference between God and His saints.

Slok VIII

He whose heart is true and whose words are true
Looketh at nobody but the one God.
Nanak, these are the marks of a man who knoweth God:

ASHTAPADI VIII

1

The man who knoweth God is ever uncontaminated,
As the lotus is untouched by the water;
The man who knoweth God is ever stainless,
As all things purified by the sun;
The man who knoweth God looketh on all men as equal,
As the wind bloweth on the rich and poor alike;
The man who knoweth God is uniformly patient,
Like the earth which one man diggeth up and another smeareth with sandal.

This is the attribute of the man who knoweth God;
Nanak, his nature is like that of fire.

2

The man who knoweth God is the purest of the pure,
As filth cannot *permanently* attach to water;
The mind of the man who knoweth God is enlightened,
Like the firmament above the earth;
To the man who knoweth God a f—riend and foe are the same;
The man who knoweth God hath no pride;
The man who knoweth God is the most exalted of the exalted;
Yet his mind is the most humble of all—
Nanak, only those are Brahmgyanis
Whom God Himself maketh so—

3

The man who knoweth God is the dust of all men's feet,
The man who knoweth God feeleth spiritual pleasure,
The man who knoweth God showeth kindness to all,
From the man who knoweth God cometh nothing evil,
The man who knoweth God ever *looketh on all* with an equal eye—
Nectar raineth from the glance of him who knoweth God—
The man who knoweth God is free from entanglements;
The way of the man who knoweth God is pure;
Divine knowledge is the food of the man who knoweth God;
The man who knoweth God meditateth on Him.

4

The man who knoweth God hath his hopes on One alone,
The man who knoweth God shall never perish,
The man who knoweth God is steeped in humility,
The man who knoweth God delighteth to show kindness to others,
The man who knoweth God is not *involved* in worldly affairs,
The man who knoweth God restraineth his wandering mind;
Very good are *the acts* of the man who knoweth God;
Everything prospereth with him who knoweth God;
In the company of the man who knoweth God all shall be saved—
Nanak, the whole world praiseth the man who knoweth God.

5

The man who knoweth God loveth Him alone;
God abideth with the man who knoweth Him;
The Name is the support of the man who knoweth God,
The Name is a halo for the man who knoweth God;
The man who knoweth God is ever watchful,
The man who knoweth God renounceth pride,
The heart of him who knoweth God feeleth supreme delight,
The home of him who knoweth God is ever happy,
The man who knoweth God dwelleth in peace and rest,
The man who knoweth God, O Nanak, shall never perish—

6

The man who knoweth God *is called* a Brahmgyani,
The man who knoweth God loveth but Him alone,
The man who knoweth God is free from care;
Pure is the doctrine of him who knoweth God;
He is a Brahmgyani whom God maketh so;
Great is the glory of the man who knoweth God.
A sight of the man who knoweth God is only obtained by good fortune;
Be a sacrifice to the man who knoweth God;
Shiv searcheth for the man who knoweth God—
Nanak, the Brahmgyani is himself God.

7

The man who knoweth God is priceless,
The man who knoweth God knoweth everything—
Who knoweth the secret of him who knoweth God?
Obeisance ever to him who knoweth God!
Even half a letter of *his praises* who knoweth God cannot be written—
The man who knoweth God is the lord of all—
Who can tell the worth of the man who knoweth God?
Only the man who knoweth God knoweth his own state;
The man who knoweth God hath no end or limit.
Nanak ever boweth to the man who knoweth God.

8

The man who knoweth God is the creator of the whole world,
The man who knoweth God liveth for ever and dieth not,
The man who knoweth God bestoweth on creatures spiritual and temporal benefits,
The man who knoweth God is the perfect being, the arranger,
The man who knoweth God is the patron of the patronless,
The man who knoweth God holdeth his arm over all,
The man who knoweth God owneth the whole world,
The man who knoweth God is himself the Formless One—
The glory of the man who knoweth God is peculiar to himself—
Nanak, the man who knoweth God is the lord of all.

Slok IX

Nanak, he is an Aparas and saveth all,
Who preserveth the Name in his inmost heart,
Who seeth God in all things,
And who every moment boweth to the Lord.

ASHTAPADI IX

1

Nanak, among millions there is scarcely an Aparas
Whose tongue toucheth not falsehood,
Whose heart loveth to behold the Bright One,
Whose eyes gaze not on the beauty of others' wives,
Who serveth holy men and loveth saints,
Whose ears hear not slander of any one,
Who deemeth himself the worst of all men.
Who by the favour of the Guru renounceth all wickedness,
Who banisheth all evil desires from his heart,
Curbeth his passions, and refraineth from the five deadly sins.

2

He is a Vaishnav with whom God is pleased,
Who is free from the influence of mammon,
Who in performing *good* acts looketh not for reward—
Of such a Vaishnav pure is the religion—

Nanak, that Vaishnav shall obtain final salvation,
Who desireth not a reward for anything,
Who is only attached to God's service and singing His praises,
Who remembereth God in his mind and body,
Who is merciful to all creatures,
Who himself holdeth fast God's name and causeth others to repeat it.

3

He is a Bhagauti who loveth God's service.
Who forsaketh the company of all wicked men,
Who removeth all superstition from his mind,
Who deemeth and worshippeth all *nature* as the Supreme Being,
Who by association with the saints washeth away the filth of sin—
Of such a Bhagauti supreme is the wisdom—
He who continually serveth God,
And dedicateth his soul and body to His love,
Who placeth God's feet in his heart—
Nanak, such a Bhagauti shall obtain God.

4

He is a Pandit who awakeneth his own mind,
Who searcheth for God's name in his heart,
Who drinketh the excellent juice of God's name—
The world liveth by that Pandit's instruction—
The Pandit who implanteth God's word in his heart
Shall not be born again.
Nanak ever maketh obeisance to that Pandit
Who understandeth the real meaning of the Veds, the Purans, and the Simritis,
Who recognizeth the great in the minute,
And who instructeth the four castes.

5

The Name, the ground spell, giveth knowledge to all;
He who among the four castes
Repeateth it, shall obtain salvation.
Some rare man obtaineth it by association with the saints.
By the favour of God, the keeping of the Name in the heart
Shall save brutes, sprites, blockhead and hard-hearted persons.

The Name is the medicine for all diseases;
Singing God's praises is beatitude and joy.
God's name is found not in any other way or by any other religion.
Nanak, he for whom such destiny was written from the first, shall obtain God's name.

6

He in whose heart is God's dwelling,
May truly be called God's slave.
The Soul of the world appeareth to his gaze,
And he hath obtained the state of God's slave of slaves.
The servant of God who believeth that He is ever near,
Shall be acceptable at His court.
His servant to whom He showeth kindness,
Shall obtain all knowledge.
The man who among all men is recluse at heart,
Thus becometh, O Nanak, a slave of God.

7

He whose heart loveth God's order
Is said to have obtained salvation during life.
The him joy and sorrow are the same;
He is ever happy and is never separated *from God,*
To him as is gold so is dross,
As is nectar so is bitter poison,
As is honour so is dishonour,
As is the poor man so is the king.
He who deemeth what cometh from God as best,
Shall, O Nanak, be said to have obtained salvation during life.

8

All places belong to the Supreme Being;
Creatures have different names according to where God placed them.
God is able to act and cause others to act;
What pleaseth Him shall ultimately be.
God extended Himself in endless waves;
The play of the Supreme Being cannot be understood.
Man's enlightenment is according to the understanding God giveth him.

The Supreme Being, the Creator, is imperishable;
He is ever, ever, ever compassionate:
By remembering and remembering Him, Nanak hath become happy.

Slok X

Many people praise Him who hath neither end nor limit:
Nanak, God created His creatures of many kinds and various species.

ASHTAPADI X

1

Many millions are His worshippers,
Many millions are engaged in religious and worldly duties,
Many millions dwell at places of pilgrimage,
Many millions wander as anchorets in the forest,
Many millions listen to the Veds,
Many millions perform excessive penances,
Many millions meditate on God in their hearts,
Many millions of poets compose verses *in His praise,*
Many millions meditate on His *ever* new names—
Even then, Nanak, they find not the Creator's limit.

2

Many millions are proud,
Many millions are in blind ignorance,
Many millions are hard-hearted misers,
Many millions are unsociable and morose at heart,
Many millions steal others' property,
Many millions bring false charges against others,
Many millions make efforts to acquire wealth,
Many millions wander in foreign lands;
Where Thou didst place man, O God, there are they:
Nanak, only the Creator knoweth His own creatures.

3

Many millions are Sidhs, Jatis and Jogis;
Many millions are Kings and enjoy pleasures;
Many millions of birds and serpents have been created;

Many millions of stones and trees have been produced;
Many millions of winds, waters, and fires;
Many millions of countries and regions of the earth
Many millions of moons, suns, and stars;
Many millions of demigods, demons, and crowned Indars.
God holdeth all things by His string,
And, O Nanak, saveth those whom He pleaseth.

4

Many millions of beings were created with the three qualities of impulse, darkness, and goodness,
Many millions of Veds, Purans, Simritis, and Shastras,
Many millions of jewelled oceans,
Many millions of animals of various descriptions;
Many millions were made long-lived,
Many millions of hills and golden mountains,
Many millions of Yakshas, Kinars, and Pishachas,
Many millions of sprites, ghosts, pigs, and tigers—
God is near all, yet far from all;
Nanak, God filleth everything, and *yet* is separate.

5

Many millions inhabit the nether regions,
Many millions dwell in hell and heaven,
Many millions are born, live, and die,
Many millions wander through many wombs,
Many millions live without exertion,
Many millions are wearied with labour,
Many millions are created wealthy,
Many millions are anxious for riches,
Wherever God pleaseth He placeth them;
Nanak, everything is in God's power.

6

There are many millions of Bairagis
Who love God's name;
Many millions search for God,

And find Him in their hearts;
Many millions thirst for a sight of God,
And find Him, the Imperishable One;
Many millions pray for the society of the saints—
They are those who love the Supreme Being.
Nanak, they are ever blest
With whom God is well-pleased.

7

Many millions of sources of life and regions *were created,*
Many millions of skies, mundane eggs,
Many millions of incarnations.
In divers shapes the world was spread out;
Many times was extension extended.
Ever and ever there is but One God—
Many millions of *creatures* were made of many descriptions;
From God they emanated and in God shall they be absorbed.
No one knoweth His limit;
Nanak, God Himself is all in all.

8

There are Many millions of His slaves
Whose minds are enlightened;
Many millions who know the Real Thing,
And ever look with their eyes on the One alone;
Many millions drink the essence of the Name,
Become immortal, and live for ever and ever;
Many millions sing the excellences of the Name,
And are absorbed in divine bliss, happiness, and tranquillity.
God watcheth over every breath of His servant,
For, O Nanak, God's servants are dear to Him.

Slok XI

The Cause of causes is the One God, there is none other.

Nanak is a sacrifice to Him who is contained in sea and land, in the nether regions and the firmament.

ASHTAPADI XI

1

The Cause of causes is capable of acting;
What pleaseth Him shall come to pass.
He who hath no end or limits
Establisheth and disestablisheth in a moment.
By His order He supporteth and holdeth the firmament;
By His order there is creation, and by His order absorption *in Himself;*
The occupations of high and low are according to his order;
By His order there are the varied phases *of nature;*
Having created, He beholdeth His own greatness—
Nanak, God is contained in all things.

2

If it please God, man obtaineth salvation;
If it please God, He maketh a stone cross *the ocean of the world;*
If it please God, He can restore the lifeless body;
If it please God, then man recounteth His praises;
If it please God, then He saveth sinners.
He Himself createth, He Himself designeth,
He Himself is the Lord of both worlds.
The Searcher of hearts sporteth and is pleased;
He causeth man to do as He wisheth.
Nanak, there is nothing seen but Him.

3

Say what can be accomplished by man;
What pleaseth God He causeth to be done;
If man had the power he would acquire all things.
God doeth what pleaseth Himself,
Through not knowing *God* man is attached to sin;
If he knew God, he would save himself from it.
The *mind* led astray by superstition wandereth in every direction,
And in a moment returneth.
God bestoweth His service on him to whom He is merciful;
Nanak, such a man shall be absorbed in the Name.

4

God the cherisher of the poor
Can in a moment make a humble worm a king;
Him who is totally obscure
God can at one render everywhere famous.
The Lord of the world will not take the accounts of those
On whom He bestoweth His favours.
Soul and body are all His property;
Every heart is full of God's light;
He made His own handiwork—
Nanak liveth by beholding His greatness.

5

Man's power is not at his own disposal;
The Cause of causes is the Lord of all.
Helpless creatures must obey orders;
What pleaseth God shall ultimately be.
Man is sometimes exalted, and sometimes debased;
Sometimes he mourneth, and sometimes he laugheth with delight and joy;
Sometimes he engageth in blame and praise,
Sometimes he is up in heaven *sometimes down* in hell;
Sometimes he is acquainted with divine knowledge,
Nanak, God Himself causeth us to meet Him.

6

Sometimes man danceth in a variety of ways,
Sometimes he sleepeth day and night,
Sometimes he is terrible in his mighty wrath,
Sometimes he is the dust of all men's feet,
Sometimes he is enthroned as a great king,
Sometimes he weareth the attire of a lowly beggar,
Sometimes he falleth into evil repute,
Sometimes he is called very good;
As God keepeth him so he remaineth—
By the favour of the Guru, Nanak speaketh the truth.

7

Sometimes as a Pandit man expoundeth *texts,*
Sometimes vowed to silence he practiseth contemplation,
Sometimes he batheth at places of pilgrimage,
Sometimes as a Sidh or Striver he preacheth divine knowledge.
Sometimes his soul wandereth in may wombs—
Is in an elephant, a worm, or a moth.
As a player he playeth several parts;
As God pleaseth so He maketh man dance.
What pleaseth God shall come to pass;
Nanak, there is none other than He.

8

Sometimes man obtaineth the saints' society,
From which He returneth not again,
And which shall not perish:
The light of divine knowledge shall then shine in his heart.
His soul and body dyed with the name of the one God
Shall ever abide with the Supreme Being.
As water blendeth with water,
So light is blended with light.
Transmigration is ended and rest obtained—
Nanak is ever a sacrifice to the Lord.

Slok XII

They who have effaced themselves and become humbly are happy,
While the very haughty, O Nanak, are consumed by their pride.

ASHTAPADI XII

1

He in whose heart is the pride of dominion,
Shall fall into hell and become a dog;
He who boasteth of his youth,
Shall become a creature of filth;
He who calleth himself good
Shall die and be born again, and wander in many a womb;

He who is proud of his wealth and property,
Is stupid and blind and ignorant;
He in whose heart God mercifully planteth meekness,
Shall obtain, O Nanak, salvation in this world and happiness in the next.

2

Not so much as a straw shall go with him,
Who, becoming wealthy, plumeth himself thereon.
He who relieth on his large army and men,
Shall be destroyed in a moment;
He who deemeth himself stronger than all,
Shall in a trice become dust;
Dharmraj shall disgrace him
Who in his pride thinketh naught of any one.
He whose pride is effaced by favour of the Guru,
Shall be acceptable, Nanak, in God's court.

3

If man do millions of good acts *but* possess pride,
He incurreth only trouble; all *his acts* are vain.
He who is proud of his various mortifications,
Shall be born again and again in hell heaven.
How shall he who, though making many efforts,
Softeneth not his heart, go to God's court?
Goodness shall not even approach him
Who calleth himself good.
Saith Nanak, pure shall be the glory of him
Whose heart is the dust of all men's feet.

4

Man hath no happiness
So long as he thinketh he can do something;
As long as man thinketh he can do something,
So long shall he wander in wombs;
As long as man deemeth any one an enemy or a friend,
So long shall his mind not be stable;
As long as man is intoxicated with the love of mammon,
So long shall Dharmraj punish him.

It is by God's grace man's bonds are burst,
And by the Guru's favour pride, O Nanak, is removed.

5

Even though man earn thousands, he will run after a lakh;
He will never be satisfied in his pursuit of wealth.
Though he devote himself to the enjoyment of many evil passions,
He will never be satisfied; he will kill himself *pursuing more.*
No one can be satisfied without contentment;
Otherwise all efforts are vain like the illusion of a dream.
All happiness is obtained by loving the Name;
But only a few obtain it by great good fortune—
God Himself is all in all, the Cause of causes;
Ever and ever, Nanak, repeat His name.

6

The Creator is the Cause of causes;
What resource hath man?
He becometh as God regardeth him—
There is only God;
Whatever was created was according to His pleasure.
He is far from all, and yet with all;
He understandeth, beholdeth, and exerciseth judgement;
He Himself is one and He Himself is many;
He neither dieth nor perisheth; He neither cometh nor goeth;
Nanak, He is ever diffused throughout creation;

7

He Himself instructeth, and He Himself understandeth;
He Himself is blended with everything;
He made His own expansion;
Everything is His, He is the Creator—
Say can anything be effected without Him?
The one God is in every place;
He Himself acteth His own parts;
He exhibiteth plays of endless kinds;
He is in the soul, and the soul is in Him;
Nanak, His worth cannot be described.

8

True, true, true is the Lord God;
By the Guru's favour some rare person describeth Him.
True, true, true is He who created all.
Among millions some rare one knoweth Thee, *O God;*
Excellent, excellent, excellent is Thy form,
Very beautiful, unbounded, and incomparable.
Pure, pure, pure is Thy Word;
Every one heareth it with his ears, and repeateth it.
Holy, holy, holy, holy
Is Thy name; Nanak uttereth it with heartfelt love.

Slok XII

He who entereth the asylum of the saints shall be saved;
He who slandereth the saints, Nanak, shall be born again and again.

ASHTAPADI XIII

1

By calumniating the saints *man's* life is shortened,
By calumniating the saints man escapeth not from Death,
By calumniating the saints all happiness vanisheth,
By calumniating the saints man falleth into hell,
By calumniating the saints the understanding is clouded,
By calumniating the saints man is without glory—
None can save him who is accursed of the saints—
By calumniating the saints man falleth from his position.
Nanak, even a slanderer shall be saved in the company of the saints,
If the merciful saints but show him mercy.

2

By calumniating the saints man's face becometh crooked,
By calumniating the saints man croaketh like a raven,
By calumniating the saints man is born as a serpent,
By calumniating the saints man is born as a creeping worm,
By calumniating the saints man burneth with thirst,
By calumniating the saints man deceiveth every one,
By calumniating the saints all man's influence departeth,

By calumniating the saints man becometh the lowest of the low;
There is no *abiding* place for him who calumniateth the saints;
But if it please the saints, O Nanak, he too may obtain salvation.

3

The slanderer of the saints is a great malefactor,
The slanderer of the saints hath not a moment's rest,
The slanderer of the saints is a great murderer,
The slanderer of the saints is accursed of God,
The slanderer of the saints loseth his dominion,
The slanderer of the saints becometh afflicted and poor,
The slanderer of the saints contracteth every disease,
The slanderer of the saints is ever separated from God,
The slanderer of the saints committeth sin upon sin;
But, O Nanak, it it please the saints, he too may obtain salvation.

4

He who slandereth the saints is ever impure,
He who slandereth the saints is no man's friend,
He who slandereth the saints shall be punished,
He who slandereth the saints shall be abandoned by all,
He who slandereth the saints is very proud,
He who slandereth the saints is ever a sinner,
He who slandereth the saints dieth and is born again,
He who slandereth the saints swerveth from happiness,
He who slandereth the saints hath no abiding place;
But if it please the saints, O Nanak, they will join him with themselves—

5

He who slandereth the saints breaketh down half way,
He who slandereth the saints succeedeth in nothing,
He who slandereth the saints shall wander in deserts,
He who slandereth the saints shall fall into the wilderness,
He who slandereth the saints is hollow within—
As the corpse of a dead man hath no breath—
He who slandereth the saints hath no root whatever;
He shall himself eat of the fruit he hath planted;
He who slandereth the saints hath no protector;

But if it please the saints, O Nanak, they will save him too—

6

He who slandereth the saints shall cry aloud,
As a fish without water wriggleth in agony;
He who slandereth the saints shall never be full,
As a fire is not satisfied with firewood;
He who slandereth the saints is left alone
Like a miserable barren sesame stalk in a field;
He who slandereth the saints is void of honesty;
He who slandereth the saints ever uttereth falsehood—
Such is the fate of the slanderer from the beginning;
Nanak, whatever pleaseth God shall take place—

7

He who slandereth the saints shall become deformed,
He who slandereth the saints shall receive punishment in God's court,
He who slandereth the saints ever gaspeth,
He who slandereth the saints is neither dead nor living,
He who slandereth the saints never hath his hopes fulfilled,
He who slandereth the saints departeth disappointed;
No one obtaineth permanence by slandering the saints—
Man is as it pleaseth God to *make him;*
No one can set aside his destiny—
Nanak, the True One knoweth everything;

8

Every heart is His, He is the Creator;
Ever and ever bow to Him;
Praise God day and night;
Meditate on Him at every breath you draw and at every morsel you eat.
Everything prevaileth that God hath done.
Man shall become as God maketh him.
God playeth His own play;
Who else can criticize Him?
He giveth His name to those to whom He is merciful;
And, Nanak, very fortunate are they.

Slok XIV

Quit devices, my good friends, and remember God, God the King;

Treasure in thy heart thy hopes in the one God, O Nanak, so shall suffering, error, and fear depart.

ASHTAPADI XIV

1

Know that all reliance on man is vain;
It is God alone who bestoweth,
By whose gifts we remain satisfied,
And not again feel thirst.
The one God alone destroyeth and protecteth;
There is nothing in man's power.
Happiness cometh from understanding the will of God;
String His name and wear it on thy neck;
Remember, remember, remember that God,
Nanak, and no obstacle shall come in thy way.

2

O man, praise the Formless One in thy heart;
O man, practise works or righteousness;
Quaff the nectar of the Name, and thy tongue shall become pure,
And thou shalt render thy soul for ever happy.
Behold God's splendour with thine eyes.
In the company of the saints *love for* all other company shall vanish.
Walk with thy feet in God's way:
Thy sins shall be erased if thou *even* for a moment repeat God's *name*.
Do God's work, hear His story with thine ears,
And thy countenance, O Nanak, shall be bright in His court.

3

Very fortunate are they in the world
Who ever and ever sing God's praises.
He who meditateth on God's name
Shall be accounted rich in the world.
Know that he shall ever and ever be happy
Who uttereth the Supreme God's name with mind and tongue.

He who recognizeth the one only God
Shall obtain knowledge of this world and the next.
He whose mind is won over to the Name,
Nanak, shall know God the Pure One.

4

Know that his thirst shall be quenched
Who by the Guru's favour knoweth himself.
The holy man who repeateth God's praises in the company of the saints,
Shall be exempt from all disease.
He who night and day singeth the one God's praises
Shall be saved even in the bosom of his family.
Death's noose shall be cut for him
Who putteth his hopes in God alone.
He whose soul hungereth for the Supreme God,
Shall, O Nanak, have no suffering.

5

He who thinketh upon the Lord God,
Is a nappy saint and wavereth not.
The servant to whom God showeth His mercy—
Say of whom shall he be afraid:
As God is, so doth He appear unto him—
Contained in His own creation.
He who is successful in his long search *for God,*
By the Guru's favour knoweth the whole reality.
When I look I *see God* is the root of all things;
Nanak, He is at once minute and great;

6

He is not born, neither doth He die;
He playeth His own parts.
Things visible and invisible, which come and go,
The whole creation is supported by the Commander,
And He Himself is contained in everything.
Employing many devices He maketh and unmaketh.
He is imperishable and infrangible;
He supporteth the universe;

He is unseen, inscrutable, and glorious.
Nanak, they whom He Himself causeth to repeat His name repeat it.

7

They who know God are glorious;
The whole world shall be saved by their spell. God's servants shall save all:
God's servants shall save all:
God's Servants shall cause sorrow to be forgotten.
They who repeat the Name under the Guru's instruction shall be happy;
The Merciful One shall blend them with Himself;
The fortunate man to whom God showeth mercy
Shall apply Himself to their service.
He who uttereth the Name shall obtain rest;
Nanak, consider him as the best:

8

Whatever he doeth is for the love of God;
He shall ever and ever abide with Him—
Whatever naturally happeneth, happeneth—
And recognize Him as the Creator.
What God doeth is pleasing to the saints;
As He is, so He appeareth *unto them*.
They shall be absorbed in Him from whom they have sprung,
And be alone deemed worthy of the treasure of happiness.
He himself giveth honour to His own;
Nanak, know that God and His servant are one.

Slok XV

God is full of all power and knoweth the affairs *of His creatures;*
I am a sacrifice to Him, O Nanak, by remembering whom salvation is obtained.

ASHTAPADI XV

1

God is the mender of what is broken;
He Himself cherisheth all creatures.
Nobody applieth in vain to Him
Whose heart feeleth anxiety for all.
O man, ever repeat God's *name;*

He himself is the imperishable Lord.
From what man doeth himself nothing resulteth.
O mortal, even though thou desire it hundreds of times,
Without God nothing shall avail thee.
Salvation, Nanak, is obtained by repeating the name of the one *God*.

2

If man be handsome, he should not be charmed thereby,
Since it is God's light that shineth in everybody.
If man be wealthy, why should be he proud *thereof,*
Since all the wealth that God hath given belongeth to Him?
Even though one be a mighty hero,
What efforts can be make without obtaining power from God?
If any one plume himself on being very liberal,
God the real Giver will think him a fool.
He whose malady of pride is cured by the Guru's favour,
Shall, O Nanak, never suffer from it again.

3

As a pillar supporteth a house,
So the word of the Guru supporteth the heart;
As a stone floateth when put into a boat,
So are mortals saved by clinging to the Guru's feet;
As a lamp giveth light in the darkness,
So man shineth on beholding the Guru;
As man can find his way in a great wilderness if *he have a guide,*
So light shall shine for him when he joineth the congregation of the saints.
I desire the dust of such saints' *feet;*
O God, fulfil Nanak's desires.

4

O foolish man, why dost thou bewail?
Thou shalt obtain what was written for thee in the beginning.
God is the dispenser of woe and weal;
Abandon others and think of Him:
Whatever He doeth gladly agree to—
Why wanderest thou astray, O thoughtless one?
O greedy moth, attached to pleasures,

What came *into the world* with thee?
Repeat God's name in thy heart,
Nanak, and thou shalt go to thy home with honour.

5

In the dwelling of the saints God's name is found—
The merchandise thou camest *into the world* to obtain.
Renounce pride, weigh *God's name* in thy heart,
And purchase it with thy life.
Lord thy merchandise, set out with the saints,
And, having freed thyself from the entanglements of the deadly sins,
Every one will congratulate thee;
Thy countenance shall be bright, and thou shalt obtain honour in God's court.
Few are the merchants *who deal in* this merchandise,
And to them Nanak is ever a sacrifice.

6

Bathe the saints' feet and *afterwards* drink the bathing water;
Dedicate thy soul to the saints;
Bathe thyself in the dust of the saints' feet,
And become a sacrifice unto them
The service of the saints is obtained by good fortune;
Sing God's praises in their company:
The saints preserve man from various dangers.
He who singeth God's praises shall taste the savour of nectar.
He who cometh to the door of the saints and seeketh their protection,
Shall, O Nanak, obtain all happiness.

7

God reanimateth the dead;
He giveth support to the hungry;
All wealth is in His glance;
But man only obtaineth what was originally destined him.
Everything is God's; He is Omnipotent.
There neither was nor shall be any but Him;
O man, ever and ever repeat His *name* day and night;
This is the most exalted and sacred duty.
He is whom God hath mercifully granted His name,

Shall, O Nanak, become pure.

8

He whose heart hath faith in the Guru
Shall remember the Lord God;
They in whose hearts is the one God,
Are called saints in the three worlds.
True are the acts and true the ways of those
In whose hearts is the truth, and who utter the truth with their mouths.
True is God's glance, true His world,
True His practice, and true His creation.
He who recognizeth the Supreme Being as true,
Shall, O Nanak, be absorbed in the True One.

Slok XVI

God hath no form, outline, or colour; He is exempt from the three qualities;
He causeth him, O Nanak, with whom He is well-pleased to know him.

ASHTAPADI XVI

1

Keep thou the imperishable God in thy heart,
And renounce human love.
There is nothing superior to God;
He is one without interruption in all things;
He is far-seeing; He is knowing.
O deep, profound, and all-wise,
Supreme Brahm, Supreme God, Gobind,
Treasure of mercy,
Compassionate Pardoner,
Nanak's heartfelt desire is
To fall at the feet of Thy saints.

2

God is the fulfiller of desires and capable of *giving* protection;
What He Hath inscribed *in mam's destiny* shall take place.
He can destroy and create in the twinkling of an eye;
None but Himself knoweth His counsel;

He is ever happy and joyous;
All things are, I have heard, in His palace;
He is King of kings and Supreme Jogi among Jogis;
In penance He is king of the penitents; in the domestic state He is an enjoyer;
By constant meditation of Him the saints obtain happiness—
Nanak, no one hath found the limit of such a Being;

3

To His play there is no limit;
All the demigods have grown weary searching for it.
What doth a son know of His father's birth?
God hath strung all things on His own string.
His servant to whom He giveth wisdom, divine knowledge and meditation,
Meditateth on Him.
They whom He leadeth astray among the three qualities,
Die to be born again, and again suffer transmigration.
The high and the low places *of the earth* are His—
O Nanak, man knoweth as God causeth him to know Him.

4

God hath various forms and various colours;
He assumeth various guises, and yet remaineth the same.
God the indestructible who hath one form,
Hath extended Himself in various ways;
He acteth various parts in a moment.
The Perfect One filleth every place;
He hath made creation in various forms;
He Himself knoweth His own worth;
All hearts are His, all places are His.
Nanak liveth by ever uttering God's name.

5

By the Name are sustained all creatures;
By the Name are supported the regions *of the earth* and the universe;
By the Name are supported the Simritis, the Veds, and the Purans;
By the support of the Name we hear *God's praises, and obtain* divine knowledge and meditation;
By the Name are supported the firmament and the nether regions;

By the Name is the whole world upheld;
By the Name are maintained all cities and houses;
By hearing the Name with attention man is saved.
He whom God mercifully attacheth to His name,
Shall, O Nanak, obtain final deliverance.

6

God's form is true, true is His place;
He is the True Spirit, He alone is Supreme;
His acts are true, His word is true;
The true Spirit is contained in everything;
His deeds are true, His creation is true;
The Root *of the world* is true, and true what springeth from it;
Pure are His acts, the purest of the pure.
Everything turneth out well for him to whom God giveth knowledge.
The true name of God bestoweth happiness;
True faith, Nanak, is obtained from the Guru.

7

True are the worlds and instruction of the saints;
True are they into whose hearts they enter.
He who knoweth how to search for the truth,
Shall obtain salvation by uttering the Name.
God Himself is true, and true is everything He hath made;
He Himself knoweth His own measure and condition.
The creation belongeth to its Maker;
He taketh counsel with none but Himself.
The measure of the Creator is not known to the creature;
Nanak, what pleaseth God prevaileth.

8

Man wondereth at the wonders upon wonders *of creation,*
But it is only he who knoweth God who obtaineth bliss.
The men of God who are enamoured with His love,
Receive under the Guru's instruction the *great* boons;
They are generous and dispellers of sorrow;
In their company the world shall be saved.

He who serveth the saints is very fortunate;
In the society of the saints man fixeth his attention on the one God.
They who sing the excellences and praises of God,
Shall Nanak, by the favour of the Guru obtain their reward.

Slok XVII

The True One was in the beginning; the True One was in the primal age.
The True One is now also, O Nanak; the True One also shall be.

ASHTAPADI XVII

1

His feet are true, and true is he who toucheth them;
His worship is true, and true is His worshipper;
A sight of Him is true, and true is he who obtaineth it;
True is His name, and true is he who meditateth on it;
He Himself is true, and so is everything He sustaineth'
He Himself is excellence and the Bestower of excellence;
The Word is true, and true is God who uttereth it;
The ears are true which hear the praises of the True One;
To him who understandeth, everything is true—
Nanak, god is altogether true.

2

He who knoweth in his heart Him whose form is true
Shall recognize the Root of all things, the Cause of causes.
Divine knowledge shall be revealed to him
Into whose heart faith in God hath entered;
He shall abide free from fear,
And be absorbed in Him from whom he sprang.
If one take a thing and blend it with another of *the same kind,*
It cannot be said to be separate from it.
A man of undersanding can understand that.
When God is found, O Nanak, *man becometh one with Him.*

3

The servant of the Lord obeyeth His order,
The servant of the Lord ever adoreth Him,

The servant of the Lord possesseth faith in his heart;
Pure is the conduct of the Lord's servant;
His servant knoweth that God is with him.
God's servant is dyed with His name,
God cherisheth His servant,
The Formless one preserveth the honour of His servant—
He is a servant to whom the Lord showeth mercy;
Nanak, such a servant remembereth God at every breath.

4

God will draw a veil over *the faults* of His servant,
And will assuredly preserve his *honour;*
He will bestow greatness on His slave,
Cause him to repeat His name,
And preserve his honour.
No one knoweth God's condition or measure—
No one is equal to God's condition or measure—
No one is equal to God's servant;
God's servant is the most exalted of the exalted.
The servant whom God applieth to His service,
Shall be renowned, O Nanak, in every direction.

5

If God infuse power into a little ant,
It can reduce to ashes armies of hundreds of thousands and millions *of men.*
God preserveth and holdeth out a hand to him
Whom He *desireth* not to deprive of life.
Though man make efforts of many kinds,
His exertions are in vain.
No one can kill or preserve but God;
He is the Preserver of all creatures.
Why art thou anxious, O mortal?
Nanak, repeat the name of God the unseen, the wonderful;

6

Ever, ever, ever repeat God's name;
Satisfy thy soul and body by quaffing its nectar.

The holy man who obtaineth the jewel of the Name,
Will look on no one but God;
He will deem the Name his wealth, the Name his beauty and delight,
The Name his happiness, God's name his companion.
He who is satisfied with the savour of God's name,
Shall be absorbed soul and body in it.
To utter the Name standing, sitting, or sleeping,
Saith Nanak, is ever the duty of the man of *God*.

7

God gave the gift to His worshipper
To utter His praises day and night.
They who serve with heartfelt love,
Shall be absorbed in the Lord.
They shall know the past and the present,
And recognize the order of their God.
Who can describe His greatness?
I know not how to describe even one of His excellences.
They who abide the whole day in the presence of God,
Saith Nanak, are the perfect men.

8

O man, take shelter with them;
Give them thy soul and body.
He who recognizeth his God
Is bountiful in all things;
In his shelter thou shalt find all happiness;
By a sight of Him thou shalt blot out all sin.
Renounce all other cleverness,
And attach thyself to His service.
Nanak, ever worship His feet,
And thou Shalt suffer no more transmigration.

Slok XVIII

He who knoweth the True Being is called the true Guru;
His disciple is saved by association with him, O Nanak, and by singing God's praises.

ASHTAPADI XVIII

1

The true Guru cherisheth his disciple,
The true Guru is ever compassionate to his servant,
The Guru will remove the filth of his disciple's wickedness—
Under the Guru's instruction the disciple will repeat God's name—
The true Guru will cut the fetters of his disciple,
If the disciple recoil from evil deeds.
The disciple to whom the true Guru giveth the wealth of the Name,
Is very fortunate.
The true Guru adjusteth this world and the next for his disciple.
Nanak, the true Guru loveth his disciple as his life.

2

The servant who dwelleth in his Guru's house,
Should heartily accept his order,
Not overrate himself,
Ever meditate on God's name in his heat,
And sell his soul to the true Guru—
The affairs of such a man shall prosper.
He who serveth the true Guru without any desire
Of reward, shall obtain the Lord.
The servant to whom God showeth favour,
Nanak, will accept the Guru's instruction;

3

The servant who fully conciliateth the Guru,
Shall know the state of the Supreme Being.
He in whose heart is God's name is the true Guru;
I am many times a sacrifice to *such* a Guru;
He bestoweth all treasure on men,
And is day and night imbued with love for the Supreme Being.
The holy man is in God and God in the holy man,
God Himself is one; of this there is no doubt.
The Guru is not obtained by a thousand devices;
Nanak, such a Guru is only found by good fortune.

4

A sight *of the Guru* is profitable; he who beholdeth him is purified;
By touching his feet man's conduct and practice become spotless;
He who on meeting him uttereth God's praises,
Shall arrive at the court of the Supreme Being.
On hearing his words the ears are satisfied;
The mind gaineth contentment and the spirit consolation.
He on whom the perfect Guru, whose spell is immortal,
Looketh with his abrosial glance becometh a saint.
His excellences are endless; his worth cannot be appraised.
Nanak, whoso pleaseth him he blendeth with himself.

5

Man has but one tongue, *God's* praises are manifold;
He is the True Being of perfect discrimination;
Mortal cannot by any words succeed in describing Him.
He is inaccessible, incomprehensible and unperturbed.
He liveth not by food, He is without enmity, the Giver of comfort;
No one hath found His worth.
Many saints continually make obeisance to Him,
And meditate in their hearts on His lotus feet.
Nanak, is ever a sacrifice to his true Guru,
By whose favour the name of such a God is repeated.

6

This divine essence only few obtain,
But they who drink it become immortal.
That being shall never perish
In whose heart the Lord of excellences appeareth.
He who taketh God's name during the eight watches,
Who giveth true instruction to his servant,
Who is not veneered by worldly love,
Who keepeth but the one God in his heart—
For him a lamp shall shine in the darkness,
And, O Nanak, his doubts, worldly love, and sorrows flee away.

7

By the perfect instruction of the saints,
Man becometh cool in *the midst* of heat;
Sorrow is put to flight, happiness resulteth,
The fear of birth and death is removed,
Fear ceaseth, man abideth fearless,
And all troubles vanish from his mind.
God showeth mercy to his own
Who in the company of the saints repeat His name.
By listening, O Nanak, to God's praises with attention
Mental stableness is obtained, and superstition and transmigration cease.

8

He whose power fascinateth the whole world,
Is without the *three* qualities, and yet possesseth all qualities.
God Himself performeth His own play;
Only he himself knoweth His worth.
There is no other than God;
He, the one Spirit, pervadeth all things without interruption;
He, the warp and the woof, is contained in all forms and colours;
He becometh manifest by association with the saints;
He who made creation infused His power into it—
Nanak is many times a sacrifice *unto Him*.

Slok XIX

Except God's worship nothing shall go with thee, *O man;* worldly things are ashes;

Nanak, the essence of wealth is the repetition of God's name.

ASHTAPADI XIX

1

In the company of the saints reflect *on God;*
Remember the one God and rest upon His name;
Forget all other efforts, my friend;
Put God's lotus feet into thy heart;'
He is the Omnipotent, the Cause of causes;
Firmly grasp His name; it *is the best* thing;

Lay up this wealth and thou shalt be fortunate.
Pure is the instruction of the saints;
Keep the hope of the one God in thy heart,
Nanak, and all thy maladies shall be healed.

2

By serving God thou shalt obtain the wealth
After which thou *now* hastest in every direction.
The happiness which thou ever desirest, my friend,
Shall be found by loving the society of the saints.
The glory for which thou performest good acts,
Shall be obtained by hastening to God for protection.
It is not by many remedies maladies are healed;
It is by administering the medicine of God's *name.*
Of all treasures God's name is the treasure;
Repeat it, Nanak, and thou shalt be acceptable in God's court.

3

Thy mind which now wandereth in every direction, shall rest
By enlightening it with God's name.
No obstacle can impede him
In whose heart God abideth.
This Kal age is hot; God's name is cool;
Remember it, remember it, and thou shalt ever be happy.
By service and love the mind becometh enlightened,
Fears depart, all hopes shall be fulfilled,
Man shall abide in the imperishable home,
Saith Nanak, and Death's noose be cut *for his escape.*

4

It is the true man who meditateth on God;
It is the falsest of the false who suffer transmigration;
But transmigration shall be effaced by serving God.
Abandon pride and *seek* the protection of the divine Guru,
So shall thy precious human life be saved.
Remember God who is the support of the soul—
Man shall not be saved by many devices,
Or by studying the Simritis, the Shastars, and the Veds.

Nanak, heartily serve God,
And thou shalt obtain thy heart's desire.

5

Thy wealth shall not depart with thee;
Why art thou wrapped up in it, O foolish man?
Son friend, family, and wife—
Say what ownership hast thou in them.
Dominion, worldly pleasure, and extensive wealth—
Say who can escape from these.
Horses, elephants, carriages, and equipages,
Are delusive shows and false displays;
Ignorant man knoweth not Him who gave them;
Nanak, he forgetteth the Name and *afterwards* regretteth.

6

Take the advice of the Guru, O silly man;
Without devotion many clever men have been lost.
Worship God with thy heart, O my friend,
And thy mind shall become pure;
Put His lotus feet into thy heart,
And the sins of many births shall depart;
Repeat His name thyself and cause others to do so;
By hearing it, and uttering it, and abiding by it thou shalt obtain salvation.
The real thing is God's true name—
Nanak, sing His excellences with devotion and love.

7

By singing God's praises filth shall be washed away,
And the poison of pride, which overspreadeth thee, shall depart.
By remembering God's name at every breath thou drawest,
Thou shalt become free from care and abide in happiness—
O man, lay aside all thy cleverness;
The true wealth thou shalt acquire in the company of the saints.
Obtain God's name as thy capital, deal with it,
And thou shalt be happy in this world and victorious in the next—
Saith Nanak, he on whose forehead such fate hath been written,
Seeth the one God without interruption in all things.

8

Repeat the name of the one God, magnify the one God,
Remember the one God, make Him thy heart's desire,
Sing the excellences of the one God who is endless;
With soul and body repeat *the name* of the one God—
God himself is the only, only, only one;
The perfect God filleth every place;
There have been many expansions of the one God.
Worship the one God, and all thy sins shall depart.
Nanak, by the favour of the Guru the one God is known by him
Whose soul and body are thoroughly imbued with His love,

Slok XX

After many wanderings, O God, I have come to Thine asylum;
Nanak's prayer, O God, is — 'Let me apply myself to Thy service.'

ASHTAPADI XX

1

I, a beggar, beg a gift of Thee, O God:
Mercifully grant me Thy name.
I crave for the dust of the saints' feet;
Fulfil my desire, O Supreme Being.
Let me ever sing Thine excellences,
And meditate on Thee, at every breath;
Let me over love Thy lotus feet,
And continually perform Thy service.
Thou art mine only shelter, mine only support:
Nanak craveth Thine excellent name.

2

In God's favouring glance there is great happiness.
But few obtain God's savour;
They who have tasted it are satisfied,
They have become perfect beings and waver not,
They are filled with the sweetness and delight of love,
And in the company of the saints feel desire *to meet God*.
They enter His asylum forsaking all others,

Their hearts are enlightened, and they fix their attention on Him day and night.
Very fortunate are they who repeat God's name;
Nanak, they who are dyed with it are happy.

3

The desires of God's servant are fulfilled;
He obtaineth pure instruction from the true Guru.
God is merciful to His servant,
And rendereth him ever happy.
God cutteth his fetters, he is emancipated,
And the ignorance from which the pain of birth and death resulteth is no more;
His wishes are fulfilled, his desires are all fulfilled;
He is blended with God and is ever present with Him.
God to whom he belonged hath blended him with Himself—
Nanak is absorbed in God's service and His name.

4

Why forget Him who destroyeth not the *effects* of labour?
Why forget Him who regardeth what is done *for Him?*
Why forget Him who gave us everything?
Why forget Him who is the life of living beings?
Why forget Him who preserveth us in the fire *of the womb?*
By the Guru's favour some rare one seeth Him—
Why forget Him who extricateth man from sin,
And joineth *with Him those who* had broken *with Him* during many births?
The perfect Guru hath taught me the real thing;
So Nanak hath meditated on his God.

5

O holy saints, do this—
Abandon all else and repeat God's name;
Remember it, remember it, remember it, and you shall be happy;
Repeat it yourselves and cause others to repeat it.
By service and love you shall cross over the world;
Without service the body shall be as dust.
From the treasure of the Name all beatitude and happiness are obtained,
And even they who are drowning obtain rest—
O Nanak, repeat the name of the Lords of excellences,

And all they sorrow shall depart.

6

The wish of my soul and body is
That the pleasures of love, affection, and desire *for God* may spring up in me;
That I may have the happiness of beholding Him with mine eyes;
And that my soul may be gladdened by washing the saints' feet.
Few there are who can obtain association with the saints,
And whose souls and bodies *are filled* with love for Thee.
Mercifully grant me one thing, O God,
To repeat Thy name by the Guru's favour.
Nanak, God's praises cannot be expressed;
He is contained in all things;

7

He is the Pardoner, compassionate to the poor,
Kind to the saints, and ever merciful.
Gobind Gopal, the Patron of the patronless,
Cherisheth all creatures;
He is the primal Being, the Creator of the world,
The support of the souls of holy men.
He shall become pure who repeateth His name,
And devoteth to Him service, affection and heartfelt love.
Devoid of virtue, low, and ignorant
Nanak seeketh thy protection, O Supreme Power.

8

He who singeth God's praises even for a moment,
Shall obtain everything — heaven, salvation, deliverance.
He to whose heart the story of God's name is pleasing,
Shall enjoy the various pleasures and greatness of a monarch.
They whose tongues continually repeat God's name,
Shall enjoy plenteous food, raiment, singing, and dancing.
Good are his deeds, glorious and wealthy is he
In whose heart the perfect Guru's spell abideth.
O God, grant Nanak a dwelling with Thy saints,
Where all happiness shall be manifested unto him.

Slok XXI

The Formless One who possesseth all qualities, and yet is devoid of them is in profound contemplation;

Nanak, what He hath made He again absorbeth in Himself.

ASHTAPADI XXI

1

Before this world in any wise appeared,
By whom were bad and good acts committed?
When God was in profound meditation,
With whom were enmity and strife?
When no colour or trace of man was seen,
Say who then felt joy or sorrow.
When there was only the Supreme Being Himself,
Where was worldly love? Who had superstition?
He Himself performed His own play;
Nanak, there was no other Creator.

2

When God was the sole master,
Say who was accounted bond or free.
When there was only the one *God,* inaccessible, limitless,
Say who was born in hell or heaven.
When God who is without attributes was in profound repose,
Say where were Shiv and his consort.
When God Himself held His own light,
Who was fearless, who feared any one?
He himself performed His own play;
Nanak, God is inaccessible and illimitable.

3

When the Imperishable One was seated on His comfortable throne,
Say where were then transmigration and destruction.
When there was only the perfect God the Creator,
Say who had any fear of Death.
When there was only the one invisible and incomprehensible God,
Whom did Chitr and Gupt call on for his account?

When there was only the pure, incomprehensible, and unfathomable Lord,
Who was then emancipated? Who was bound with fetters?
God is wonderful in Himself;
Nanak, it was He Himself created His own form.

4

When there was only the pure Being, the Lord of men,
And there was no filth of sin, say what was *the need* of ablution.
When there was only the bright, formless, and undisturbed One,
Who was held in honour and who in dishonour?
When there was only the Lord of the world,
Say who was the victim of deceit and fraud.
When God's light was contained in Himself,
Who felt hunger? who satiety?
The Creator is the Cause of causes;
Nanak, the Creator is beyond calculation.

5

When God's glory was contained in Himself,
Who was then mother, father, friend, son, or brother?
When He Himself was versed in all accomplishments,
Where did any one see the Veds and Muhammadan books?
When God kept His designs to Himself,
Who thought of favourable or unfavourable omens?
When He Himself was far and He Himself was near,
Who was Master and who was slave?
Man is astonished at the wonders of creation:
Nanak, only god Himself knoweth His own condition.

6

When the undeceivable, the impenetrable and the inscrutable One was contained in Himself,
Who felt the influence of mammon?
When there was no one to offer obeisance to God but Himself,
The three qualities had not yet entered *the world*.
When there was only the one God,
Who was free from care, who felt care?
When God was content with Himself,

Who preached and who listened?
God is totally infinite, the most exalted of the exalted:
O Nanak, He Himself is His own parallel.

7

When God made this illusion of the world,
He diffused the three qualities in it, demerits and merits began to be spoken of;
Some suffered hell and others enjoyed heaven.
God made the snares and entanglements of mammon,
Pride, worldly love, doubt, excessive fear,
Woe and weal, honour and dishonour,
And delivered different kinds of doctrines.
God Himself performeth and beholdeth His own play;
When He collecteth the stage properties, O Nanak, He alone remaineth.

8

Where there are saints of the Invisible, there is He Himself.
When God extended Himself, the saints became glorious;
He Himself is the arbiter of both states;
God's glory is peculiar to Himself;
He Himself performeth plays, amusements, and frolics;
He enjoyeth pleasures *and yet remaineth* separate *from* them;
He attacheth whomsoever He pleaseth to His name,
And causeth whomsoever He pleaseth to play the play *of the world.*
He is incalculable, unfathomable, uncountable, and unrivalled—
His slave Nanak speaketh as He causeth him to speak.

Slok XXII

O Lord of men and lower animals, Thou art contained *in everything;*
Nanak, the one God is *everywhere* extended; where is there another seen?

ASHTAPADI XXII

1

Thou Thyself art the speaker, Thou Thyself the hearer;
Thou art one, and Thou art many.
When it pleased God, He created the world;
And when it pleased Him, He absorbed it in Himself.

Without Thee, O God, nothing is done;
Thou holdest the whole world on Thy string;
He whom God Himself instructeth,
Obtaineth the true Name,
Looketh on all with an equal eye, knoweth the truth,
And is, O Nanak, victorious over the universe.

2

Men and the lower animals are in the power of Him
Who is compassionate to the poor and the Patron of the patronless.
No one can destroy whom God preserveth;
He whom God forgetteth is *already* dead.
Why should any one leave God and go to another?
The one bright Monarch is over all.
Know that He in whose power are the ways of all creatures,
Is with thee whether at home or abroad.
The Ocean of excellences is endless and illimitable;
The slave Nanak is ever a sacrifice *unto Him.*

3

The perfect compassionate God filleth every place:
He is merciful to all,
And knoweth His own affairs.
The Searcher of hearts is contained in everything,
And cherisheth creatures in divers ways.
Whatever creatures He made meditate on Him.
He blendeth with Himself whosoever pleaseth Him,
Performeth His service, and singeth His praises.
He who hath hearty faith in Him,
O Nanak, recognizeth the one God, the Creator.

4

The hopes of him who is attached to the name of the one God,
Shall not be in vain.
Service is the duty of the servant;
He who obeyeth God's order shall obtain the supreme state,
Than which nothing more exalted can be conceived.
He in whose heart the Formless One dwelleth,

And who night and day worshippeth the Guru's feet,
Shall burst his fetters and be free from enmity:
He shall be at ease in this world, happy in the next,
And, O Nanak, God will blend him with Himself.

5

Be joyous in the company of the saints;
Sing the praises of God who is the Primal Joy;
Meditate on God's name the real thing;
Save thy human life so difficult of attainment;
And sing the ambrosial words of God's praises—
That is the way to save thy soul.
He who beholdeth God ever near him,
Shall be delivered from his ignorance, and his spiritual darkness dispelled.
Hearken to instruction, and treasure it in thy heart,
So shalt thou, Nanak, obtain the reward thy heart desireth.

6

Arrange both this world and the next for thyself
By clasping God's name to thy heart.
Perfect is the teaching of the perfect Guru;
He in whose heart it dwelleth assayeth the truth.
With thy soul and body attentively repeat God's name,
And sorrow, pain, and fear shall depart from thy heart.
O dealer, deal in the true merchandise of *the Name,*
And thy cargo shall go to heaven with thee.
Put the prop of the one God into thy heart,
Nanak, and thou shalt not again suffer transmigration.

7

Where can any one go far from God?
Thou shalt be saved by meditating on the Preserver.
All his fear shall depart who uttereth the name of the Fearless One,
And he shall be saved by God's mercy.
He whom God preserveth shall not feel misery;
By repeating God's name his mind shall be happy,
His anxieties shall depart, his pride be erased,
And there shall be none equal to him—

Nanak, all his affairs shall succeed
Over whom the brave Guru watcheth.

8

The world shall be saved by beholding *the Guru,*
Whose understanding is perfect, whose glance is nectar,
And whose lotus feet are incomparable.
Profitable is a sight of him, beautiful his form,
Blessed his service, and acceptable his servant.
He in whose heart the Searcher of hearts,
The Supreme Being, dwelleth is happy,
And Death shall not approach him.
Nanak, he who in the company of the saints meditateth on God
Becometh immortal, and obtaineth the immortal rank.

Slok XXIII

The Guru hath given the eye-salve of divine knowledge by which the darkness of ignorance is dispelled;

The mind of him, O Nanak, who by God's favour meeteth the saints is enlightened.

ASHTAPADI XXIII

1

In the company of the saints I have seen God within me;
God's name to me is sweet—
All things of various colours and divers forms
Are in the heart of the one God.
God's name is the nine treasures and ambrosia
For him in whose body it findeth a resting-place.
Where there is deep meditation, the unbeaten sound *is heart;*
The wonder and marvel of it cannot be described.
He to whom God showeth Himself, beholdeth Him,
And, O Nanak, obtaineth understanding.

2

The Endless One is with thee whether at home or abroad;
He is contained in every heart,
In earth, heaven, and nether regions;

In all worlds He is the Perfect Cherisher;
In forest, glade, and mountain He is the Supreme Being;
As He ordereth so are *His creatures'* acts.
In wind, water, fire,
And in every direction is He contained;
There is no place where He is not.
Nanak, by the Guru's favour obtain happiness;

3

Consult the Veds, Purans, and Simritis, *and thou shalt know*
That the one God is in the moon, the sun, and the stars.
Everybody speaketh with the voice of God.
Who is unwavering and never wavereth.
He playeth His play with all His appliances;
He cannot be obtained by purchase, His attributes are priceless;
His light is in all things.
He holdeth the warp and woof of the world.
Nanak, this is the creed of those who
By the Guru's favour are freed from superstition.

4

In the sight of the saints everything is God;
In their hearts is all faith.
It is *only* good words the saints hear;
They love God who is contained in all things.
The rule of the saint who knoweth God is to speak the truth to everybody;
Whatever happeneth he taketh for the best,
For he recognizeth God as the Cause of causes.
God dwelleth within as also without man;
Nanak, on beholding Him all men are fascinated.

5

He himself is true; true is everything that He hath made:
Everything was created by God.
If it please Him He expandeth Himself,
If it please Him His form alone remaineth.
His manifold power cannot be seen;

He blendeth with Himself whomsoever He pleaseth.
What can be described as near Him and what distant,
Since He Himself filleth all space?
Nanak, God causeth that man to understand Him
Whom he teacheth that He himself is within him.

6

God Himself abideth in all the elements;
He beholdeth all things with His own eyes;
The whole creation is His body;
He Himself heareth His own praises;
He hath made transmigration as a play,
And rendered Maya subservient to Him.
Included in everything, He yet remaineth distinct.
Whatever order is to be given, He giveth Himself;
By His order man cometh, by His order man goeth;
Nanak, when it pleaseth Him, He blendeth man with Himself.

7

Whatever cometh from Him is not evil;
Say hath any one except Him done anything.
He Himself is good; His acts are very good;
He Himself knoweth His own mind;
He Himself is true, and true is everything that He supporteth;
The warp and woof of the world He hath blended with Himself;
His condition and measure cannot be described;
If any one else were *like Him,* he would know how to describe Him.
Nanak, by the favour of the Guru
It is known that all God's acts must be accepted.

8

He who knoweth Him must always be happy,
And God will blend him with Himself.
He in whose heart God dwelleth is wealthy,
Of high family, honoured, and obtaineth salvation during life.
Hail hail, hail! a man hath come
By whose favour the whole world shall be saved.
The object of his coming was

That through him the Name might be remembered.
He was saved himself and he saved the world:
To him, Nanak, I ever make obeisance.

Slok XXIV

He who worshippeth the perfect God whose name is perfect,
And who singeth the praises of the perfect One, O Nanak, obtaineth the perfect One.

ASHTAPADI XXIV

1

Hear the instruction of the perfect Guru—
Regard the Supreme Being as ever near thee;
Repeat His name at every breath,
And the anxiety of the heart shall depart.
Abandon the fleeting wave of desire,
And heartily pray for the dust of the saints' feet.
Renounce pride, make supplication,
And thus shalt thou in the company of the saints cross the ocean of fire.
Fill thy storehouses with divine wealth,
Nanak, and bow before the perfect Guru.

2

By repeating God's *name* in the company of the saints,
Thou shalt obtain rest, comfort, peace, and happiness.
Drink the nectareous essence of God's praise,
And thou shalt avoid hell and save thy soul.
Think in thy heart of the one God
Who hath one form but many manifestations.
Gopal, Damodar, compassionate to the poor,
Destroyer of pain, completely merciful—
Remember, remember for ever His name;
Nanak, it is the support of the soul.

3

The saints' words are the holiest hymns;
Priceless rubies are those gems;
He who heareth them and liveth according to them shall be saved;

He shall be saved himself and save others;
Profitable his life and the lives of his associates,
Whose heart is touched by divine love.
He for whom the unbeaten music or rejoicing playeth,
Shall on hearing it be happy, and sing God's *praises.*
God shineth in the countenance of the holy man;
Nanak, in his company men are saved.
Hearing that God is able to give shelter, I have come to seek it.
God hath mercifully blended me with Himself.
No hatred remaineth me; I have become the dust of all *men's feet;*
And I have in the saint's company obtained God's nectareous name.
The divine Guru was pleased with me,
And the service of his servant hath been rewarded.
By hearing God's name and repeating it with my tongue
I have become freed from entanglements and sin.
God hath Himself kindly shown me compassion,
And, O Nanak, my cargo hath arrived at its haven.

5

Praise God, my dear saints,
With attentive and composed minds.
In the Sukhmani are composure and God's praises and name.
He who hoardeth it in his heart shall become wealthy,
And all his desires shall be fulfilled;
He shall become a distinguished person, renowned throughout the world;
He shall obtain the highest place of all,
And shall not again undergo transmigration.
Nanak, he who obtaineth the Sukhmani,
Shall depart after earning the wealth of God's *name.*

6

These advantages shall be obtained by him who reciteth *the Sukhmani,*
And heartily heareth Guru Nanak's words in praise of the Name:
Rest, peace, wealth, the nine treasures,
Understanding, divine knowledge, all spiritual power,
Wisdom, devotion, union with and meditation on God,
The best divine knowledge, the most excellent ablutions,

The four desirable objects, mental enlightenment,
Contempt of all things, though in the midst of them,
Beauty, cleverness, knowledge of the truth,
And the *power of* looking on all men as equal.

7

If any one heartily utter this precious *hymn*,
He shall obtain salvation in every age.
It containeth the sound of God's name,
Which the Simritis, Shastars, and Veds repeat.
God's name is the sum-total of all faith;
It dwelleth in the hearts of His saints.
Millions of sins are erased in the company of the saints,
And by their favour man escapeth Death.
They on whose foreheads God recorded such destiny,
Have, O Nanak, entered the asylum of the saints.

8

He in whose heart this Sukhmani dwelleth or who listeneth to it with love,
Shall remember the Lord God;
The pain of birth and death shall be removed from him;
His human life so hard to obtain shall that moment be saved;
His renown shall be spotless and his speech nectar;
The one Name shall be contained in his heart;
Sorrow, disease, fear, and doubt shall not exist for him;
His acts shall be pure, he shall be called a holy man,
And his fame shall be the most exalted of all.
Nanak, such are the merits of the composition called Sukhmani.

Lunar Days

The advantage of devotion:

My sorrow hath fled and my doubt departed since I have taken God's shelter.

Nanak hath obtained the fruit his heart desired by singing God's praises.

He who singeth, he who heareth, he who meditateth on God;

He who preacheth and he who fixeth the Name in his heart, shall be saved;

His sins shall be cut away, he shall become pure, and purged of the filth of various births;

His countenance shall be bright in this world and the next, and worldly love shall not affect him;

He who praiseth God is wise, a Vaishnav, a possessor of divine knowledge,

Wealthy, a hero, and of reputable family.

The Khatris, Brahmans, Sudars, Vaisyas, and Chandals shall be saved by remembering God.

Nanak is the dust of the feet of him who knoweth his God.

Guru Ki War I

The fate of those who forget God:

Where shall they who have totally forgotten God find an arm to grasp?

Nanak, God potent to act and cause to act hath ruined them.

The fate of murderers adulterers, and robbers:

Men take halters at night and go to *strangle* others, but God knoweth such persons.

Concealed in places they leer at other men's wives.

The break into houses *even* difficult of access, and enjoy wine for its sweetness:

But they shall afterwards regret their respective misdeeds.

The angel Azrail will press them like millfuls of sesame.

The fate of idolaters and ingrates:

It is the servants of the True King who are acceptable;

Nanak, the fools who serve other Gods pine away and die.

The destiny God wrote in the beginning cannot be effaced.

The wealth of God's name is Nanak's capital; ever meditate on it.

In terrible hell there is much suffering; it is the abode of the ungrateful.

God smiteth them, Nanak, and they die a miserable death.

Gauri Ki War II

Man is happy at all seasons when remembering God:

Nanak, that is delightful day when God cometh into the mind.

Accursed is the season, however pleasant, when the Supreme Being is forgotten.

God is man's best friend:

Nanak, contract friendship with Him who hath everything in His power.

They are accounted false friends who go not a step with one.

Miscellaneous aphorisms of the Guru:

I have seen every place; there is none beside God.

Nanak, they who have met the true Guru, have attained their object.

The condition of this perishable world is as a flash of lightning.

Whoever repeateth the Lord's name, Nanak, is beautiful.

Men have searched the Simritis and the Shastras, but no one hath found God's worth.

He who meeteth the society of the saints enjoyeth divine pleasure.

True is the name of the Creator; He is a mine of jewels.

The mortal, on whose forehead such destiny hath been written, remembereth God.

O God, grant Nanak, Thy guest, the true Name as his travelling supplies.

Man appeareth to be happy, but his heart is anxious, and his avarice never departeth.

Nanak, without the true Name, no one's sorrow departeth.

They who have not loaded truth to carry with them, shall be plundered.

Nanak, they who meeting the Guru recognize the one God shall be congratulated.

They who part friendship with God are worthless:

They who are separated from their Lord, O Nanak, are entangled in the knot of doubt,

And useless and the beautiful fruit borne by the akk plant.

They who forget God suffer the pain of transmigration:

They who forget God die, but cannot die altogether;

They who turn away from God, *are in agony* like a thief on the stake.

Blest are they who ever remember God:

Nanak, blest are they perfect are they, and saints are they,

Who remember the spell of God's name at every breath they draw.

The following reproach was addressed to a Musalman priest:

Thou wanderest about all day under the pressure of hunger:

How shalt thou escape falling into hell, if thou remember not thy Prophet?

The following is repeated as a grace before and after meals:

The beggar beggeth for alms 'Give me, Or dear One;

Giver, Benefactor, I have ever remembered Thee.'

God's unequalled storehouses are never exhausted.

Nanak, unequalled is the Word which hath arranged everything.

Remember the Word and you shall be happy here and hereafter:

O beloved, learn the Word; it shall protect you from transmigration:

Your faces, saith Nanak, shall become bright, and you shall ever be happy remembering the one God.

Man should not pray for worldly advantages:

That is the best begging which beggeth for the one God;

Except the Lord's name, Nanak, all words are sinful.

The condition of him who loves and is beloved by God:

He in whose heart the love of God dwelleth is like the golden earth studded with gems of grass.

Nanak, all his affairs become easy with whom the true Guru is pleased.

The covetous go wherever they expect gain:

The kite wandereth in every direction—over water, mountain and forest,

But only resteth where it seeth carrion.

The Guru's devotion to God:

I have made Him a friend who is versed in all arts;

I sacrifice to Him may soul: He is the wealth of my body and soul.

O beloved, if Thou take *my hand,* I will never forsake Thee.

They who forsake God are evil and fall into hell's forments.

Love the Omnipresent:

O silly woman, dispel thy doubts, and love thou the only dear One.

Whithersoever thou goest, there is He present.

A hypocrite can never be equal to a saint:

Persons only fitted to play at bat and ball *like children,* mount horses and handle guns.

Animals which fly like barn fowl wish to be on a par with swans.

Salvation is obtained by repeating, hearing, or even writing God's name:

He who repeateth God's name with his tongue, and heareth it with his ears, is saved, my friend.

The hand which writeth God's praises with love is pure.

Such have obtained all the merit of bathing at the sixty-eight places of pilgrimage;

They have crossed over the ocean of the world and subjugated the fortress of evil passions.

Nanak, such attach men to the infinite God's skirt and service, and save them.

God will save His servant:

He who hath God hath no further desires;

Nanak, all who touch His feet are saved.

Asa

Mammon affects not saints but only the worldly:

Maya devoureth him who loveth her;

She greatly terrifieth him who seateth her down in peace.

Brethren friends, and families are at variance on beholding her;

But now by the Guru's favour she is under my control.

Sidhs, Strivers, demigods, and men

Are bewitched on beholding her; except the pious all are deceived by her deceit.

Some who wander as ascetics are in love with her;

Others as family men amass wealth, but they cannot make her their own.

Others who call themselves continent are greatly troubled by her.

God hath preserved me from her by attaching me to the Guru's feet.

She leadeth astray the penitents who practise penance.

Pandits have been seduced by her into every form of greed.

Maya hath bewitched earth and heaven.

My true Guru hath given me his hand and saved me.

Maya acteth as a servant to the holy man.

With clasped hands she waiteth on him and respectfully saith,

'What thou orderest I shall do;

But, O saint, I cannot approach thee.'

The condition of those who have renounced worldly love:

My beloved hath separated me from my mother-in-law:

My husband's younger brother's wife, and my husband's elder brother's wife have died a grief and sorrow.

I no longer heed my husband's eldest brother,

Since my clever and wise Spouse hath protected me.

Hear, O ye people, I have obtained the essence of love.

The true Guru hath given me God's name, and I have killed and destroyed mine enemies the evil passions.

In the first place, I have renounced the love of pride;

Secondly, I have renounced the customs of men;

Thirdly, I have renounced the world, and deem an enemy and a friend the same.

Fourthly, having met the Guru I recognize the excellences of the final state.

I have assumed an attitude of contemplation in the cave of rest.
God appeared as light and played for me unbeaten music;
I have obtained great joy by meditating on the Guru's word.
Attached to my Beloved, I have become a blest and happy wife.
The slave Nanak herein uttereth divine wisdom;
He who heareth and acteth *accordingly* shall be saved,
Shall be absorbed in God,
And not again suffer transmigration.
Holiness is described under the allegory of perfect woman:
A house is adorned by the presence of
A woman who is virtuous and devotion incarnate,
Whose beauty is incomparable, and conduct without reproach.
Some rare holy man may find her:
On meeting the Guru I have found such a well-behaved woman:
She sheddeth luster on feasts and marriages.
As long as she lived with her father,
Her husband wandered about very lonely.
When I served and conciliated the true man,
He brought her to my house, and I obtained all happiness.
She possesseth the thirty-two good qualities; true and holy are her offspring:
She is obedient, accomplished and beautiful,
She fulfilleth the wishes of her husband and her lord;
She comforteth in every way her husband's younger and elder brothers' wives;
She is the best of the household;
She giveth counsel to her husband's younger and elder brothers.
Blest is the home in which she hath appeared
O Nanak, its inmates pass their time in perfect happiness.

The interference of Maya, or worldly love in human affairs, and how she is to be overcome:

If I form any plan, Maya alloweth it not to mature:
She standeth near virtue and continence to repulse them;
She weareth many guises and assumeth many forms;
She alloweth me not to dwell at home, but maketh me wander in different places.
She is the mistress of my house, and alloweth me not to dwell therein.
It I try to do so, she quarrelleth with me.
She was sent by God in the beginning as a ruler.

She hath subdued the nine regions and all worlds.

At the banks of sacred waters she relinquisheth not her hold on Jogis and Sanyasis,

While they grow weary of reading the Simritis and studying the Veds.

Where I sit, there she sitteth with me;

She forcibly entereth every abode.

Even by entering a low asylum I cannot save myself from her.

Say, my friend, to whom shall I have recourse?

Having heard of the true Guru's teaching I have come to him.

The Guru hath fixed God's name in my heart as a spell.

I now may dwell in my own home singing the praises of the Eternal One.

Nanak hath met God, and is free from anxiety.

My house is now mine own, and its former mistress and ruler

Is under my control; the Guru hath made me a courtier of God.

The Guru versifies an address made to him by a Sikh:

Having glanced at foreign countries I have come here for traffic.

I have heard, O Guru, thou hast an incomparable and profitable thing,

To purchase which I have tied virtues in my dress and brought them as my capital.

Having beheld the jewel, my heart hankereth after it.

O merchant, a dealer hath come to thy door.

Exhibit your goods, so that we may effect a bargain.

God hath sent me to the merchant.

Priceless thy jewel and priceless thy capital.

I have found a well-disposed friend to act as broker.

Now that I have made my purchase my mind is easy.

I have no fear of thieves, of wind, or of water.

Quietly have I purchased, and quietly do I take away my purchase.

When the true Name is gained, there is no regret.

I shall take my purchase home safe and sound.

I have made a profit and am happy.

Thanks to the perfect merchant, the bestower,

Such a bargain some rare pious man hath made.

Nanak taketh home profitable goods.

The following was addressed to a hypocritical Brahman:

O Brahman, people make thee offerings and worship thee

Thou takest from them and yet deniest that they give thee.

Thou shalt regret thy conduct at the Court

Where thou shalt have to appear.

Such Brahmans as contrive evil

For the innocent shall be lost, O my brethren.

With covetousness in their hearts they wander about like mad dogs;

They slander others, and bear the load of their sins on their own heads.

O brahman, thou art plundered by mammon, yet thou reflectest not

That in many ways thou art led astray through error.

Thou wearest many religious dresses before men,

But thy heart is besieged by evil passions.

Thou preachest to others, but art ignorant thyself.

Such a Brahman shall nowhere be acceptable.

O foolish Brahman, remember God

Who, beholdeth thee, heareth thee, and abideth with thee.

Saith Nanak, if such be thy fate,

Renounce pride and cling to the Guru's feet.

The fate of the slanderer:

The slanderer roareth and screameth,

He forgetteth the primal God the Supreme Being, and obtaineth the reward of his acts.

Any friend he may have he shall take with him *to hell.*

Vainly the slanderer taketh on himself a load as that of a boa-constrictor, and burneth himself in the fire.

Nanak telleth what taketh place at God's gate.

God's saints are ever happy; they are in ecstasies singing His praises.

Pride mars man's good qualities:

In the first place, thy caste is good;

Secondly, thy lineage is honoured;

Thirdly, thine abode is beautiful;

But the pride of thy heart marreth thy beauty.

O handsome, shapely, wise, and clever man,

Excessive pride and worldly love have ensnared thee.

Very clean is thy kitchen.

Thou bathest, adorest, and appliest crimson frontal marks.

Thou pratest of divine knowledge while thou art dissolved in pride.

The dog covetousness ruineth thee in every way;

Thou dressest and enjoyest thyself;

Thou performest religious ceremonies to be honoured of men.

While thou sprinklest over thy body perfumed distilled aloe wood and sandal,

The pariah wrath is thine evil companion.

All other creatures are thy water-carriers.

In this world thou issuest thine own coin.

Thou hast gold, and silver, and copper;

But thy lust hath destroyed thy virtue.

The soul which God mercifully regardeth.

Shall be delivered from its prison,

That body which meeteth the company of the saints shall taste the relish of God's name,

And, saith Nanak, produce good fruit.

Then shalt thou be like a happy married woman endowed with all comeliness and happiness;

Then shalt thou be all-beautiful and wise.

The Guru preaches is brief sermon on humility:

The framework of the body hath been skilfully constructed,

Yet know for certain that it shall become dust.

Remember thine origin, O thoughtless fool;

Why art thou proud of such a thing?

Thou art a guest on three sers of corn a day;

All thine other property thou hast only as a trust.

Thou art ordure, bones, and blood wrapped up in skin:

Is it of this thou art proud?

If thou know One Thing thou shalt be pure;

Without knowing it, thou shalt be ever impure.

Saith Nanak, I am a sacrifice to the Guru,

Through whom God the omniscient Being is obtained.

The Guru's impatience to meet God:

Separated from my Spouse one ghari appeareth to me as a day, yea, as many days.

My mind is distressed until I meet my Beloved.

Separated from my Spouse one moment appeareth to me a day; yea, it never passeth.

Excessive is the desire of my heart to behold Him; is there any such saint as will cause me to meet my Beloved?

The four watches of the day *appear to me* as the four ages of the world.
When night cometh I think it will never end.
The conspiracy of the deadly sins hath kept me from my Beloved.
Wandering and wandering I weep and wring my hands.
At last God hath shown Himself to His servant, Nanak,
Who having seen Him hath obtained supreme happiness.

Instead of worshipping God at home man performs vain devotion abroad:

Man forsaking the love of God, becometh intoxicated with the love of worthless objects
He hath what *he wanteth at* home, yet he goeth abroad *to seek it:*
He listeneth not to the true ambrosial Word.
Attached to false scriptures, he wrangleth *with the holy*.
Taking the wages of the Lord he serveth some one else.
With such qualities is mortal clothed.
He hideth himself from Him who is ever with him.
He prayeth again and again for what is useless to him.
Saith Nanak, O God, compassionate to the poor,
As it pleaseth Thee so cherish me.

The intoxication of devotion:

He who drinketh the essence of God is ever imbued with it;
The effect of all other essences is but for a moment.
He who is intoxicated with God's essence is ever happy;
Anxiety is produced by all other essences.
He who drinketh God's essence is inebriated and intoxicated;
All other essences are worthless.
The value of God's essence cannot be described:
It is found in the saints' shop;
But nobody can purchase it even with millions of rupees.
The Guru giveth it to him who hath obtained *his favour*.
Nanak having obtained its relish from the Guru,
And tasted it, hath become astounded.
Nanak having become accustomed to its taste
Cannot by any means relinquish it in this world or the next.

The Guru prays for God's protection:

Beside Thee, O Lord, I have none other; Thou art in my heart;
Thou art my friend and my companion; why should my soul be afraid?

Thou art my shelter; Thou art my hope.

Sitting or standing, sleeping or waking may I not forget Thee O God, at every breath I draw!

Protect me, protect me, O God, in Thine asylum! terrible is the ocean of fire.

Giver of happiness to Nanak; true Guru, we are Thy children.

God preserves His saints from worldly love, which is a malignant fever:

God hath saved His servant,

My mind is reconciled to the Beloved; my fever hath poisoned itself and died.

I feel not cold or heat when I sing the praises of God's name.

My vomiting totally ceased when I took the protection of God's lotus feet.

By the favour of the saints, God hath been kind to me and given me assistance.

Nanak ever singeth the Treasury of excellences, and thus dispelleth doubt and sorrow.

The Guru's instruction is medicine for the mind diseased:

I have taken God's name as my medicine;

I have been cured, my pain hath departed.

My fever hath left me through the perfect Guru's instruction

I have become glad, my sorrows have all fled.

Nanak, all animals obtain happiness

By meditating on the supreme God in their hearts.

The Guru fears not the death of his body:

The time *of death,* which man desireth not, shall arrive.

Without God's order how shall the fire *of fear* be put out, however much we try?

The body is dissolved by water, fire, and earth,

But the soul is neither young nor old, O my brethren.

The slave Nanak hath entered the sanctuary of the saints,

And by the Guru's favour the fear *of death* is far from him.

The advantage of saintly association and devotion:

By association with the saints, in whom God's light for ever shineth,

Man obtaineth a dwelling at God's feet.

O my soul, ever repeat God's name,

So shalt thou obtain comfort, peace, and happiness; and all thy sins shall depart.

Saith Nanak, ye whose acts are perfect

Shall on meeting the true Guru obtain the perfect supreme Being.

O my True Guru, Holder of the play of the world, preserve Thy child.

Give me sense ever to sing Thy praises, my God, inaccessible and endless.

When a mortal is in his mother's womb he abideth under the support of the Name;

He is happy, he remembereth God at every breath, and the fire *of the womb* affecteth him not;

So, O man, cease to covet others, goods and others' wives, and to slander others.

Relying on the true Guru, worship in thy heart God's lotus feet.

The houses, mansions, and places which thou beholdest—of these none shall depart with thee.

As long as thou livest in this Kal age, Nanak, remember Gold's name.

Everything is false save devotion to God:

Empire, property, youth, mansions, fame, comeliness, and youthful beauty,

Great wealth, elephants, horses, and rubies purchased with hundreds of thousands,

Shall be of no avail in God's court hereafter; the proud must depart without them.

Why apply thy mind to any but the one God?

Standing, sitting, sleeping or waking ever and ever meditate on Him.

They who were victorious in the great decorated and beautiful arenas, and in the contests of the battle-field,

Who loudly boasted that they had the power of killing, capturing, or rleasing,

Left everything and departed on the very day the order of the Supreme Being arrived.

Man performeth ceremonial works of many descriptions, but the Creator he knoweth not.

He preacheth, but he practiseth not; he knoweth not God's word.

Naked he came, naked shall be depart; *his act are impure* as when the elephant throweth dust on its head.

Ye good saints and friends, hear me all—false is this world.

Fools have died in agony speaking of their belongings.

On meeting the Guru, Nanak hath meditated on the Name; the true Name hath saved him.

Few are wakeful in God's service:

The whole world is fast asleep in error and silly occupations;

Only some rare servant of God is awake.

Man is absorbed in greatly fascinating mammon who is dearer to him than life:

Few are they who forsake her.

Some rare holy man is attached

To God's incomparable lotus feet, and the instruction of His saints.

Nanak, they who are very fortunate, and to whom God showeth favour,

Are awakeful in the company of the saints, and become imbued with divine knowledge.

The fate of the slanderer:

The slanderer who washeth away the filth of the sins committed by the slandered in various births, shall obtain his deserts.

He shall have no happiness here, no enterance into God's court *hereafter*, and he shall be tormented in the realm of Death.

The slanderer hath lost his life in vain.

He cannot succeed in anything, and hereafter shall not find a place.

Such is the fate of the wretched slanderer: what can the poor creature do?

He shall be ruined where he shall have no protector: to whom shall he appeal?

There is no salvation anywhere for the slanderer: such is the will of God.

The more the saints are slandered, the happier are they.

Thou, O God, art the prop, Thou art the helper of the saints.

Saith Nanak, God protecteth His saints, and the slanderer He consigneth to the stream.

The following was addressed to a hypocritical Sanyasi:

He who washeth his body while he hath filth in his heart shall lose *his happiness* in both worlds.

Here he suffereth from lust, wrath, and worldly love; hereafter he shall sob and weep.

The way to worship God is different. The serpent is not killed by striking its lair on the outside, neither doth the deaf man hear the Name.

The hypocrite while abandoning his worldly occupations knoweth not of devotion;

He applieth himself to criticism of the Veds and the Shastras, but knoweth not the real means of union with God.

As a bad coin is discovered when examined by a money-changer,

So the Searcher of hearts knoweth everything; how shalt thou hide thyself from Him?

The false are at once ruined by their falsehood, deception, fraud and hollowness.

Nanak uttereth this most varily; see and remember this in your hearts.

The wonders wrought by the Guru's teaching:

By the Guru's instruction, a low Chandal woman becometh a Brahmani and a Sudar woman attaineth the highest rank;

The craving desire for terrestrial and celestial enjoyments is extinguished and destroyed.

The cat of the house hold is now differently trained; on seeing mice it feareth them.

The Guru hath subject the lion to the goat; the dogs eat grass;

A hut hath been raised without pillars in which the homeless find a home.

Without a setter jewels are set and a marvellous precious stone placed among them.

It is not by clamour the plaintiff succeedeth; by silence he obtaineth justice.

Man dead to God while enjoying wealth, and seated upon *costly* carpets, *now knoweth* that what appeareth to the eye quickly vanisheth.

He who saith he knoweth, knoweth nothing; but he who *really* knoweth is well-known.

Saith Nanak, the Guru hath given me nectar to drink, and on tasting it I am happy.

The Guru's dependence on God:

Where Thou, O Lord, art, what fear is there? whom shall I praise but Thee?

Where I have only Thee I have everything; there is none but Thee.

O father, I have seen that the world is poison.

Preserve me, O Lord of the earth; Thy name is my support.

Thou knowest the whole state of my mind; to Whom shall I go to tell it?

Without the Name the whole world hath gone mad; when it obtaineth the Name it becometh sane.

What shall I say? to whom shall I tell my condition? what I want to say must be told to the Lord.

What Thou hast done prevaileth; ever and ever my hope is in Thee.

If Thou grant greatness, it is to Thine own greatness; let me everywhere meditate on Thee.

O God, Thou art ever the Giver of happiness to Nanak; Thy name alone is my strength.

The Guru acknowledges his obligations to God:

When I forget Thee, every one vexeth me; when I remember Thee, men do me service.

I know none but Thee, Thou true, invisible, and in scrutable One.

When I think of Thee, Thou art always merciful; what is the wretched crowd then to me?

Say whom shall I call bad or good? All men are Thy creatures.

Thou art my prop; Thou art my support; Thou givest me Thy hand and protectest me.

He to whom Thou showest mercy can suffer no ill.

Only that is happiness and that greatness which is pleasing to God.

Thou are wise, Thou art ever kind, O Lord; if I obtain Thy name, I am happy.

In Thy presence this is my humble representation; my soul and body are totally Thine.

Saith Nanak, whatever distinction I possess is Thine; no one knoweth my name.

The following represents a conversation between a Sikh and a devout lady who had asked him the questions contained in the first part of the hymn. The conversation was versified by the Guru.

Thou hast escaped worldly love, impurity, and sloth; by whose favour was it done?

Worldly love one greatly fascination thou feelest no longer; whither hath gone thy sloth?

By what arduous mortification hast thou escaped from lust, wrath, and pride,

Which have ruined godly men, demigods, demons, beings possessed of the three qualities, and the whole world?

A forest fire consumeth much grass; some rare green Shrub *like thee* hath escaped.

I cannot describe such an omnipotent being; his praises cannot be expressed.

In this chamber of lamp-black thou hast not been besmirched; nay, thou hast assumed a spotless colour.

The Sikh's reply:

The great spell of the Guru hath taken its dwelling in my heart, and I have heard the wonderful Name.

God hath mercifully looked on me with favour, and attached me to His feet.

Through love and service Nanak hath obtained happiness in the association of the saints.

The following represents another conversation between the same lady and the Sikh:

Thy red jacket becometh thee;

Thou art pleasing to the Lord, and thou winnest His heart.

Who hath given this bloom *to thy face?*

What dye hath given thee thy bright complexion?

Thou art beautiful, thou art a happy wedded wife.

In thy house is thy Beloved, in thy house is good fortune.
Thou art chaste, thou art distinguished,
Thou art pleasing to thy Beloved, thou possessest superior knowledge.

The Sikh's reply:

I please my Beloved, wherefore I have this bright complexion.
Saith Nanak, God hath looked on me with a favouring glance.
Hear, my friend, this is the reward of my toil,
That God Himself decketh and adorneth me.

Man is happy on meeting God, as a woman on meeting her husband:

When Thou wert distant, I greatly suffered;
Now that I have contrived to meet Thee,
My female companions cease to taunt me.
My suspicions have fled; by the Guru I am united with my Beloved.
My Beloved hath approached and placed me on the couch;
I no longer need what people say
In my temple is the light of the word.
My Spouse is joyful and happy.
Through the destiny recorded on my forehead my Beloved hath come home to me,
And Nanak hath found lasting wedded bliss.

The Guru, while associating with the world, ever thinks on God:

My soul is attached to the true Name;
My love for men is but artificial guise;
My ties are only external: I smile on every one,
But I am separate from them as a lotus from the water.
I converse with everybody,
But I keep my heart with God.
I appear very formidable,
But *in reality* my heart is the dust of every one's feet,
The slave Nanak hath found the perfect Guru;
He hath shown me the one God both in my heart and in nature.

However great man's pleasures, he is, as it were, dead without devotion.

Man may enjoy pleasures in the vigour of youth,
But without the Name he is blended with the dust.
He may wear *costly* earrings and *fine* clothes;

He may have a comfortable couch, and be proud thereof;
He may have elephants to ride and a golden umbrella over his head;
But without the worship of God he is, *as it were,* beneath the earth.
Man may enjoy many beautiful women,
But without the essence of God all relishes are insipid.
Deceived by mammon man is led into sin and evil,
But he is saved, O Nanak, by entering the sanctuary of the merciful God.

The saints are likened to a garden, the Guru to a gardener:

There is a garden in which many trees are planted;
They bear the ambrosial Name as fruit.
So contrive, O man of God,
That thou mayest obtain the rank of nirvan.
Around the garden, my brethren, are poisonous pools; within it is nectar;
There is one gardener to irrigate;
He tendeth the leaves and branches;
He bringeth many vegetables and planteth them therein;
They all without exception bear fruit.
He who hath received the ambrosial fruit of the Name from the Guru,
Crosseth over the world's ocean according to the slave Nanak.

The Guru prefers the spot where the saints congregate to any place of pilgrimage:

If I go on a pilgrimage *I see* men boasting;
If I inquire of Brahmans, *I find* them immersed in mammon.
O my friend, show me that place
Where God's praises are ever sung
By meditating on evil and good according to the Shastras and Veds,
Man again and again descendeth to hell and ascendeth to heaven.
In the family man's life there is anxiety, and in the hermit's pride.
The soul is entangled in religious ceremonies.
He who by God's favour hath his mind under control,
Shall be saved, O Nanak, by the Guru's instruction.
Sing God's praises in the company of the saints:
The place where they dwell is obtained from the Guru.

Let God be ever present to man in all his avocations:

Whether standing, sitting, or sleeping, meditate on God.
Taking the walks sing God's praises.

With thine ears hear the ambrosial World.

By listening to it thy heart shall be glad, and all thine infirmities and troubles depart.

While working,, travelling, or *wandering by the* rivers' shore repeat Gods' name.

By the Guru's favour drink God's nectar.

He who day and night singeth God's praises

Shall not fall in Death's way.

By touching the feet of him who forgetteth not *God's name.*

During the eight watches of the day, O Nanak, emancipation is obtained.

God's kingdom is for the lowly:

The lowly man whom nobody knoweth

Shall be honoured by everywhere repeating God's name.

I crave for a sight of Thee; grant it, O my Beloved:

Who hath not been saved by serving Thee?

The whole world washeth the dirt of his feet

Whom nobody would approach.

The man who is useless to everybody

Is invoked *as a saint* by the Guru's favour.

In the company of the saints, the mind that sleepeth awaketh;

Then, O Nanak, the Lord is dear.

The omnipresence of God expressed by different metaphors:

God is himself the tree, and its extended branches.

He watcheth His own field.

Wherever I look there is the one God;

He is in every heart.

He himself is the sun and the expansion of its rays.

He is at once concealed and manifest.

He is described as possessing all qualities and no qualities.

Both descriptions together apply to the one God.

Saith Nanak, the Guru hath dispelled my doubts and fears,

And I behold the Blissful one everywhere.

The Guru's self-depreciation:

I know no tricks and devices of speech,

But day and night I repeat Thy name.

I possess no merits—not even one.

O God, Thou doest, and causest *all things* to be done.
I am fool, blockhead, ignorant, and thoughtless,
Long for Thy name in my heart.
I have performed no works of devotion, penance, or mortification;
I have only adored Thy name in my heart.
I know nothing; I have little wisdom.
Nanak representeth, Thou art, O God, my shelter.

The relation of the creature to the Creator:

Thou art my lake, I am Thy fish;
Thou art my Lord, I am *the beggar* at Thy gate.
Thou art my Creator, I am Thy worshipper.
I have found Thy sanctuary, O God of profound excellence.
Thou art my life, Thou art my support.
On beholding Thee I bloom like the lotus.
Thou art my salvation, and mine honour; Thou art the Acceptor of *the holy*.
Thou art Almighty, Thou art my strength.
Nanak's supplication to God is—
May I night and day repeat Thy name, O Lord of excellences!

The Guru one day visiting his sacred tank saw mourning in one house and rejoicing in another. Upon this he composed the following:

Mourners practise falsehood;
They laugh while mourning for others.
One man dieth *and there is weeping for him;* in the house of another there is singing.
One man weepeth, another laugheth.
From youth to old age
Man attaineth not his object; then he regretteth *lost opportunities*.
The world is subject to the three qualities,
And therefore man passeth through hell and heaven.
Saith Nanak, that man's birth is fruitful, and he is acceptable
Whom God hath applied to the repetition of His name.

A man had a dream which he related to Guru Arjan. He thought he had fallen into a well and tried to ascend by the well-rope. Two mice, one black and the other white, were gnawing it away. In the well was a venomous serpent which he feared would sting him. In this dilemma and drop of honey fell into his mouth from a tree which grew over the well, and he awoke. The following was composed by the Guru on the subject of the dream:

Night and day mice gnaw the rope.

He who falleth into the well eateth sweets.

The night passeth away in thinking and reflecting.

Man while considering the various pleasures of the world never thinketh of God.

Deeming the tree's shadow immovable he buildeth his house *beneath it;*

But Death's noose is *round his neck,* and Maya aimeth her arrow at him.

The sandy shore which is exposed to the waves

The fool considereth to be permanent.

He who repeateth the Sovereign God's name in the society of the saints,

Shall, Nanak, live for ever singing God's praises.

The following was addressed to a dead body:

With the soul thou didst play.

With the soul thou didst meet every one.

Everybody desired thee with the soul;

Without it no one wisheth to see thee.

Where is that soul now?

Without it thou art in a sad plight;

With it thou wert master in thine own home.

With it thou wert distinguished,

With it thou wert fondled;

Without it thou wert left in the dust.

With it thou hadst honour and greatness,

With it thou hadst relations with the world,

With it thy framework *was tricked out* in various ways;

Without it thou hast become clay.

The soul neither dieth nor is born;

It acteth subject to God's orders.

O Nanak, it is God who having fashioned *the body* uniteth and separateth *the soul* from it—

He Himself knoweth His own power.

The attributes possessed in common by God and the saints:

God doth not die, nor do we fear *death;*

He doth not perish, nor do we grieve.

He is not poor, nor are we hungry;

He feeleth not pain nor do we.

There is no destroyer but God;
He liveth and giveth us life.
He hath no entanglements, nor have we;
He hath no *worldly* occupations, nor have we;
He hath no impurity, nor have we—
When he is glad, we are ever happy—
He hath no anxiety, nor have we;
He is not defiled *by the world,* nor are we;
He feeleth no hunger, and we no thirst.
If He is pure, we are so also.
We are nothing, He is the only Being:
He alone is the beginning and end.
O Nanak, the Guru hath dispelled and shattered our doubts.
We and God, having become united, have assumed the same colour.

The advantages of loving the Lord:

By love for the Lord happiness is ever obtained,
By love for the Lord we feel no misery,
By love for the Lord the filth of pride is washed away,
By love for the Lord man is ever pure.
Hear, my friend, bear love and affection to God,
Who is our life and soul and the support of every heart.
By love for God all treasure is obtained,
By love for God the pure Mame entereth the heart,
By love for God man is ever honoured,
By love for God anxiety is erased,
By love for God man crosseth the terrible ocean,
By love for God man feareth not Death,
By love for God all are saved,
By love for God He goeth with us.
No erring man may by himself meet God.
He to hom God is merciful joineth the society of the saints.
Saith Nanak, I am a sacrifice unto Thee, O God;
Thou art the shelter and strength of the saints.

The proud and rich oppressor is brought to his level by death:

Man becoming a king, exerciseth dominion;
Committing oppression he acquireth wealth;

Amassing and amassing he filleth his coffers;
But God taketh his wealth from him and bestoweth it on another.
The body is an unbaked earthen vessel with water therein,
Yet man becometh very proud of it.
He becometh fearless and reckless,
And never thinketh of the Creator who is with him.
He raiseth and collecteth armies,
But when the breath leaveth him he becometh ashes.
He possesseth lofty mansions, seraglios and queens,
Elephants and teams of horses to delight his heart,
A large family of sons and daughters;
But through love of them the fool dieth in great affliction.
He who created him, destroyeth him.
Pleasures and enjoyments are like a dream.
He is emancipated, he possesseth empire and wealth,
O Nanak, to whom the Lord is merciful.

The condition of the regenerate:

The order of the Beloved is sweet to me;
My Spouse hath divorced my co-wife *who obeyed not His order.*
My Beloved hath decorated me His happy married wife,
And slaked the burning of my heart.
It is well that I did the bidding of the Beloved;
I have known what happiness and tranquillity are with Him.
I am the handmaiden, the servant of the Beloved
Who is indestructible, inaccessible and infinite.
I will take a fan and wave it over my Beloved.
The five deadly sins which tormented me have fled.
I am not of high family, nor am I beautiful;
I know not how I have pleased my Spouse.
Though I am helpless, poor, and unhonoured,
My Spouse hath taken my hand and made me His queen.
When first I saw my Beloved Friend,
I obtained happiness and tranquillity, and blest was my married life.
Saith Nanak, my desires have been fulfilled.
The true Guru hath united me with God, the Lord of excellences.

The following is a description of Maya, or worldly love:

On her forehead is a frown, her look is sour,

Bitter is her speech, rude her tongue;

She is ever hungry, she thinketh God is distant *and seeth her not*.

Such a female hath the one God created.

She hath devoured the whole world except those whom the Guru hath protected, my brethren.

Casting a net of deception she watcheth till the whole world *fall therein*.

She hath bewitched Brahma, Vishnu, and Shiv.

Only the pious who love the Name have not been dishonoured by her.

Men grow weary performing fasting, vows, and expiations;

They wander to the banks of sacred streams over the whole earth;

But only those who have sought the true Guru's shelter are saved.

The whole world is bound by the love of Maya.

The obstinate and the foolish are consumed by pride.

Guru Nanak hath taken mine arm and protected me.

God's praises; His name man's only support:

I am a purchased slave; Thou, O Lord, art my true Master;

My soul and body, yea, everything is Thine.

O Lord, Thou art the honour of the unhonoured; I put my trust in Thee.

Know that he who hath other support than the True One is feeble.

Thine empire is boundless; no one knoweth its limit.

He who meeteth the true Guru, walketh according to Thy will.

Device and cunning are of no avail.

Receive, O man, the happiness which the Lord being pleased conferreth on thee.

Even though thou perform millions of ceremonies, they will not avail thee.

The slave Nanak hath made the Name his support and forsaken all other calling.

The following was addressed by the Guru to his mother:

If the invisible and infinite Lord dwell a little in my heart,

O may mother, my troubles, pains, and infirmities shall all vanish.

I am a sacrifice to my Master.

My soul and body are very happy repeating His name.

I have heard a little regarding that true Lord.

I have obtained happiness upon happiness. O my mother which cannot be estimated.

On beholding Him with mine eyes I was pleased, and began to long for Him.

O mother, I am without excellences, yet God Himself hath attached me to His skirt.

God is totally beyond the Veds and the books of the world; Nanak's King hath openly manifested Himself.

Magnification of the Lord who ought to be served and remembered by His frail creatures:

Hundreds of thousands of saints worship Thee, uttering 'Beloved, Beloved!'

In what way shall I who am without virtues and sinful meet Thee, O my life?

Thou art my prop, O Lord, Sustainer of the earth, and merciful God;

Thou art the Lord of all; the whole creation is Thine.

Thou art ever the Helper of the saints, and they behold Thee ever present.

They who are without the Name die lamenting.

Transmigration is at an end for those who embrace the Lord's service.

What shall be the condition of those who forget the Name?

The whole world is like trespassing cattle.

Saith Nanak, O God, do Thou Thyself cut off my shakles and blend me with Thee.

Instruction to the human race:

O man, forgetting all other things, think only of the one God;

Put aside false pride and offer Him thy soul and body;

Praise thou the Creator during the eight watches of the day.

I live by Thy gifts, O God show mercy unto me.

O man, do that work by which thy countenance may be bright.

O God, he on whom Thou bestowest truth becometh attached to it.

O man, construct such a house as shall never fall.

If thou put the one God in thy heart, thou shalt never die.

God is dear to those who are pleasing to Him;

And by the Guru's favour, O Nanak, they praise Him the Ineffable.

The bliss of those who devote their thoughts of God:

What men are they who forget not the Name?

They are as God; know that there is no difference between Him and them.

The souls and bodies of those who meet Thee, O Lord, are happy.

They obtain happiness; all their sorrows are dispelled by the favour of the saints,

By whom are saved all countries and worlds.

They are perfect saints in whose hearts Thou, O God, dwellest.
He whom Thou acknowledgest is acknowledged.
He is illustrious, accepted, and famous everywhere.
O true King, fulfil Nanak's desire
To adore and remember Thee day and night at every breath.

Man ought ever to attend to his devotions:

O thou, the prey of sloth, why sleepest thou forgetting the Name?
How many float away *to perdition* on this river of life!
O man, embark on the boat of God's feet and cross over.
During the eight watches of the day sing God's praises in the company of the saints.

Thou enjoyest various pleasures, but they are empty without the Name.
Without God's service thou shalt weep thyself to death.
Thou dressest, eatest, and perfumest thyself and rubbest on batna,
But, without remembering God's name, thy body shall assuredly depart and become dust.

This world is very difficult to cross: only a few know this.
They who seek God's protection, O Nanak, shall be saved; this is God's law.

The Guru calls upon his saints to join him in worship and arrive at a state of exaltation:

Come my friends, let us meet and enjoy every relish;
Having met let us repeat God's ambrosial name so that our sins may be blotted out.

Meditate on the Real Thing, O ye saints, that no troubles may befall you.
The pious are on the alert, and have destroyed all the thieves.
Take wisdom and humility as your viaticum, and destroy the sin of pride.
True is the shop, perfect the traffic; deal in the ware of the Name.
They who offer up their souls, bodies, and wealth are held in honour.
They who are pleasing to their Lord enjoy themselves.
Fools of weak understanding who drink wine become whore-masters.
They who are saturated with God's elixir, Nanak, are the true drinkers.

The Guru, as handmaiden of the Lord, offers Him homage:

The God whose handmaiden I am, is the most exalted of all:
Everything whether small or great is His.
My soul, my life, and my wealth are admittedly the Lord's.
I am accounted the handmaiden of Him through whose Name I have become pure.

O Thou, who art independent and full of joy, Thy name is a jewel and a diamond.

She whose Lord Thou art, roameth satisfied and ever happy.

Ye friends and companions of my association, implant in me right understanding,

That I may serve the saints with love, and thus obtain God's treasure.

All are handmaidens of God; all call Him Master,

But it is only she whom God adorneth, O Nanak, who abideth in happiness.

The duties of the holy handmaiden:

Become the handmaiden of the saints and learn thy duties:

The highest of all virtues is not to deem thy Spouse afar.

Dye thy soul with the beautiful madder of God's name.

Abandon devices and cunning, and know that God is with thee.

Make obedience to thy Spouse's words thine ornaments;

Chew forgetfulness of the world as thy betel;

Make the Guru's instruction thy lamp, and spread the couch of virtue.

Stand with clasped hands all day long, and thou shalt meet the sovereign God.

She who is pleasing to the Creator possesseth all discretion and ornaments;

She is endowed with peerless beauty, O Nanak, and is a happy wife.

The advantages conferred by the Guru:

As long as I have mental doubts I stray in devious paths:

When the Guru dispelled my doubts I obtained rest.

The evil passions which tormented me have left me through the Guru:

I have escaped from them, and they have escaped from me.

Man is entangled from the moment he thinketh that *worldly things* are private property.

I have escaped from entanglements since the Guru dispelled my spiritual ignorance.

Man suffereth as long as he knoweth not the will of God.

He is happy when, meeting the Guru, he recognizeth God's will.

I have no enemy to torment me, nor doth any one appear to me to be evil.

The servant who serveth the Guru, O Nanak, is a slave of the Lord.

Devotion is pleasing to the Lord and procures the fulfilment of desires:

Sing God's praises and thou shalt obtain great happiness, comfort, and delight.

If the true Guru give His name, evil influences shall be removed.

I am ever and ever a sacrifice to my Guru;

I devote myself to the Guru by meeting whom I have obtained my real object.

He who remembereth not God believeth in good and bad omens.

Death approacheth not him who is pleasing to the Lord.

The Name is superior to all gifts, charity, devotion and penance.

All his desires shall be fulfilled who repeateth God's name.

His fear is no more, his errors and worldly love have fled, and he seeth none but God.

Nanak, if the supreme Being preserve, no sorrow shall befall us.

The Guru sings God's praises on every occasion:

I sing God's praises at home, I sing them abroad, I sing them awaking in the morning.

I who, deal in God's name, have obtained it as my viaticum *from the Guru,*

And completely forgotten all things beside.

The perfect Guru hath given me the gift of the Name; it is my only support.

In woe I sing *God's praises,* in weal I sing them; on my way I remember them.

The Guru hath firmly fixed the Name in my heart and slacked my thirst.

I sing *God's praises by* day, I sing them by night, I sing them with my tongue at every breath.

The faith that God is with us whether alive or dead resulteth from association with the saints.

Bestow this gift, O God, upon Thy slave Nanak, that he may clasp to his heart the dust of the saints' feet,

That he may hear of God with his ears, behold Him with his eyes, and put the Guru's feet on his forehead.

Man must die at last, and his only hope is in God:

The body which thou deemest permanent is only a two days' guest.

Children, wife, home, all thy property—the love of all these things is transitory.

O man, why laughest thou?

If thou look attentively, these things are like an enchanted city; profit is only obtained by worshipping God.

Clothes worn on the body fall to tatters after two or four days;

However much thou runnest upon a wall, thou shalt at last arrive at its end;

Salt at once melteth if put into a pitcher of water;

So when the order of the Supreme Being arriveth, the soul must depart in a trice.

O man, thy walking, thy sitting, and thy breathing are all counted.

Ever sing God's praises, Nanak, and thou shalt be saved under the shelter of the true ?Guru's feet.

The blessings obtained when God mercifully grants the true Guru;

When God is merciful,

What is reversed becometh straight, and slanderers and enemies become friends.

The jewel of *divine knowledge* shineth in the darkness, and the impure understanding becometh purified.

When I met the true Guru I obtained happiness, prosperity, and the fruit of God's name.

No one knew me, despicable that I was, *but now* I have become famous throughout the world.

Formerly no one would allow me to associate with him, *but now* all men worship may feet.

I used *formerly* to go about begging for paise, *but now* all the thirst of my heart is quenched.

I who could not endure reproach from any one, have now become patient through the society of the saints.

What praises of Him who is totally beyond reach can be uttered by a single tongue?

Thy servant Nanak is in Thy sanctuary; make him Thy salve of slaves.

Man is slow to virtue, but swift to vice:

O fool, thou art very slow to thy profit, but to thy loss thou hastenest.

O sinner, thou makest not good bargains, but art attracted by worthless things

O True Guru, my hope is in thee.

O Supreme God, Thy name is Purifier of sinners; I have come to Thy shelter.

O man, thou listenest to foul language and art entangled in it, but in repeating the Name thou art indolent.

Thou greatly delightest in slander, and art wrong-headed.

Thou covetest thy neighbour's wealth, son, and wife, and like a mad dog eatest what ought not to be eaten.

Thou hast no love for the true faith; on hearing the truth thou becomest angry.

O compassionate to the poor, merciful Lord God, Thy name is the support of the saints.

O God. Nanak hath gladly entered Thine asylum; be mindful of Thine own honour.

An exhortation to man to abandon worldly love:

Thou clingest to perishable things; worldly love hath bound thee.

Thou thinkest not whither thou shalt have to go: through pride thou hast become blind.

O man, why not abandon the world and worship God?

Thou dwellest in a frail chamber: the diseases of all the passions affect thee.

While talking of thy wealth day and nights pass away; every moment life groweth shorter.

As men are led away by sweet savours, so art thou by false and filthy occupations.

Thy senses are attached to the pleasures of lust, wrath, avarice, and worldly love;

Therefore, the Supreme Being hath caused thee to wander again and again in births.

When He who removeth the sorrows of the poor becometh merciful, all happiness is obtained on meeting the Guru.

Saith Nanak, if thou day and night meditate on God He will heal all thy maladies;

So, my brethren, repeat God's name.

And He who removeth the sorrows of the poor, shall become merciful, and the pains of birth and death vanish.

For the unworthy pleasures of a moment man forfeits his future happiness:

For the fleeting pleasure of lust, thou shalt suffer misery for endless time.

For the enjoyment of a ghari or two, thou shalt repent again and again.

O blind one, remember the Lord God;

Thy time hath approached.

Thou art misled on beholding even for a moment the beauty of the akk, the nim, and the colocynth.

As is companionship with a serpent so is *an intrigue with* thy neighbour's wife.

For worthless objects thou committest sin, but the real thing is neglected by thee.

Thou lovest what thou shalt have to abandon and thou quarellest with thy friends.

This is the case with the whole world, but only he who hath the perfect Guru shall be saved.

Saith Nanak, when man is purified, he shall cross over the terrible ocean of the world.

Man cannot conceal his sins from God:

What men do in secret God seeth, though fools and block-heads deny it.

They reap the reward of their own acts and regret them afterwards.

My God knoweth all man's devices beforehand.

Deceived by error O man, thou triest to hide thine act from Him, but afterwards thou shalt have to confess thy heart's secrets.

Man applieth himself to what God hath applied him: what can any mortal do?

Pardon me, O lord, supreme God; Nanak is ever a sacrifice unto Thee.

The mortal sins, though potent, can be subdued by the saints:

The five deadly sins subdue the four castes and the four stages of life, and trample on the six religious systems.

They have bewitched and deceived the beautiful, the accomplished, the lovely, and the wise.

Is there any puissant here or champion to seize and destroy them?

He who can pass his life killing and destroying them, is perfect in this age.

They form a great tribe who cannot be controlled and who will not flee; they are a mighty and obstinate army:

But, saith Nanak, he who is under the protection of the society of the saints crusheth them.

Sweet is the society of the saints:

My beloved, *the society of the saints* is a stream of nectar;

The Guru diverteth it not from my heart even for a moment.

On beholding and touching it great pleasure and delight are obtained:

It is dyed with the Creator's dye.

Death never approacheth him who meeting the Guru uttereth the Name even for a moment:

God, O Nanak, embraceth and claspeth him to His heart.

The occupation of the saints:

Good is the society of the saints:

Every watch, every hour, every moment they sing God's praises and speak of Him;

Walking, sitting, or sleeping they sing His praises; their souls and bodies are absorbed in His feet.

I am small, Thou, O God, are great; Nanak knoweth Thy sanctury.

Meditate on God who has done and will do so much for man:

The soul, mind, body, life—all pleasures and enjoyments are given by God;

He is the Relation of the poor and the Bestower of life; He is potent to save those who seek His protection.

O my soul, meditate on God's name.

In this world and the next the one God who accompanieth thee is the Helper; fix thy love on Him alone.

Men ponder on the Veds and Shastras to secure deliverance;

But superior to all religious ceremonies and observances is the utterance of the Name.

Lust, wrath, and pride depart on meeting the true divine Guru.

They in whose hearts he fixeth God's name and worship best perform His service.

O Compassionate One, I seek the protection of Thy feet; Thou art the honour of the unhonoured.

Thou, O God, art the Support of my soul and life; Thou at Nanak's strength.

The advantage of the saints' society and God's love:

Without the society of the saints man ever wavering suffereth great misery:

By love of the one Supreme God the profit of God's essence is earned.

Men grasp the unreal:

O madmen, ye have fallen asleep.

Ye are intoxicated with worldly love, families, and sensual enjoyments, and embrace fleeting pleasures.

Desires which are false, joy and delight which are a dream the perverse deem real.

They discover not at all the secrets of the wealth of the ambrosial Name which is with them.

Nanak, they whom God mercifully keepeth in the company of the saints, obtain His protection.

The Guru grasps the real:

The love of that Dear One for me!

Not gold, or gems, or pearls, or rubies; no, no, no!

Not empire, not fortune, not authority, not enjoyments—

none of these do I desire.

In worshipping the feet of the saints and taking their protection I find supreme happiness.

All Nanak's heart-burning was dispelled

When he obtained the love of the Beloved.

The Guru makes God manifest:

O God, the Guru hath shown Thee to mine eyes.

In this world and the next in every heart art Thou, O Bewitcher.

Cause of causes, Supporter of the earth, Thou alone art beautiful.

Nanak devoteth himself to meeting and beholding the saints; he sleepeth in complete happiness.

The Guru prays God to crown his devotion:

Bringing service to a successful issue,
O God, I have gladly come to Thee.

He who putteth God's feet into his heart and obtaineth the boon of the Name is successful.

This is his happiness here and hereafter; preserve him by association with saints.

Nanak, meditate on the Name, sing God's praises, and thou shalt be easily absorbed in Him.

The longing of the holy for God:

O God, Thy feet are beautiful;
God's saints find the *in their hearts.*

They who dispel their pride and practise worship, sing God's praises with the greatest zest:

They long for the one God; they thirst to behold Him; none else pleaseth them.

O God, have mercy upon me; what is the helpless creature? Nanak is a sacrifice unto Thee.

The Condition of the holy is contrasted with that of the listless and the proud:

He who forgetteth God is already dead;

He who meditateth on the Name shall obtain all the advantages thereof, and be happy;

He who practiseth pride, though he be called a king, shall be caught like a parrot, insnared in a trap.

Saith Nanak, he who meeteth the Guru shall become immovable.

The Guru describes the condition of the worldly:

He who sleepeth in the intoxication of sin and worldly love hath no understanding.

It is only when Death lifteth him up by the hair that he shall come to his senses.

They who are attached to the poison of avarice and the other deadly sins acquire wealth by oppressing others.

They are intoxicated with pride in what is destroyed in a moment, and, demons that they are, know not God.

The Veds, the Shastras, and holy men cry out, but the deaf hear not.

They utterly lose their game, and the fools regret what is lost.

All the tax they pay shall be by way of punishment, and it shall not be credited in God's court.

O men, the work by which God would cast a veil over your sins you have not performed.

Since the Guru hath shown me that the world in such as it is, I have sung the praises of God alone.

Having renounced all pride in his strength and skill, Nanak hath entered Thine asylum.

What the holy gain by devotion:

By dealing in the name of God

The saints and holy men are propitiated, the Beloved is obtained, His praises are sung, and the music of the five instruments is played.

When I obtained God's favour I obtained a sight of Him, and am now imbued with His love.

By serving the saints I conceived love and affection for my darling Master.

When the Guru fixed divine knowledge in my heart, I rejoiced that I should not be born again.

I have obtained tranquillity and the treasure of God within me,

And renounced all the wiles of the lust of my heart.

For a long time my soul hath been very thirsty:

O God, grant me a sight of Thee, show Thyself unto me.

Embrace poor Nanak who hath entered Thine asylum.

The Guru in his humility and sense of dependence in God prays to Him:

Would that some one would destroy the strong fortress *of sin,*

Save me from desires, avarice, deception, worldly love, and error;

And that the diseases of lust, wrath, avarice, and pride would leave me!

May I in the company of the saints love God's name, sing His praises,

Meditate on Him day and night,

And capture and raze the rampart of error!

Nanak, the Name is my treasure.

The Guru instruct a disciple:

Abandon lust wrath, and covetousness,

And remember God's name in thy heart.

The worship of God is a profitable work.

Forsake the sins of pride, worldly love, and falsehood, and ever utter God's name.

O man, attach thyself to the feet of the saints.

Awake and remember the feet of the Lord God

Who is compassionate to the poor, the Purifier of sinners, and the Supreme Being.

Serve God, O Nanak, and thy lot shall be perfect.

The play of the world:

God hath exhibited this play consisting of rejoicing and mourning, joy and sorrow.

One moment man feareth, again he feareth not, and other times he pursueth his fancies;

One moment he enjoyeth pleasures, and again he abandoneth them;

One moment he practiseth Jog, penance, and worship of many kinds, and again he wandereth in error:

And sometimes, O Nanak, God of His mercy applieth man to His love by association with saints.

The Guru continues his instruction:

Take the protection of the one God,
Utter the hymns of the Guru,
Obey the order of the True One,
Receive the treasure *of the Name* in thy heart,
And thou, O man, shalt enter into happiness.
He who in life is dead
Shall cross the terrible ocean.
Call him the fearless
Who is the dust of all men's feet.
O man, the instruction of the saints
Removeth all anxieties.
Sorrow can never approach him
Whose happiness is in the Name.
All men obey him
Who listeneth to God's praises.
Nanak, profitable is his advent into the world,
And he is pleasing to the Lord, O my soul.

The Guru prays to the Lord of the unowned:

God is for him
Who hath nobody besides.
He who knoweth the state of his heart
Knoweth everything.
Save me who have fallen—
This, O my soul, is Nanak's prayer.

The Guru's message to his soul:

O *my soul,* who hast come from afar,

Hear my message.

Everybody hath abandoned the things

To which thou art attached.

The were as a dream for those

Who repeated God's name.

They who leave God and attach themselves to others Hasten to transmigration.

It is only they who repeat God's name

Who shall continue to live.

He to whom God is merciful,

O Nanak, becometh His worshipper.

Asa Ashtapadi

Man must make his choice between God and mammon:

When I please the five *virtues,* I displease the five *sins.*

When I put the former into my heart, I dispossess the latter.

In this way the city *of my body* is peopled, O my brethren.

Trouble departed from me when I grasped the divine knowledge of the Guru.

The Guru hath made a fence round the true religion:

Meditation on the divine knowledge of the Guru is a strong thorny gate.

O my brethren and friends, sow the field of the Name,

And make the perpetual service of the Guru your traffic.

Make all your shops out of peace and rest and happiness.

The wholesale dealer, the retail dealers, form a company in the one God's name.

Where the true Guru hath set God's seal

Neither infidel-tax, nor fine, nor poll-tax is levied.

Load and dispatch your cargo of the Name,

So shall you, under the Guru's instruction, return home with a profit.

The wholesale dealer is the true Guru; the retail dealers are his disciples;

The stock-in-trade is the Name; the remembrance of the True One is the account kept.

O Nanak, everlasting is God's city;

He who serveth the perfect Guru shall abide in it.

Asa Birhara

Worship God alone and you shall be happy:

Remember the supreme God, O my dear friend, and sacrifice thyself for a sight of Him.

O my dear friend, why abandon Him, whose memory causeth sorrow to be forgotten?

I would sell this body to the saint, O my dear friend, if he caused me to meet the Beloved.

The pleasures and attractions of sin are insipid; I have abandoned them, O mother.

Lust, wrath, and covetousness forsook me, O my dear friend, when I fell at the true Guru's feet.

They who are imbued with God go not elsewhere, my dear friend;

They who have tasted God's essence, O my dear friend, are satisfied and contented.

They who seize the skirt of the saint, O Nanak, shall cross over the terrible ocean.

Asa Chhant

Jubilation on spiritual victory:

Joy! great joy! I have seen God.

I have tasted, I have tasted His sweet essence.

His sweet essence hath rained on my heart: through the kindness of the true Guru I have obtained composure.

Since the five enemies fled, my home hath become habitable, and I sing a song of rejoicing.

The holy saint being my intercessor, I am comforted and satisfied with the ambrosial World.

Saith Nanak, when I saw God with mine eyes my heart was gratified with Him.

Highly adorned are my beautiful gates:

My continual guests are the beloved saints.

When I did homage to them and served them, they adjusted mine affairs.

God Himself is the Groomsman, He Himself is the Birdesman, He Himself is the priest, He Himself is the God of marriage.

He himself adjusteth His own affairs; He Himself sustaineth the world.

Saith Nanak, when the Bridegroom sitteth at home with me adorned are my beautiful gates;

The nine treasures in abundance then enter my house,

And I obtain everything, everything by meditating on the Name.

By meditation on the Name with composure and devotion God is ever my Helper.

My cares are at an end, my transmigration hath ceased, and my mind no longer feeleth anxiety.

When I call out God's name, spontaneous music playeth, and there is a scene of wondrous splendour.

Saith Nanak, when the Beloved is with me, I obtain the nine treasures.

All my brethren and friends became overjoyed

When I on meeting the Guru conquered in the very toilsome struggle of the arena;

When on meeting the Guru I repeated God's name, I conquered and the walls of the fortress of error were demolished.

I obtained the wealth of many treasures, and God stood by to assist me.

He whom God hath made His own possesseth divine knowledge, and is conspicuous among men.

Saith Nanak, the brethren and friends of him on whose side standeth God rejoice.

How man should love God:

When water and milk are placed over a fire, the water alloweth not the milk to burn; O men, in that way love God.

As the bumble-bee becometh entangled and intoxicated by the odour of the lotus, and leaveth it not even for a moment,

So relax not a whit thy love for God; dedicate to Him all thine ornaments and enjoyments.

Man in the company of the saints hath no fear of what is called the way of death where wailings are heard.

Sing and meditate on God's praises, and all thy sins and sorrows shall depart.

Saith Nanak, chant the song of God, O man, love Him and bear Him such affection in thy heart

As a fish beareth water; it hath not a moment's happiness out of it; such love bear God, O man.

The chatrik thirsty for raindrops chirrupeth every moment 'Rain, beautiful cloud!'

So love God, give Him thy soul and fix all thine attention on Him.

Be not proud, seek God's protection, sacrifice thyself for a sight of Him.

The Woman who hath true love for the Guru and with whom he is well pleased, shall meet her parted Spouse.

Saith Nanak, chant the song of the eternal God; love Him,

O my soul, and bear Him such affection

As the love of the sheldrake for the sun; she feeleth much anxiety as to when she shall behold the day.

As the kokil in love with the mango sweetly singeth, so love God, O man:

Love God, be not proud, all are but guests of a single night.

Now why art thou, who camest and shalt depart naked, attached to and enamoured of the world?

By entering the asylum of the feet of the pious, the worldly love thou feelest now shall depart, and stability be thine,

Saith Nanak, sing the chant of the Merciful Being, O man, and love God *as the sheldrake* watcheth for the day.

As the deer at night hearing the sound of the bell giveth its life; so, O man, bear love to God.

As a wife in love with her husband waiteth on her beloved; so give thy heart to thy Darling:

So give thy heart to thy Darling, enjoy Him, and thou shalt obtain all happiness and bliss.

My friend, my Beloved, we have met after a very long time, and I have clothed myself in red.

When the Guru became the mediator, I saw God with mine eyes; none appeareth to me like my Beloved.

Saith Nanak, chant the song of the compassionate and fascinating One; O man, grasp God's feet and such love bear thou Him.

The great God to whom all creation is subject cannot be obtained by idle pilgrimages and ablutions:

Of roaming and searching from forest to forest and of many ablutions I have become very weary.

Nanak, when I met the holy man, I found God in my heart,

Whom countless munis and penitents seek for,

Whom millions of Brahmas worship, and whose name is uttered by men of divine knowledge;

To meet whom the Bright One; men perform devotion, penance, mortification, religious ceremonies, worship, many purifications and adorations,

Wander over the earth, and bathe at places of pilgrimage.

O God, men, forests, glades, beasts, and birds all worship Thee.

The merciful beloved God is found, O Nanak, and salvation obtained by meeting the society of the saints.

Millions of incarnations of Vishnu and of Shiv with the matted hair

Desire Thee, O merciful One; for Thee their souls and bodies feel endless longing.

The Lord is infinite and unapproachable, He is the all pervading God and Master.

Demigods, Sidhs, the crowd of celestial singers meditate on Thee; the Yakshas and Kinars utter Thy praises.

Millions of Indars and various gods repeat Thy name,

O lord, and hail Thee.

Thou art the Patron of the patronless, saith Nanak;

Thou art the compassionate; associate me with the saints that I may be saved.

Millions of Devis and Lakshmis serve Thee in divers ways.

Invisible and visible beings, wind, water, day and night adore thee.

The stars, the moon, and the sun meditate on Thee; the earth and the heavens sing Thy praises.

All the sources of production and all articulate creatures ever meditate on Thee.

The Simritis, the Purans, the four Veds. and the six Shastras repeat Thy name.

Nanak, through the society of the saints meet the Purifier of sinners, to whom the saints are dear.

As much as God communicated to me, so much doth my tongue utter.

They who serve Thee unknown to me are without number.

Thou art the all-pervading, indefinable, unfathomable Lord; Thou are within and without all things.

We are beggars all, Thou alone art the Giver; Thou art not far away; nay, Thou art present and manifest.

Thou art in the power of Thy saints; how can their praises be recounted who meet Thee?

May Nanak obtain the boon and honour to be allowed to place his head on the saints' feet!

God confers bliss on those who love Him:

Abiding is the marriage state of the saint; her Spouse neither dieth nor departeth.

She who hath God for her Husband shall ever enjoy Him.

The Lord is indestructible and invisible; He is ever young and stainless.

He is not distant; He is ever present; He filleth every direction for ever and for ever.

He is the Lord of the soul from whom proceed salvation and wisdom; I love the love of that Beloved.

Nanak expoundeth what he knoweth from the Guru's instruction; abiding is the married state of the saint; her Spouse neither dieth nor departeth.

She who hath God for her Spouse enjoyeth great bliss.

Happy is such a woman, she is completely honoured:

She enjoyeth honour, greatness, and happiness, she singeth God's praises, and is ever with her great Lord.

She hath all perfections, the nine treasures; her homes is never empty, it containeth everything.

The married state of her whose speech is honeyed and who obeyeth her Beloved, shall ever be permanent.

Nanak expoundeth what he knoweth through the Guru's instruction—she who hath God for her Spouse enjoyeth excessive bliss.

Come, my companions, to the holy man, and let us apply ourselves to his service.

Let us lay aside our pride, grind *his corn,* and wash his feet.

Let us efface and not parade ourselves, and our troubles shall depart.

Let us take the Guru's protection, obey him, and be happy with whatsoever he doeth.

Let us do him the lowest service, dispel care, be wakeful and stand before him with clasped hands day and night.

Nanak expoundeth what he knoweth from the Guru's instruction; come, my companions, to the holy man, and let us apply ourselves to his service.

He on whose forehead such destiny hath been written applieth himself to the saints' service.

The desires of him who hath obtained the company of the saints shall be fulfilled.

In the company of the saints are loved of God and remembrance of His name.

The sins of superstition, worldly love, and duality all are abandoned by him,

In whose heart dwell peace, composure, and devotion; he singeth God's praises with joy and delight

Nanak expoundeth what he knoweth through the Guru's instruction—he on whose forehead such destiny hath been written, applieth himself to the saints' service.

The Guru gives way to self-depreciation:

I am a sinner, devoid of understanding and virtue, friendless and low,

Foolish, hard-hearted, of mean birth, steeped in the mire of worldly love,

Enveloped in the filth of error, and in acts of pride and arrogance—the thought of death entereth not my heart.

Through spiritual ignorance I am entangled with domestic enjoyments and worldly love.

Youth fadeth away, age increaseth, Death which hovereth over me bideth his time.

Nanak representeth, my hope is in Thee, O God; preserve me, lowly though I be, in the asylum of Thy saints.

I have wandered in many births and have suffered great pain in wombs.

Deeming enjoyments and gold delicious, I have become entangled with them.

Through transmigration I have been born innumerable times, and have wandered through many lands.

Now I have taken God's protection, and obtained all comfort from His name.

O Protector, beloved Lord, by me nothing was or shall be effected.

Nanak hath obtained happiness, comfort, and joy through Thy mercy, and hath crossed over the ocean of the world.

God hath saved nominal saints: what fear have the real saints?

In any case carefully listen to God's praises.

By carefully listening to His word man obtaineth divine knowledge and the wealth of His name.

He becometh imbued with God's love and singeth His praises.

Were the earth to become paper, the forests pens, and the wind a writer,

The end of the Endless One could not be described; Nanak hath grasped the protection of His feet.

The inward satisfaction obtained by devotion:

Day and night become pleasant by remembering God's name.

By love to His lotus feet wickedness and sin depart;

Pain, hunger, and poverty flee away, and man's path appeareth clear.

When we meet the society of the saints and love the Name, the heart's longings are satisfied.

By beholding God, man's desires are fulfilled and his whole family saved.

Day and night, night and day, O Nanak, it is joy to remember God's name.

The Guru prays for grace to remember God:

To utter God's name in the company of the spotless saints is a holy thought.

O God, saith Nanak, bestow mercy on me, that I may not forget Thy name for a moment!

The virtues of the man of pure life are conspicuous and God renders him happy. This chant is sung by Sikhs at marriages:

The stars glitter on a clear night.

Holy men the beloved of my Lord are awake;

The beloved of my Lord are ever awake, and remember His name night and day.

They meditate in their hearts on His lotus feet, and forget Him not for a moment.

They renounce the mental sins of pride and worldly love and efface the pain of wrong-doing.

Nanak representeth, the servants of God, the dear saints are ever awake.

My couch hath splendid trappings.

In my heart joy hath sprung up since I heard that my Lord was approaching.

One meeting my Lord I have entered on happiness and am filled with the essence of joy and delight.

He embraced me; my sorrow fled; my soul, mind, and body all bloomed afresh.

I have obtained my heart's desires by meditating on God; the time of my union with Him I account auspicious.

Nanak representeth, when he met the Bearer of prosperity, the essence of all pleasure was prepared for him.

My companions meeting me asked me to described my Spouse.

I was so filled with the sweets of love that I could not speak.

The attributes of the Creator are deep, mysterious, and boundless; the Veds have not found His limit.

She who meditateth on the Lord with devotion and love, who ever singeth His praises,

And is pleasing to her God, is full of all virtues and divine knowledge.

Nanak representeth, she who is dyed with the colour of God's love shall be easily absorbed in Him.

When I began to sing songs of joy to God,

My friends became glad, my troubles and mine enemies fled away,

My happiness and comfort increased, I rejoiced in God's name, and He Himself bestowed mercy on me.

I clung to His feet, and being ever wakeful I met Him.

Happy days came I obtained peace with all treasures and was blended with God.

Nanak representeth , the saints of God are ever steadfast in seeking His protection.

Why should man fall away from God for the sake of short-lived pleasure?—

Rise and go, O traveller, why delayest thou?

Thine appointed time is complete; why covetest thou what is false?

Thou covetest what is false, and by the deceit of Maya thou committest innumerable sins.

O wretched man, Death hath sought thee; thou shalt be overcome by him, and thy body shall be a heap of ashes.

Thou shalt depart leaving thy property and youth; no more shalt thou have clothing and food.

Saith Nanak, thine acts shall accompany thee, their effects cannot be effaced.

Instead of pleasure there ever resulteth pain from the commission of sin.

Lo! as the deer is snared on a moonlight night,

So the sins thou hast committed shall not forsake thee; they shall lead thee away with a halter round thy neck.

Thou art deceived by a mirage; thou embracest an unsubstantial lover;

Thou art intoxicated with avarice, greed, and conceit; thou art brimful of pride.

Nanak, man like the deer is destroyed by his ignorance, and his transmigration ceaseth not.

The fly is caught in the sweets—how can it take flight?

The elephant falleth into a pit—how can it escape?

It will be difficult for her to escape who remembereth not her Spouse even for a moment.

Her sufferings and punishment cannot be reckoned; she shall obtain the fruit of her own acts

What she hath done in secret shall become manifest; she shall be ruined in this world and the next.

Nanak, without the true Guru the proud self-willed man is ruined.

God's servants live by clinging to His feet.

The Lord embraceth those who seek His protection.

He giveth them strength, understanding, divine knowledge and meditation; He Himself causeth them to utter His name.

God Himself is the society of His saints: it is He who saveth the world.

The Preserver ever preserveth those whose acts are pure;

Nanak, they shall never go to hell; God's saints are under His protection.

Man cannot hide his sins from God:

What man doeth either by day or night shall be recorded on his forehead.

He from whom man seeketh to conceal his acts is with him and seeth them:

The Creator is with him and seeth them; why committeth he sin?

Do good acts, repeat the Name, and thou shalt never go to hell.

During the eight watches of the day repeat God's name, and it shall accompany thee.

Ever worship in the company of the saints, O Nanak, and the sins thou hast committed shall be blotted out.

By violence and fraud thou fillest thy belly, O ignorant fool,

Although God the Giver continueth to give thee everything

The Compassionate Lord is ever the Bestower; why forget Him?

Join the society of the saints and boldly worship God, so shall thy whole family be saved.

The Name is the support of the sidhs, the strivers, the gods, the munis, and the saints.

Nanak representeth, ever worship God the sole Creator.

Cheat no one; God assayeth everything.

They who practise falsehood and deception shall be born again in this world,

While those who have meditated on the one God have crossed over its ocean;

Having abandoned lust, wrath, and blame of the blameless, they have entered the sanctuary of the Lord.

God pervadeth sea and land, the nether regions, and the firmament: He is exalted, inaccessible and infinite.

Nanak representeth, God is the prop of His servants: H lotus feet are their support.

Lo! the world is a phantom city; nothing is durable.

The enjoyments of the world shall not accompany thee.

God is ever with thee; remember Him day and night.

Beside the one God there is none: burn the love of worldly things.

Deem that God in thy heart as they friend, thy youth, thy wealth, thine all.

Nanak representeth, he who obtaineth God by great good fortune entereth on happiness and rest.

The effect of worldly love on man and other animals:

The illusion of mammon is terrible, the illusion of mammon is terrible; alas! great is its intoxication, it perverteth men's natures, and their lives, alas! pass in vain.

In the deep and awful forest, in the deep and awful forest, alas! the thieves of the soul rob the house in broad day-light, and night and day eat the *plunder*.

By night and day they eat the plunder; life passeth away without God; come to me, O God, Thou Lord of mercy.

Without the companionship of the Beloved many births and deaths have taken place, and there is no salvation.

I am without family, beauty, distinction, or divine knowledge; who is my cherisher but Thee, O God?

With clasped hands Nanak hath entered Thy sanctuary; O beloved Lord, grant him salvation.

Alas! as a fish out of water, a fish out of water dieth by separation from it, so hom can I live without the Beloved?

The deer faceth the arrow, it faceth the arrow, alas! it sacrificeth its life while absorbed in the pleasure of listening *to the hunter's bell*.

Love to the Beloved hath sprung up within me: I have abandoned the world to meet Him: curses on the body which remaineth for one moment without Him!

Mine eyelids close not; I am absorbed in the love of the Dear One; my mind anxiously looketh for Him night and day.

They who are imbued with God's love and intoxicated with the Name, lose all fear, doubt, and worldly love.

Bestow mercy and compassion, O Thou compassionate, all pervading God, that Nanak may be absorbed in Thy love.

The bumble-bee is humming, the bumble-bee is humming; alas! intoxicated with the savour and odour of the honey of the flowers, it entangleth itself in its love for the lotus.

The heart of the chatrik thirsteth, the heart of the chatrik thirsteth; its heart longeth for the beautiful cloud-drops; when it drinketh all its fever departeth.

O Destroyer of fear, O Destroyer of sorrow, come to me: my soul and body feel for Thee excessive love.

Beautiful, clever, wise Lord, with what tongue shall I utter Thy praise?

Take me by the hand, give me Thy name: he on whom Thou lookest with favour hath his sins erased.

Saith Nanak, he who beholdeth God the Purifier of sinners feeleth no pain.

I think of the Lord, I think of the Lord; me friendless preserve in Thine asylum : I delight to meet Thee who giveth delight to my soul.

I meditate on Thy beautiful form, I meditate on Thy beautiful form; my soul longeth for a knowledge of Thee, O God, who preserveth the honour of Thy suppliants.

God who bestoweth full honour and destroyeth sorrow hath fulfilled all my desires.

Happy was that day when God embraced me: on meeting my Spouse my couch was adorned.

God casting a glance of favour on me, all my sins have been erased.

Nanak representeth, my desires have been fulfilled. I have found the Bearer of prosperity, the Treasury of excellences.

Gujari

The necessity of the Guru:

Men perform devotional exercises and the six religious acts *of the Hindus;* worldly people are steeped in such things;

But without the Gùru the filth of pride leaveth not their hearts, and they lose their game.

O my God, mercifully preserve me.

Out of millions some rare man is a servant of God; all others are worldly.

The Shastras, the Veds, the Simritis, all have I searched; they all utter one cry:

'Without a guru none obtaineth salvation;' observe and consider this in thy mind.

Were one to bathe at the sixty-eight places of pilgrimage and wander over the whole earth,

Were one to perform various purifications day and night, all would be darkness without the true Guru.

Running hither and thither, I traversed the whole world, but now I have arrived at God's door.

Good hath removed my sinful desires and enlightened my understanding: Nanak is saved under the Guru's guidance.

Man through his perversity is ever doing what he ought not to do:

Man proposeth to go to the west, but he is led away to the east.

God in an instant establisheth and disestablisheth; He holdeth in His hands the result of man's designs.

Human devices are of no avail:

What my Lord deemeth fit shall continue to be.

Men who go forth with the object of acquiring territory and amassing money, die on the way.

Their armies, officers, and servants—all shall they leave and depart to the city of Death.

Through obstinacy man asserteth himself and deemeth there is none other like himself.

The food which blameless persons have reprobated and laid aside he eateth again and again.

He to whom God is kindly disposed and merciful shall have his shackles cut off.

Saith Nanak, he who hath met the perfect Guru is acceptable, whether he be a family man or an anchoret.

The advantages of devotion and charity:

They who repeat the priceless Name shall have their shackles cut off;

They shall be freed from the sins of lust, wrath, worldly love, and the disease of pride.

They who joining the company of the saints sing God's praises,

Shall have their hearts purified by the favour of the Guru and obtain the highest of all happiness.

I have adopted this as my worship—to deem good whatever God doeth:

To consider friends and enemies as the same is an index of the way to God.

He filleth every place, wherefore I go nowhere.

He is in every heart, uninterruptedly in all things; he is immersed in love and dyed with love.

When God is merciful and compassionate, man arriveth at the abode of the Fearless.

In one moment his troubles and anxieties are at an end, O Nanak, and he becometh absorbed in God.

Man ought to trust to God alone:

Every one to whom I address myself is full of his own troubles;

But he who heartily adoreth the Supreme God shall cross over the terrible ocean.

None but the great God can remove this distress and sorrow.

Whoever forsaketh God and becometh a worshipper of others, shall find his honour, dignity, and reputation decrease.

They who are acquaintances and relations for the sake of mammon are of no avail.

God's slave, even though he be of lowly birth, is exalted; in his company man obtaineth whatever his heart desireth.

Even though man have thousands and millions of viands obtained by sin, yet shall his hunger not be satisfied thereby.

By remembering the Name there appear endless lights by which the Unseen is manifested.

Wandering and wandering I have arrived at Thy Door, O destroyer of fear, sovereign God.

Nanak desireth the dust of the saints's fact; in it he findeth his happiness.

All worldly possessions are temporary; the Name alone is permanent:

Man first dwelleth in his mother's womb; leaving it he cometh into the world.

He then desireth splendid houses, beautiful gardens, and mansions; but none of these shall go with him.

Vain is every desire of the covetous.

The perfect Guru hath given me God's name; it is a thing that becometh my soul.

Man is attached to and rejoiceth in the company of dear friends, relations, sons, brethren and wife;

But when the last moment hath arrived, Death seizeth him while they look on.

By unworthy means man amasseth wealth, gold, silver and copper;

But he really only gaineth his hire as a labourer; everything else passeth to others.

Horses, elephants, chariots man acquireth by violence and calleth his own;

But when there is a long journey before him, they will not travel a step with him.

The Name is my wealth, the Name maketh me happy as a king, the Name is my family and helper.

God gave Nanak the wealth of the Name which shall never perish or transmigrate.

Men of the lowest castes have by devotion obtained celestial bliss and glory:

Those who have lapsed God hath purified and made his own; every one boweth before them.

No one now asketh their caste or their tribe; men bet the dust of their feet.

Such O God, is *the effect* of Thy name!

Thou art the Lord of all creation; Thou specially assistest Thy servant.

In the company of the saints, Nanak hath obtained wisdom; singing God's praises is his support.

In this way God's servants Namdev, Trilochan, Kabir, and the tanner *Rav Das* obtained salvation.

God is unknowable:

O God, none there is who understandeth Thee; how may we know Thee?

Shiv Brahma, and all the munis have not been able to realize Thy state.

The story of God is recondite and deep.

God Cherishes His servants, and they sing His praises:

God's servant hath no worldly wisdom, resource, or cleaverness;

As occasion offereth, he meditateth on God.

It is God's function to love His saints;

He cherisheth and fondleth them as His own children.

God's saints sing His praise as their devotion, penance, mortification, and religious ceremonies.

Nanak hath entered the asylum of the Lord; he hath obtained there the fearless boon of happiness.

The Guru enjoins worship and saintliness:

My beloved friends, worship God day and night; make not the slightest delay.

Serve the saints with love; put aside pride and obstinacy.

The entrancing merry God is my soul and honour;

He dewelleth in my heart; my mind is fascinated as I behold His sports.

By remembering Him my mind is happy, and its rust is rubbed off.

The importance of meeting *God* cannot be described; Nanak, it is beyond everything.

Only the really holy man is free from worldly love:

Men call themselves Munis, Jogis, and learned in the Shastras, but *Maya* hath them all under her control.

The mind is lost in astonishment at her subjection of the three gods and the three hundred and thirty millions of demigods.

She is potent and continueth to pervade the whole world.

Her secret is obtained by the Guru's favour; no one besides knoweth it.

Ever conquering she hath subdued all places, and enmeshed all the world;

Saith Nanak, she misleadeth not the holy man, but becoming his handmaiden claspeth his feet.

The Guru humbles himself before God:

Small is the power of mother, father, brother, son, and kinsman.

Though various forms of mammon are seen, yet none shall go an inch with one.

O God, I have none but Thee.

I am helpless, devoid of merits; possessing non I have come to Thee.

I am a sacrifice again and again to Thy feet; in this world and the next Thine is the power *to save*.

In the company of the saints Nanak hath obtained a sight of Thee; to none else oweth he obligation.

God's omnipotence:

In a moment Though established and disestablishest; Thy worth cannot be appraised.

Thou turnest a king into a beggar in a moment, and into the lowly Thou infusest splendour.

O ye people, ever mediate on your God.

Why are ye anxious and solicitous regarding the things which perish in a moment?

O God, Thou art my prop, my perfect True Guru; I have fallen under Thy protection.

I, Nanak, am heedless, silly, childish; reach me Thy hand and save me.

A supplication to God:

It is Thou who conferrest gifts on all; do Thou abide in my heart.

He in whose heart Thy lotus feet are contained, hath not the darkness of doubt.

O my Lord, where I remember Thee, there art Thou *present*.

O Thou who cherishest all, have mercy on me that I may ever praise Thee;

That I may remember Thy name at every breath and long for Thee only.

Nanak's prop is the Creator; he hath renounced the hopes he had in others.

No evil can befall him whom God protects:

Nanak Seeketh Thy protection, O Creator; Thou, O God, art the support of the soul.

What can the world do to him whom Thou aidest and protectest?

The Guru humbles himself and prays to God for mercy:

I have never fixed my attention on God.

I have passed my life in worldly occupations and not sung the name of the Treasury of excellences.

I have by deception exerted myself in various ways to amass money kauri by kauri.

How much sorrow was debited to me when I forgot God and was eaten up by the arch fascinator *mammon!*

Be gracious, O Lord, and take not mine acts into account.

O God, Thou art compassionate and benign, and ocean of clemency; Nanak hath come under Thy protection.

The advantages of meditating on God:

By the Guru's favour I have meditated on God, and all my doubts have vanished.

Anxiety, ignorance, and fear have left me, and my sins are at an end.

God's name is dear to my soul.

Having met the saints, I have under their instruction meditated on God in the most sinless way.

Devotion and the performance of various ceremonies are forfitable when the Name is remembered.

When Thou didst graciously protect me, my desires were fulfilled.

May I never at any time forget God the omnipotent!

How can I describe Thy various attributes? They are innumerable and ever ineffable.

Thou art the Remover of the sorrows of the poor, the Saviour compassionate and merciful.

The immovable dignity is obtained by remembering the Name; Nanak hath firmly grasped Thy protection.

Ashtapadi

God's praises, and supplications unto Him:

O Lord, King of men, Friend of the poor, Purifier of sinners,

Dispeller of fear and terror, Abode of mercy, Treasury of excellences, profitable is Thy service.

O god Gopal, great Gobind,

I have taken the protection of Thy feet, Thou merciful God, cause me to cross the terrible ocean of the world.

Dispeller of lust and wrath, Burner of pride and worldly love, Murari, Honey of the soul,

Sustainer of the earth, set aside my transmigration and preserve mine honour, Thou Primal Joy.

Many burn in their desire for mammon; but by the Guru's spell divine knowledge is obtained in the heart, *and they are healed*.

Prick *the bubble of* my pride, O Thou full of mercy, and dispel my anxieties, O Thou Eternal Being.

O man, remember the Omnipotent every moment, and calmly apply thyself to the contemplation of God.

O compassionate to the poor, ever happy, who fillest all space, I beg the dust of Thy saints' feet.

From the evils of worldly and sensual love, and from the sins of hope and desire *preserve us*.

Preserve the faith and remove doubt from our hearts; save us, O Formless One!

Even they who are without raiment become well attired from the treasury of God's storehouses.

The stupid, the senseless, and the fools become virtuous and patient by God's favourable glance.

Thou shalt obtain salvation while alive by repeating the name of the Lord of the world, remembering Him, and having faith in Him in Thy heart.

The belief that God is compassionate and merciful to His creatures and pervadeth everything is the rule of the saints.

God showeth Himself to hose who hear His praises and utter His name.

Saith Nanak, O God, Saviour of sinners, receive me in Thine embrace.

Gujari Ki War II

When Gods is pleased, man obtains every boon:

When Thou art pleased, O Kind and Incomprehensible One, Thou dwellest in my heart.

When Thou art pleased, O Kind One, I obtain the nine treasures in my own home.

When Thou art pleased, O Kind One, I act according to the Guru's instruction.

When Thou art pleased, O Kind One, Nanak shall be absorbed in the True One.

Kings without piety are not held in honour:

How many sit on thrones and have many musical instruments played for them!

But without the true Name, Nanak, nobody's honour hath been preserved.

The demigods and priests do homage to God:

Men standing with the Veds and the books of the Musalmans meditate on Thee, O God.

They who are prostrate at Thy door cannot be counted.

Brahma and Indar on their thrones meditate on Thee.

Shiv, Vishnu, and the avatars proclaim Thy praises.

Moslem priests, Prophets, Shaikhs, and saints *utter Thy name*.

God the warp and woof is woven into every heart.

By falsehood man passeth away, by honesty he abideth.

Man applieth himself to those duties to which God appointed him.

They who are slow to devotion must eventually suffer:

Man is slow to goodness, but a tiger to evil.

Nanak, to-day or tomorrow the feet of the heedless shall fall into a trap.

God loves man despite his sins:

However evil our ways, Thy love for us, O God, is not hidden.

Saith Nanak, Thou O Lord, the true Friend, hast overlooked our sins of thought.

Man is saved by humbling himself before God:

Countless sinners become pure by fixed their attention on God's feet.

He, O Nanak, on whose forehead such destiny hath been written, obtaineth God's name for the sixty-eight places of pilgrimage.

The following is uttered by Sikhs when they put on new clothes:

Thou, O God, hast given me the raiment of love to preserve mine honour.

O my Lord, Thou art wise and far-seeing; Nanak knoweth not Thy worth.

By remembering Thee, I obtain everything, I find nothing difficult.

Nanak, he whose honour the true Lord protecteth can be dishonoured by no one.

God is the raft to ferry man over the dangerous ocean of the world:

The river is deep; I cannot ford it; *yet I must because* I love Thee.

My heart is sewed to Thy feet, O God, saith Nanak; Thou art the raft and the boat.

The saints are the Guru's friends:

They, a sight of whom banisheth evil inclinations, are my friends.

Nanak, I have searched the world all over; there are few such persons.

Long for the Omnipotent:

Nanak, long for that God who is the support of all;
By whose power the earth resteth upon water, and timber containeth fire.

The Guru prays to God who is potent to bestow:

All Thou hast made is dependent on Thee alone.
What Thou madest in the beginning prevaileth in the world.
I am astounded on beholding Thy astounding might.
Thy slave hath come under Thy protection; act and I shall be saved.
All wealth is in Thy hands to give it to whom Thou pleasest.
He to whom Thou art merciful repeateth Thy name.

Men read religious books without spiritual advantage:

The broth is stirred with spoons, but they know not its flavour.
Nanak, those men are the best who are imbued with the relish of God's love.

The Guru is convinced of the unity of God:

When my Beloved was kind to me, I searching found
One Creator; Nanak, no other can be seen.

Sin may be avoided by remembering the Guru's instruction:

Take aim with the arrow of truth and bring down sin.
Remember the Guru's instruction, Nanak, and no sorrow shall befall thee.

He who forgets God can never prosper:

Millions of obstacles are in his way who forgetteth the Name:
He croaketh day and night, Nanak, like a raven in an empty building.

The life of an anchoret is not necessary to salvation:

Nanak, I have met the true Guru, and my union with God is accomplished.
Even while men laugh, and play, and dress, and eat, salvation can be obtained.

The favours conferred by the Guru:

Hail! hail to that true Guru who hath demolished the fortress of doubt!
Congratulations to that true Guru who hath united me with God!
The Guru hath given me as a medicine the inexhaustible treasure of the Name.
It hath cured the great and terrible disease of *spiritual ignorance.*
In obtaining the wealth of the Name. I have found a great treasure;
And by recognizing myself I have won this priceless human life.

The praises of the Guru the omnipotent being cannot be expressed.

The Guru is the supreme Brahma, illimitable, invisible and inscrutable.

Effort encouraged by the Guru:

O man, by striving and earning enjoy happiness.

Nanak, by meditating on God, meet Him and thine anxieties shall vanish.

God destroys slanders and protects the holy:

God at once destroyed the slanders and suffered them not to live for a moment.

He caught them and yoked them to birth, for He could not endure the torments of His slaves.

He dragged down the slanderers by the hair of their heads, and sent them on the road to Death.

He threw them into hell, where they groaned in agony;

But God, true that He was, O Nanak, embraced and protected His saints.

Devgandhari

The intoxication of devotion:

Thy servant, O God, is intoxicated with Thine elixir.

He who obtaineth the store of the essence of love, for saketh it not to go elsewhere.

While seated he repeateth God's name, while sleeping he repeateth God's name, he taketh God's essence for his food.

Bathing in the dust of the saints' feet is equal to ablution at the sixty-eight places of pilgrimage.

Profitable is the life of God's servant who hath made God a father of good children.

Nanak, he who recognizeth the all-pervading God, taketh all with him and saveth them.

The following is sung at banquets and also when the Granth Sahib is brought to the temple in the early morning:

O God, this is the desire of my heart:

That Thou, the Treasure of mercy, the Compassionate, shouldst make me the slave of Thy saints;

That I should touch their feet in the morning and behold them night and day;

That I should devote my body and soul to their service and sing God's praises with my tongue;

That I should ever abide with the saints and remember Thee at every breath I draw.

The Name is my sole support and wealth; from it Nanak obtaineth delight.

The Guru's delicious sensation on meeting God:

O Beloved, Thy words are nectar.

O my Beloved, very beautiful, Bewitcher of the soul, Thou art in everything and yet distinct.

I long not for empire, I long not for salvation; my soul loveth Thy lotus feet.

There may have been Brahma, Shiv, Sidhs, Munis, and Indar, but I desire only a sight to Thee.

O Lord, I have come helpless to Thy door, and, weary that I am, have entered the asylum of Thy saints.

Saith Nanak, I have met God who beguileth the heart; my soul is refreshed and happy.

The unity of God:

Know that there is only one God:

Know Him to be one through the Guru's instruction.

Why wander? wander not, my brethren; God is surely contained in every place.

As the fire which is in timber cannot be made available without skill,

So God's door is not obtained without the Guru.

Abandon pride in the company of the saints;
Thus, saith Nanak, shall the Primal Treasure be obtained.

The Guru deprecates evil communications:

Turn away, O my soul, turn away,
Turn away from the apostate.

False is the love of the false; abandon it, O my soul, and thou shalt be saved: thou shalt not be saved in the company of the apostate.

As any one who entered a house filled with soot would become black,

So whoever associated with the apostate would become defiled; but he who meeteth the Guru shall escape from Maya, and flee *from evil association*.

O merciful One, Ocean of mercy I crave this boon of Thee, not to bring me face to face with the apostate.

Make Nanak Thy slave of slaves, and his head shall roll under the saints' feet.

Bihagra Chhant

The following was composed in reply to a question how God could be worshipped:

I have seen one miracle of God, O my beloved; what He doeth is perfect justice.

God appointed the world as a beautiful arena, my beloved, where all men come and go.

He who created the earth made men's coming and going.

God inviteth some who meet the true Guru to His palace; others wander astray in error.

Thou alone, O God, knowest Thine own limit; Thou art contained in everything.

Varily speaketh Nanak—hear, O saints, God dispenseth perfect justice.

Come and meet me, O companions, my beloved; let us worship God's name.

Worship the perfect true Guru, my beloved; let us smooth the way to death.

Having under the Guru's instruction smoothed the arduous road, we shall obtain honour in God's court.

They whom God so predestined fix their attention on Him day and night.

Pride, egotism, and worldly love depart when we associate with the holy man.

Saith the slave Nanak, salvation is obtained by worshipping God's name.

O saints, my beloved, let us unite and with clasped hands worship the Imperishable Being.

I have examined many forms of worship, my beloved; *but they are all vain*; let us devote our souls and bodies *all to Him*.

When soul, body, and wealth belong to the Lord, what offering shall we make Him?

The compassionate God embraceth him to whom He showeth mercy.

He on whose forehead such destiny was written loveth the Guru.

The slave Nanak saith—let us by association with the saints worship God's name.

I have returned, O my beloved, from searching in every direction; and have found God in my own home.

God hath made *this body* as a temple, O my beloved, and He is contained therein.

The Lord God is contained in everything; He becometh manifest by the Guru's instruction.

Darkness is dispelled, and troubles removed when the Guru Hath caused the essence of God's nectar to trickle into the mouth.

Wherever I look, there and in every place is the Lord, the Supreme Being.

Saith the slave Nanak, on meeting the true Guru, I have found God on returning home.

The exquisitely pleasurable feeling of union with God:

O pleasant night, grow long as I love the Dear One;

O unpleasant sleep, grow short that I may ever touch His feet.

I long for the dust of His feet, and I ever beg for His name for the love of which I have abandoned the world.

Forsaking my very evil inclinations, I have become imbued with the love of the Dear One and intoxicated without wine.

I have met the Dear One on the right way; He hath taken my arm, and I have become absorbed in His love.

Nanak imploreth Thee, O Lord, to extend him the favour to continue attached to Thy feet.

O my friends and companions, let us remain attached to God's feet.

Our hearts feel great love for the Dear One; let us pray for His service.

Let us go and meet the saints of God, meditate on Him, and we shall obtain His service.

Let us forsake the sins of pride and worldly love, and dedicate to Him our bodies, wealth and souls.

God is the great Being, all-prervading, of perfect excellence; on meeting Him all error and fear depart.

Nanak representeth, hear my counsel; my companions, let us ever and ever repeat God's name.

God's spouse is a happy wife, and enjoyeth every pleasure;

She shall not become a widow; her Spouse is long-lived.

She is never unhappy, she meditateth on God; blest and fortunate is she.

She sleepeth in peace and rest; her sins are blotted out, and she awaketh in the delight and love of the Name.

She remaineth absorbed in God's love; His name is her jewels; the words of the Dear One are to her sweet and pleasing.

Nanak representeth, I have obtained my heart's desire; I have met God who is a long-lived Spouse.

He in whose soul and body God the Primal Joy is contained,

Hath at home songs of rejoicing and millions of pleasures.

God, may Spouse, is infinite, compassionate, the Possessor of wealth, the SAviour of sinners.

God, the Extender of mercy, is He who causeth man to cross the terrible ocean.

God embraceth him who seeketh His protection; this is the function of the Lord.

Nanak representeth, I have found God as my Spouse, and He ever indulgeth in dalliance with me.

Dark is the night and difficult the road. There is none to light man's way and guide him but God:

Thou who art imbued with love for many worldly things shall find thy way difficult.

O sinner, there is none to help thee;

No helper is thine; thou shalt ever regret it.

Thou utterest not God's praises; shall these days ever return?

As leaves separated from the tree shall not grow again thereon, *so shall Thy relations and friends part from thee,* and thou shalt proceed alone on thy way to Death.

Nanak representeth, without the name of God man ever wandereth in distress.

O man, thou practisest deception in secret, but God who knoweth everything knoweth thee.

When Dharmarj taketh thine account, thou shalt be pressed like a bundle of sesame.

O mortal, thou shalt suffer the penalty of thine acts, and wander in many wombs.

Imbued with the love of the arch fascinator, thou shalt lose the jewel of thy human life.

Thou wert clever at everything else except repeating the one God's name.

Nanak representeth—they for whom it was so destined are attracted to superstition and worldly love.

The ungrateful are separated from God and have no mediator.

The all-cruel myrmidons of Death shall seize them;

Shall seize and lead them off, and they shall obtain their deserts on account of their love for the arch fascinator.

They never repeated God's praises under the Guru's instruction, so their breasts shall be applied to the hot pillar.

Man is ruined by lust, wrath, the pride; he loseth his senses and then regretteth.

Nanak representeth—without repeating God's name man faileth to meet Him.

There is none but Thee, O God, the Preserver.

It is Thy function to save sinners.

I seek Thy protection, O saviour of sinner, Master, Ocean of mercy, compassionate:

O Creator, Cherisher of every heart, rescue me from the blind well.

Thou art my Protector, cut away my heavy fetters, and give me the Name as my sole support.

Nanak imploreth—O God, compassionate to the poor, reach me Thy hand and save me.

The day when God blended me with Himself was fortunate:

All happiness then appeared, and misery remained far apart.

Comfort, ease, joy, and delight ever accrue from singing God's praises.

In association with the saints worship God with love, and thou shalt not again rush through births.

God graciously embraceth man according to the result of former acts.

Nanak representeth—when God is met, man never again wandereth in transmigration.

Prayer and praise of God:

Hear my supplication, O my Lord God,

Though I am full of millions of sins, nevertheless I am Thy slave.

O Thou Dispeller of grief, merciful, fascinating, Destroyer of trouble and anxiety,

I seek Thy protection, protect mine honour; Thou art in all things, O spotless One,

Thou hearest and beholdest us; Thou art with us all, O God; Thou art the nearest of all to us.

O Lord, hear Nanak's prayer, save the slave of Thy household.

Thou art ever omnipotent; we are poor and beggars.

O God, save us who are involved in the love of mammon.

Bound by covetousness and worldly love, we have committed various sins.

The Creator is distinct and free from entanglements; man obtaineth the fruit of his acts.

Show us kindness, Thou purifier of sinners; we are weary of wandering through many of womb.

Nanak representeth—I am the slave of God who is the Support of the soul and life.

Thou art great and omnipotent; my understanding is feeble.

Thou cherishest even the ungrateful; Thou lookest equally on all.

Unfathomable is Thy knowledge, O infinite Creator; I am lowly and know nothing.

Having rejected the gem *of Thy name,* I have amassed kauris; I am a degraded and silly being.

By the commission of sin I have amassed what is very unstable and forsaketh man.

Nanak hath sought Thy protection, O omnipotent Lord; preserve his honour.

When I sang God's praises in the association of the saints,

He united me, who had been separated from Him, with Himself.

By ever thoroughly singing God's praises, He who is happiness itself becometh manifest.

My couch, when God accepteth me as His own, is adorned by Him.

Having dismissed anxiety I am no longer anxious, and suffer no further pain.

Nanak liveth beholding God and singing the praises of the Ocean of excellences.

Wadhans

God holds His court in every heart, but the screen that conceals it can only be rent by piety:

Very exalted is His court;

It hath no end or limits.

Hundreds of thousands and millions hasten,

But they can never reach His court.

What is that auspicious hour when God is met?

Hundreds of thousands of saints worship Him.

Hundreds of thousands of great penitents do penance unto Him.

Hundreds of thousands of Jogis practise Jog.

Hundreds of thousands of great enjoyers enjoy enjoyments;

But God *is not thus found;* He dwelleth in every heart: only a few know it.

Is there any friend who can rend the screen between Him and us?

If that friend be kind to me, I will make efforts *to meet God,*

And sacrifice my body and soul unto Him.

After many wanderings I have come to the saints,

And all my sorrows and doubts are dispelled.

God hath invited me to His court to quaff nectar.

Saith Nanak, my Lord is the most high.

The love of the saint for the Beloved:

My heart desireth to meet the True Guru; how shall I find Him, my dear?

Even though hundreds of amusements be afforded a child, it cannot live without milk.

The hunger of my heart departeth not, O my boon companion, even though hundreds of dishes be served before me.

My soul and body feel love for the Beloved; how shall my heart be satisfied without beholding Him?

Hear, O my friend and beloved brother, introduce me to the Friend and Giver of happiness.

He who ever repeateth to me God's words knoweth all the secrets of my heart.

I cannot abide for a moment without *God,* and I cry for Him as the chatrik for water.

What excellences of Thine, O God, shall I recount? Thou preservest men without merits like me.

My boon companion, I am waiting for my Spouse; when shall I behold the Beloved with mine eyes?

All my pleasures and amusements are forgotten; without my Beloved they are of no account.

This vesture becometh me not; I know not how to adorn myself.

I make obeisance to those companions of mine who enjoy their darling Beloved.

I have made all decorations, O my boon companion, but without the beloved they are of no avail.

When my Spouse speaketh not to me, O my companion, my youth passeth all in vain.

Blessed, blessed are the happy wives, O my boon companion, who are united with their Spouse.

I am a sacrifice to such happy wives, O my boon companion, and I ever wash their feet.

As long as duality and superstition were in my heart, I thought God distant;

But when I met the perfect true Guru, O my companion, all my hopes and desires were fulfilled.

I obtained the highest happiness, O my boon companion, and discovered that my Beloved was everywhere.

Nanak hath obtained divine pleasure, O my boon companion, by touching the true Guru's feet.

Wadhans Chhant

The following is sung at marriages after the usual circumambulations are completed:

O my God, my hopes and desires have been fulfilled.

I am without merits; all merits are Thine;

All merits are Thine, O my Lord; with what mouth shall I praise Thee?

Thou hast not considered my merits or demerits; Thou hast at once pardoned me.

I have obtained the mine treasures; congratulations resound and unblown trumpets play.

Saith Nanak, I have found a good Spouse and home, and all my anxieties art at an end.

Sorath

Prayer and worship are not to be addressed to idols and demigods, but only to the Creator:

To whom else shall I pray? whom else shall I worship, since it is God who created all?

The different persons who appear the greatest of the great shall all be blended with the dust.

The fearless, the Formless, the Destroyer of fear will grant all happiness and the nine treasures.

O beloved God, I am satiated with Thy gifts.

Why should I flatter wretched man? What need I from him?

He who meditateth on God possesseth everything; God hath appeased his hunger.

The Giver of happiness conferreth such wealth as shall never be exhausted.

The true Guru hath introduced me to God; I am now happy and absorbed in bliss.

O my soul, repeat the Name, worship the Name, utter the Name night and day.

Hear the instruction of the saints and all Thy fear of death shall depart.

They to whom my God is merciful are attached to the Guru's words.

Who can appraise Thy worth, O God? Thou art compassionate to all creatures.

Whatever Thou doest prevaileth; what can we poor children do O God?

Preserve Thy slave Nanak, as a father cherisheth his son.

Man's life hangs by a frail thread; his only hope is in God:

Sons, kinsmen, the wife of thy household are attached to thee for thy wealth.

None of them will assist thee at the last moment; their love is all false.

O man, why pamperest thou thy body?

It shall vanish like a cloud of smoke; worship the one beloved God.

Thy body is disposed of in three ways—it is thrown into the river, to the dogs, or burnt to ashes.

Man deeming himself immortal sitteth at home and for getteth the Cause of causes.

God fashioned beads of many sorts and strung them together on a frail string.

That string shall break, O wretched man, and then shalt thou regret.

Meditate day and night on Him who created thee and adorned thee.

Appendices

APPENDIX - I

FAMILY AND LIFE WORK

Guru Arjan Dev—Fifth Guru of the Sikhs (1563-1606)

Father—Guru Ramdas Mother—Mata Bhani

Fourth Guru of the Sikhs

Guru Arjan Dev

Place of birth—Goindwal Date of birth — 15 April 1563

Name before Guruship — Arjan Dev

Religion — Sikh

Married to Mata Ganga Daughter of Shri Krishanchand Marriage Date — 1579 (16 Years)

Son

(Guru) Hargobind (1595)

Education

Place — Goindwal, Amritsar Subjects — Punjabi, Religions, Sanskrit, Arithmetic

Period — 13 years

Profession

Family business—None

Fifth Guru of Sikhs

Meeting with Guru

The Persuasion — Guru Ramdas Time Period — 18 years.

Reasons — Son — youngest

Son of Guru Ramdas

The Guru Period

Place of residence—Goindwal, Amritsar

Period of Guruship — 15 Sept. 1581—30 May 1606 (25 years)

Teachings

1. Unity of God; 2. Worship only Nirgun aspect of God; 3. Daily Prayers; 4. Prayers to include a request, a thanks and an appeal.

Contribution to Sikhism

1. Transformation of Sikh sect to Religion;
2. Compilation of Guru Granth Sahib;
3. Construction of Harimandir Sahib;
4. Conversion of Sangatias to Masands;
5. Construction of 4 other Shrines;
6. Change of profession of the Sikhs (from Agriculture to Business).

Related Gurdwaras

Total = 12

Location = Kartarpur (3), Goindwal (1), Tarantaran (1), Amritsar (1), Chharta (1), Lahore (5).

Hymns

Total = 2218

Recording in Guru Granth Sahib—

In 30 Raags (Except Raag Jai Jai Vanti)

Language/s used — Punjabi, Sanskrit, Sindhi, Lehndi

Sakhis/Source

1. Mohsin Fani—Author Dabistan
2. Bhai Gurdas
3. Bhat Swayas

Important Names

1. Emperor Jehangir
2. Prince Khusrav
3. Chandu Shah
4. Sulahi Khan

The Departure

Place of death — Lahore

Date/year — 30 May 1606

Other Points to Remember

1. First Guru at the young age of 18
2. First Son-Guru
3. First Guru born in Sikh family
4. First martyr of Sikh history

Guru Arjan Dev—The Fifth Guru of the Sikhs

		Guru Age
1563	Born at Goindwal	
1579	Marriage with Mata Ganga	16
1581	Anointed as the fifth Guru of the Sikhs	18
1588 (28 Dec.)	Foundation stone of Harimandir by Mian Mir	25
1595	Birth-Guru Hargobind	32
1598	Emperor Akbar's visit at Goindwal	35
1601	Started compilation of Guru Granth Sahib	38
1603	Visited Baba Mohan for the collection of Mohan Pothis	40
1604	Completion and installation of Guru Granth Sahib at Harmindir	41
1605	Emperor Akbar's stay at Batala, inspection of Guru Granth Sahib and gift of estates and gold coins for the spread of word of God as contained in Granth Sahib	42
1605 (October)	Prince Khusrau's (Akbar's son) visit	42
1606	Martyrdom at Lahore	43

Construction of Gurdwaras

1586	Harimandir sarovar surfaced	23
1588	Completed Sanntokhsar	25
1588	Founded Harimandir	25
1590	Taran Taran — Sarovar started	27
1593	Kartarpur (Jallandar) founded	30

1596	Taran Taran-Harmindir founded	33
1597	Chherta Sahib Gurdwara founded	34
1597	Gobindpur founded	34
1599	Baoli Sahib at Lahore founded	36
1602-3	Ramsar (Amritsar) founded and completed	39-40